PARTNERS IN FAITH

Partners in Faith

A PROGRAMME OF ADULT FAITH DEVELOPMENT

Written by
Ciarán Earley OMI
and
Gemma McKenna

THE COLUMBA PRESS
DUBLIN 1991

First edition, 1991, published by
THE COLUMBA PRESS
93 The Rise, Mount Merrion, Blackrock, Co Dublin, Ireland

Origination by The Columba Press
Posters devised by Ciarán Earley OMI
and prepared for publication by Eimear O Boyle
Printed in Ireland by
The Leinster Leader

ISBN: 1 85607 032 8

ACKNOWLEDGEMENTS

Many of the ideas in this programme derive from a wide source of readings, studies, and experiments with which we have been in contact over the years. As far as possible, those specifically referred to or drawn from have all been acknowledged, either within the text or here below. Some suggested background reading is mentioned below, where relevant. We are grateful to those publishers who have given us permission to use their copyright material. If we have inadvertently missed any copyright holders, we offer our apologies and invite them to get in touch with us so that things can be put right in future editions. We would also like to express our indebtedness to all those other writers, teachers, thinkers and practitioners whose work has contributed so fundamentally to our own growth and to the programme.

SESSION TWO: We have drawn on some of the ideas of Fr Denis Edwards, *The Human Experience of God*, Gill & Macmillan, 1983, and Fr John Shea, *Stories of God*, Thomas Moore Press, 1980, for this session.
SESSION THREE: Dermot A. Lane, *The Experience of God*, Veritas, Dublin, 1981. Handout 4 based on Arthur Baranowski, *Praying Alone and Together*, St Anthony Messenger Press, 1988. Supplementary Material 1 was submitted by the Tallaght group at *Partners in Faith*. The diagram on p 14 is derived from Martin A. Lang, *Acquiring Our Image of God*, Paulist Press, 1983. Stories in Supplementary Material 3 are from Edwards, *The Human Experience of God*.
SESSION FOUR: Some of the material on Moses is derived from Carlo Montini, *Through Moses to Jesus*, Ave Maria Press, 1988, Second Meditation. Handout 7 is taken from *NIV Serendipity Bible for Study Groups*.
SESSION SIX: Walter Brueggeman, *The Prophetic Imagination*, Fortress Press, 1985. Other ideas for this session have come from the writings of Carlos Mesters, especially *Os Profetas – E A Saude Do Povo*, and *Os Dez Mandmentos*.
SESSION NINE: The Psalm on page 49 is taken from Brandt & Coreta, *Psalms Now*, Concordia, 1986. Supplementary Material 1 is taken from Flynn & Thomas, *Living Faith*, Sheed & Ward USA, 1989.
SESSION TEN: We are indebted to Fr Albert Nolan OP for some of the ideas in this session, from a talk by him at Milltown Park, Dublin, in 1989. The tale on p 57 and Handout 16 are derived from *Gateway Series: No. 3 Cry the Poor*, St Columban's, Navan.
SESSION THIRTEEN: Loughlan Sofield & Carroll Juliano, *Collaborative Ministry*, Ave Maria Press, 1987. Our model for the Seven Step Method is based on material from the Lumko Missiological Institute, South Africa.
SESSION SEVENTEEN & EIGHTEEN: Anne Hope & Sally Timmel, *Training for Transformation* 1, 2, & 3, Mambo Press, Zimbabwe, 1984. Ideas for this session have also been drawn from Gerard Kirkwall and Colin Kirkwall, *Living Adult Education*, Open University Press, 1989, the source also of the cartoons and photograph on page 92.
SESSION TWENTY-TWO: Eamonn Bredin, *Disturbing the Peace*, The Columba Press, Rev. ed., 1991. The diagram of the synagogue is from Albert Rouet, *A Short Dictionary of the New Testament*, Paulist Press, 1982.
SESSION TWENTY-SIX: Many ideas in this session come from Arthur Baranowski, especially his *Creating Small Faith Communities*, St Anthony Messenger Press, 1980, and also from our own reflection on small christian communities within the Irish context.
SESSION TWENTY-SEVEN: We found two books helpful in this session: Alfred Lapple, *The Catholic Church, A Short History*, Paulist Press, 1982, and Gerald Foley, *Empowering the Laity*, Sheed and Ward USA, 1986.

Contents

About this book

You have picked up this book probably because you are interested in adult faith development and/or small faith groups. If that is the case, we are delighted, because we put this book together for people like you.

Four years ago, a group of us got together to begin a project called 'Partners in Faith', with people from different parishes in the Archdiocese of Dublin. Four years later, having run the course with people from thirty-six parishes, we now offer you the material, the methods and the reflections that have emerged from the whole process.

The Pastoral Department of the Dublin Institute of Adult Education has a mandate to initiate pastoral projects and to communicate the results to others. Our last Book, *Actions Speak Louder* (The Columba Press, 1989), came out of just such a process.

We offer this book in a spirit of dialogue. We know that if we were different kinds of people, if we had more resources, if we had more time, etc., this might be a better work. However, as Gabrielle Stuart of Mount Oliver has pointed out, there is a kind of pride involved in waiting till you have the perfect piece of work, the most excellent. If we keep waiting, there will be no chance of dialogue, of either affirmation or criticism. We, therefore, put the fruit of three years of struggle before you, hoping that it will further the dialogue about adult faith development in our country.

How the Project began
Part of our mandate within the Institute is to develop pastoral projects within a framework of action, evaluation and communication. Four years ago, as a result of Pastoral Department meetings, we decided to take on the challenge of adult faith development in and through small faith groups. The reasons for this are based on our own convictions about the church: we believe that there is need for new ways of being church, and also for a renewed consciousness of the judaeo-christian message. This can happen more effectively within small faith groups, with a more radical biblical sense of mission. Later, we saw the need to give people a group approach to action.

First of all we had to form a team to lead the process. We two were joined by Michael Reidy, diocesan priest, Director of Studies at the Institute. Eamonn Bredin, of the diocese of Kilmore, and author of *Disturbing the Peace* (The Columba Press, 1985 & 1991), and lecturer at Mount Oliver, was more than willing to collaborate with us. John O'Brien CSSp, whom we often refer to as our 'mobile theological unit', was, at the time, immersed in the struggles of the people in Fatima Mansions in Dublin, and had just completed his doctorate in theology at the Gregorian University in Rome. He accompanied us throughout the entire first year. Obviously, there was an imbalance in the team, with one woman and four men. You can imagine how, with such a diversity, the initial meetings were pretty stormy as we struggled to set general aims, develop a framework within which to work, and then actually set about working. There was initial confusion about roles. Between us, we had to work out who were the designers, the leaders, the facilitators, the consultants, the lecturers, the animators, the maintainers, etc., and it took a long time for the necessary distinctions to emerge.

Basic Agreements

(a) Experience of christian community

We all agreed that we wanted the process to be an experience of christian community. We hold that christianity is a communitarian religion: we are called to conversion *individually* and to salvation *collectively*. If we, as christians, propose to the world that it be characterised by the values of participation and communion, then we must show these values in our church structures and activities. This is why we decided to invite people to participate as members of groups who would undertake group actions on the course.

We decided to invite six groups from six different parishes on Wednesday nights. Each group consisted of five people. During the sessions, we would invite groups to take on small tasks at the service of the wider group, and also, during the year, to plan and lead a major learning event for all on the course.

(b) Essential judaeo-christian message

Having agreed on the structures of participation, we then had to decide on the theological content of the course. We wanted to offer people a version of the kerygma that would inspire and motivate. Obviously, this would be in line with the church's traditions. The personal convictions of the leading learners came into play: though we follow different lifestyles and theological emphases, we did manage to create an 'agreed vision' out of which to proceed. The sessions of the programme reveal this vision.

(c) Bias towards action

The 'Partners in Mission' movement has influenced all of us, so we greatly appreciate the 'psycho-social' method and approach of Paolo Freire. This led us not only to communicate a method for group action, based on Freire's approach, but also to enable the participants to actually use it on the course. This has become a very exciting part of the 'Partners on Faith' experience, when 'ordinary' people can use their own gifts to identify the concerns of others and to plan and execute a response to those needs.

(d) Reflection on experience

Reflection on one's own concrete experience is basic to the approach used in 'Partners in Faith'. People are invited to focus on the themes as embodied in their experience, and to say their own word as it emerges from their reflection. They are then presented with material which affirms, challenges or stretches their own thoughts and, from the resultant dialogue, they are encouraged to express their creativity in different ways. This leads to a new level of consciousness. Each night is a variation on this approach.

(e) Confidence-building

Because of the options above, we do not explicitly set out to spend time on what is called 'personal development'. People who come on the course are already managing their homes, relationships and work, pretty well. We believe that the confidence they need, for developing as members of small faith groups or teams, will come from participation and practice on the course, and from the affirmation they receive from the leading learners, their group companions and the wider group. By the end of the course, people have a good sense of themselves and their capabilities as christians.

Ciarán Earle
Gemma McKenna
Dublin Institute of Adult Education
Summer 199

Participants in 'Partners in Faith', 1988-1991

The participants are listed under the names of their parishes, in alphabetical order, rather than in chronological order of the years in which they participated. Where more than one group attended from a single parish, the names in the different groups are separated by a line space.

1. Ayrfield:
Breda Keean
Phyllis Byrne
Kay Morgan
Bill Galgey

2. Balally:
Aline Molony
Sr Attracta Gaffney
Roy Finnegan
John Sexton
Marie Webb R.I.P.

3. Balcurris:
Audrey Meehan
Ann Hayes
Sr Bernadette O'Reilly
Mary Kiernan

4. Ballymun:
Margaret Byrne
Lilian O'Brien
Tomas Maher
Sr Irene Baily

5. Beaumont:
Tony Bolton
Colette Higgins
Anne Morris
Sean Dempsey

6. Blakestown
Jimmy Green
Annette Hannon
Catherine Byrne
Pat Farrell
Fr Bernard Thorne

Gerry Cassidy
Rita Fagan
Jacqueline Dunne
Br Eugene Traynor
Jim Nolan

7. Cabinteely:
Dot Carr
Ellen McKean
Josephine McMullan
Moira Flavin
Caoimhe Máirtín

8. City Quay:
Josephine O'Reilly
Jimmy Whelan
Catherine Fox
Fr Eamonn Crosson

9. Clondalkin:
Bernadette Goldsbury
David O'Leary
Kate McHale

10. Clontarf:
Thelma Bradley
Bernadette Daly
John O'Connell
Phelim O'Reilly
James Sherran

11. Corduff:
Breda Jennings
Mick Shanley
Patricia Deane
Fr Mick Sullivan
Eddie Clarke

12. Darndale:
Mena Hourigan
Pat Kiely
Mary Good
Sr Nora O'Neill
Fr Oliver Barry

Gerry Kiely
Eileen Walsh
Sr Maria Crowley
Angela McLaughlin
Betty Lalor
Nancy Gorman

13. Donnycarney:
Jacinta Kennedy
Joe Murray
Eamonn Mooney
Fr Liam Lacey

14. Finglas West:
Joan Doherty
Brendan Butler
Cathy Ryan
Sr Concepta Smiddy
Charles Bowden R.I.P.

15. Finglas South (Rivermount):
Kay Whelan
Leslie Smartt
Harry Murphy
Carmel O'Sullivan
Ann Gibney
Fr Paddy Mullery

16. Francis Street:
Dick Harper
Rita Kavanagh
Mary Keane
Sr Rosarii
Clare Hughes

17. Gardiner Street:
Mary Fay
Dennis Murphy
Mary Ryan
Christopher McLaughlin
Fr Patrick Hume

Martin Cumberton
Nuala Fagan
Sr Siobhan Noctor
Jim Corcoran
Cecilia Armstrong

18. Greenhills:
John Shelly
Alice O'Toole
Denis Sexton
Helen Gorman
Eugene Myler
Fr Tom Basquel

19. Halston Street:
Sr Maisie Hayden
Sr Nuala
Tony Jennings
Maureen Miley

20. Kilmore West:
Henry Quinn
Kathleen Farrell
Enda Madden
Paula Madden
Totsy Redmond
Sr Magdalen

21. Lucan:
Diane Birnie
Gerry O'Reilly
Angela Masterson
Fr Eoin Cooke
Ronan O'Connor
David Lynch

22. Meath Street:
Ann Ryan
Anne Mooney
Fr Philip Kelly

Sandra Darley
Catherine Graham
Fr Ben O'Brien
May Finnerty

23. Navan Road:
John Dowdall
Mary Ward
Maureen Goodwin
Eithne Fitzsimons

24. North Wall
Bernie Sheridan
Marie O'Reilly
Eva Donnellan
Phil Hynes
Sr Ann Roche
Sr Sandra McSheaffrey
Fr Johnny Stokes

25. Portmarnock:
Cecilia Agnew
Brendan Redmond
Frank Walsh
Rita Walsh
Sr Margaret Tarrant
Stephen

26. Rialto:
Fr Brian Murtagh
Ronan Ashe
Susan Gannon
Phyllis Glynn
Carmel Connell

27. Sean McDermott Street:
Liam Sheridan
Susan Bradley
Roddy Lyndsey

28. Silloge:
Marie Kelly
Kathleen Day
Sr Gabriel Morgan
Paddy Connelly
Mick Cantwell

29. Springfield:
Mary Murray
Mary Flanagan
Ann O'Rourke
Carmel Fletcher
Mary O'Connor
Sr Anne-Marie O'Shaughnessy

Carmel Page
Tricia Ronan
Sylvia Halpin
Fr Gabriel O'Dowd
Mary Brady

Tony McDermott
Sr Maura Walsh
Mary Munds
Fr John McLaughlin

30. St Aengus:
Anne Lavella
Phyllis Lambe
Michael Buffini
Fr Martin Crowe

Vincent Healy
Anne Parkes
Sr Margaret Mary Fox
Breda Baker
Br Eamonn OP

31. St Martin's:
Vera Thackaberry
Margaret Dennehy
Maureen Monahan
Ann White
Marie Byrne
Sr Máire Corbett

31. St Martin's (continued):
Ann Finnegan
Dolores Connelly
Jacinta Tanguy

Lorraine Duignan
Frances Cussen
Fr Archie Byrne

32. Jobstown:
Sr Ruth Harnett
Nancy Donoghue
John Donoghue
Eileen Conway
Kathleen Fox
Vera Dillon
Bernadette Cahill

33. Firhouse:
John Caulfield
Paul Buggy
Theresa Saab
Mary Davey
Fr Con Sayers

34. Killinarden:
Joan Boyle
Patrick Nicholl
Patrick Walsh
Bernie Rowley
Sr Phyllis

SESSION ONE

First Gathering of groups

Aims
• To create an atmosphere of welcome and ease.
• To help people begin to get to know each other.
• To outline what *Partners in Faith* is about and respond to reactions.
• To pray together.

Materials
Name Tags.
Flash Cards.
Handouts 1 & 2.
Tape recorder and appropriate music.
Candle.
Six sheets newsprint 18″ square, magic markers, blutak.

Time-Table
1.	7.45	Arrival and distribution of name tags.
2.	8.00	Getting Acquainted.
		Stretch break.
3.	9.00	Presentation: What is *Partners in Faith* About?
4.	9.15	Buzz session and feedback.
5.	9.30	Handout 2.
6.	9.35	Prayer.
7.	9.55	Distribution of Folders.
8.	10.00	Conclusion.

Suggested Procedure

1. Arrival
As people arrive coffee and tea are being served. Chairs are arranged in small clusters around the room. People take a name tag.

2. Getting Acquainted
Welcome everybody. Give a brief outline of what's going to happen in the session (cf. Aims and Time-Table). To help people get acquainted and feel at ease we have found these activities helpful:

Paul Jones: Ask three groups to form an inside circle facing outwards and the other three groups to form an outside circle facing inwards. Play some music and ask each person to move towards the left in time to the music. Stop the music after a short while. Individuals facing each other tell something about themselves. (Name, place, family, interests). When they are finished restart the music and repeat the pattern three or four times.

Self-introduction: Everyone in turn, in one large circle, says their name, where they come from, something about their family and what they are interested in.

Describing our place: Each group gathers together and does a brainstorm on what is interesting about the place they come from. They then select three or four things they consider interesting to present to the whole group.

The leaders record the contributions on six small sheets of newsprint (18″ sq.) on which the names of the parishes have been written. These are placed on the wall and referred to by the leaders, stressing what's common, differences, themes, as a way of affirming the participants in their local identity.

B R E A K

3. Presentation
What Partners in Faith is about
A leader, using flash-cards containing the main headings below, presents the following points on what Partners in Faith *is about. This is also the content of Handout 1.*

1. Small faith communities
Small Faith Communities are an important way of being the church now and in the future. They are characterised by mutual support, faith sharing, gospel reflection, prayer, study and outreach.

2. Experience of Christian Community
In order to equip people to be small faith communities, Partners in Faith sets out to give participants a lived experience of christian community integrating the elements mentioned above. In all sessions they will inter-react with one another, share experience and ideas, be affirmed and challenged by presentations and gradually take on tasks with and for the group.

3. Essential Biblical message
Participants are given an opportunity to explore their own faith and have it affirmed, challenged, deepened and stretched by the core biblical message of God and God's dream for people as revealed through Moses and the Prophets, Jesus and the community called church.

4. Method for Group Action
In order to experience what it's like for a group to make a difference to the world around it they will, with step by step guidance, learn a method of identifying and responding to needs and actually use it on the course.

5. Confidence-Building
Through participation in the sessions they will find themselves gradually growing in confidence because here they will have a safe setting in which to say their own word, try out tasks, work in a team and discover their own abilities.

6. Faith in Action
Partners in Faith aims:
1. to help all get clear what they stand for and what they are called to do.
2. to support all in keeping faith deep, alive and active through being members of small faith communities.

4. Buzz Session and Feedback
After the presentation people are then asked to reflect for a few moments quietly on: 'What do I feel now? What do I think? What questions are coming up?' In their groups they share their feelings, thoughts and questions. Someone makes a summary of the main points. In a plenary session each group gives their feedback and the leaders respond appropriately.

5. Handout 2
A leader distributes and comments on Handout 2 which names the themes for the first term.

6. Prayer
Theme:
Partners in Faith

– Introduction (improvise in accordance with mood.)
– Quiet music
– Reading: Luke 24:13-35
– Reflection (link the reading with the session and the course)
– Prayers (ready-made and open)
– Concluding prayer.

7. Distribution of Folders
Distribute folders in which people can keep handouts etc. Encourage people to write down thoughts and feelings that strike them as a result of the first session.

8. Conclusion
Collect the name tags before people leave.

Handout 1

What Partners in Faith is about

1. Small faith communities are an important way of being the church now and in the future. They are characterised by mutual support, faith sharing, gospel reflection, prayer, study and outreach.

2. Experience of Christian Community

In order to equip people to be small faith communities, *Partners in Faith* sets out to give participants a lived experience of Christian community integrating the elements mentioned above. In all sessions they will inter-react with one another, share experience and ideas, be affirmed and challenged by presentations and gradually take on tasks with and for the group.

3. Essential Biblical Message

Participants are given an opportunity to explore their own faith and have it affirmed, challenged, deepened and stretched by the core biblical message of God and God's dream for people as revealed through Moses and the Prophets, Jesus and the community called church.

4. Method for Group Action

In order to experience what it's like for a group to make a difference to the world around it, they will, with step by step guidance, learn a method of identifying and responding to needs and actually use it on the course.

5. Confidence-Building

Through participation in the sessions, they will find themselves gradually growing in confidence, because here they will have a safe setting in which to say their own word, try out tasks, work in a team and discover their own abilities.

6. Faith in Action

Partners in Faith aims:
1. To help people get clear what they stand for and what they are called to do.
2. To support people in keeping faith deep, alive and active through being members of small faith communities.

Handout 2

Sessions 1 – 12

Session One: Introduction to Partners in Faith
Session Two: Moments of Mystery
Session Three: Images of God
Session Four: The God of Moses
Session Five: God's Dream for People
Session Six: Emergence of the Prophets
Session Seven: Prophets Today
Session Eight: Spirituality: The Positive Way
Session Nine: Spirituality: The Negative Way
Session Ten: Spirituality: The Creative Way
Session Eleven: Spirituality: The Transformative Way
Session Twelve: Review and Celebration

SESSION TWO
The Mystery Dimension of our Lives

Aims
- To help people get to know each other better.
- To introduce people to Team Tasks and the idea behind them.
- To explore the experience of mystery in life as a starting point for religion.

Materials
- Handout of the pen-portraits which the groups did in exercise (c) last week.
- Handout on Team Tasks and a rota for the term.
- Blutak, magic markers.

Time-table
1. 7.45:   Getting more acquainted
2. 8.05:   Team Tasks
3. 8.15:   Guided reflection: The experience of Mystery
4.   Sharing in area groups.
5.   Plenary Session.
           Break
6. 9.30:   Presentation.
7. 9.45:   Buzz Session and Feedback.
8. 10.00: Prayer.
9. 10.15: Conclusion.

See Supplementary Material on page 9 before starting.

Suggested Procedure

1. Getting more acquainted
Welcome, (Name Tags)
People are asked to introduce themselves again.
Distribute the pen portraits of each area drawn up at last week's session.
Pair off the groups. Ask each group to enlarge on what is in the portraits about their area and say what the people are like. Encourage them to ask questions of one another.
All of this is to break down barriers and get people into a relaxed mood with one another.

2. Team Tasks
The leader explains the idea of the Team Tasks, distributes Handout 3 on the Team Tasks and a proposed rota (See Handout 3).

3. Guided reflection
Introduction
In this session we begin with a very basic question: how does religion come about? The word 'religion' comes from the Latin 'religare' which means to 'link together'. How do people and God come to link up with each other? It's an old truth that all knowledge begins with human experience and so it is with people's faith in God.

Human experience is simply the inter-action between the 'I' at the core of my being and the different worlds around the 'I' – the personal, interpersonal, wider society and all of creation. And inter-acting with these worlds through touching, sensing, feeling, thinking, choosing and acting is human experience.

Since time began people have identified key moments in their human experience when they have had a sense of a presence greater than themselves, of something beyond us but of which we are a part. We can be experiencing an event, say the birth of a child, and it may happen that we become aware indirectly of the source of life, the giftedness of life. We find it hard to put this experience into words. So we describe it as a moment when we were in touch with the mystery of life. We are overwhelmed by a sense that there is more than ourselves involved, something more than we can account for.

These deeper moments can be seen as doorways or gateways to the one we call 'God'.

Let's reflect in this session on our experience of life in order to see if we can identify special moments or occasions when we realised that there was something more to life. It will be like looking at a bright hillside and suddenly or eventually becoming aware of the sun, the source of the brightness.

Guided Reflection
Relax...put yourself in a comfortable position...feet on the floor...loosen your shoulders,...relax your legs...gently close your eyes...go into yourself...tune into your breathing... became aware of your body.

Now go back in your mind's eye ...to the home where you were brought up....imagine the most familiar room...table... fireplace... chairs....pictures on the wall....

Recall the face of your mother, her eyes...the lines on her face...the face of your father... brothers... sisters... grandparents.... the people around in your home...

Remember the other people who came and went in your home...aunts...uncles...cousins...neighbours....how did you relate to them?

Imagine the street or road outside your home...the houses ....fields...park....trees....shops....playground.

As you see the images of people, places, happenings, try and recall any moment when you have a sense of something different,..a sense of wonder...of something beyond... greater.....

***

Recall going to school...the classroom...the desks... the teachers....other students...classes... feelings....

Think of the people you got to know...school pals... friends....enemies....

Remember those times ...of study...exams...games... doubts ...fears....

At the same moment you became aware of your body changing...you began to take note of the opposite sex... meetings...

***

A time comes when you have to figure out what you are going to do with your life...who you are....sooner or later you seek out work...something to do...you decide what you are going to do with your life...earn your keep....change jobs... do training...

You meet many people ...one day someone special...heart beats faster...you decide on marriage or to stay alone...you leave home...

For a moment try and recall any time which was special ... when there was an extra dimension...

***

You may have changed homes... gone to different places.. to live and work...different environment and scenery...

There are times when everything in your work and life seems grand. Then...there are times when the going is rough.

Seasons come and go...autumn leaves...winter cold..summer holidays...perhaps the sea, beach, mountains, rivers, places to play and rest.

The time when a child is born

A time when sickness hits you or your family....others show care.

A time when a parent or someone close to you dies.

A time when relationships break down or a depression sets in.

A time when you moved into wider circles...you got involved with other people...community activites....

You remember a time of conflict...of rows...of separation.... or forgiveness...

You remember special moments in the wider world....men in space, the Pope's visit...violence in the North... elections...hunger, Live-Aid...the World Cup... Gulf War...

Let your imagination run through the people, places, happenings in your one and only life...and try to focus on one special moment when you became aware that there was something more to life...something greater...you had that sense of mystery.

Remember where it was, who was there, what happened, what you were feeling...

4. Sharing in area groups

Ask that someone co-ordinate the group so all will have a chance to speak. Ask the participants to share as much or as little of the moment they remembered with each other. It's important that each person has time to share and is listened to respectfully.

5. Plenary Session

When they have finished, ask one person in each group to note what was said, using this formula to report:
>   One person experienced mystery on the occasion of...
>   Another on the occasion of...
These occasions are listed on newsprint. If time permits, individuals are invited to say more about their experience.

BREAK

6. Presentation

The mystery dimension of our lives

The leader can draw on what has been coming up in the groups as well as using some of the ideas suggested here. Points can also be illustrated by photographs

When I want to understand how religion begins I must return to human experience. Since time began people have identified key moments when they have had a sense of something beyond, the sense of a presence greater than us but of which we are a part.

We can remember these special moments of mystery which serve as gateways or doorways to the one we call 'God'. For instance, the moment of **childbirth**. How many people on the occasion of the birth of a child feel a sense of gratitude. They realise what a gift life is and they get in touch with the giver of life. They have co-operated in the creation of a new human being and they feel the presence of the creator of all being. It often happens too at the moment of the **death** of a dear one, a parent, a spouse, a friend, that people feel in the darkness of loss and powerlessness that there is Someone there holding/supporting us in the sorrow. This sense of protective presence leads us to peace and the conviction that we will one day be united with the loved one who is no longer with us.

It can happen sometimes that when our hearts have hardened – maybe in hatred against someone – we feel trapped in anger and bitterness because of someone's words or actions. Logic and justice say we should keep our distance, and keep our hearts stonily closed, but then, for no obvious reason, we are drawn to reach out in **forgiveness** to that person. It's a moment of mystery when we find room for that person again and we are in touch with compassion.

Sometimes it's when our life has fallen through and we have a deep sense of **failure**. When our plans and dreams fall apart. At this moment we realise that life is larger than our little corner – that we don't have the last word – and we find ourselves reaching out in trust to begin again or to yield to something beyond us – in hope.

Of course one of the greatest moments of mystery is when it dawns on us how much we are **loved**. Maybe we have taken someone for granted. They are always there and some day it becames clear what a gift it is that I am loved by this person, particularly when I don't seem in any way to deserve it. It's then I get the sense of the gift of love and the Source of all love.

There are other occasions when a sense of mystery breaks through: in the beauty of **nature**, a moment of **creativity** when one realises one's own **vulnerability**, even when one feels **loneliness** or **alienation**. These significant moments can lead us to a great presence within and beyond our life experience.

The journey of faith begins with the conviction of an all powerful and faithful presence to which we are related.

It begins with these glimpses of Mystery which we can discover as gracious and loving.

7. Buzz Session

Buzz: Ask: What strikes you from what you've heard now and before (thoughts, feelings questions...)? Then provide chance for all simply to hear each other. The leaders need to note with sensitivity the insights, questions, doubts of the participants and decide if and when they will arrange a response either within the course or outside it.

8. Prayer

Theme: *Human Experience of God*
Music:
Scripture Text: Wisdom 13:1-9 (Or other appropriate text).
Reflection: Faith as attending and responding to the presence of God as revealed in life.
Prayers.

9. Conclusion

Remind the groups about the Team Tasks and about keeping personal notes.

Handout 3

Team Tasks

Partners in Faith sets out to be an experience of Christian community which is about people knowing each other and caring for and supporting one another. The getting to know one another happens when people participate in the different activities. The other aspects of caring for and serving one another happen in two ways:

Informally, when spontaneously people see a need and respond to it.

Formally, when a small group takes on certain tasks at the service of the whole group.

Six needs of the whole group have been identified which the six groups can take care of in weekly rotation. By taking on these tasks people will grow in confidence in saying and doing things and learn certain skills:

1. Report Team

This team reminds us of what happened at the previous session and helps us tune into the next one. To make the report each one on the team recalls what went on and one person (give everyone a chance) writes a summary containing:

1. The main theme/topic of the session
2. What we did
3. The key ideas or concerns mentioned
4. Some of the comments or questions people had.

We in turn, after carefully going over the whole story from the beginning, have decided to write an ordered account for you. Luke 1:3.

2. Commentary Team

This team reflects on what went on in all aspects of the session – atmosphere, activities, presentation, materials, participation, etc. – from their different angles. Someone makes a short summary of the comments for the next session (not more than ten sentences). The following phrases indicate what to look for:

'It was good that....'
'Something that struck me/us was...'
'It was very important that...'
'A question that came up for us was....'
'It would have been better if...'
'We suggest that....'

As long as we have the opportunity, let all our actions be for the good of everybody. Galatians 6:10

3. News Team

This team helps us reflect on God's presence in the reality around us. Before the next session the News Team:

1. Pick one item of news (either an event, a situation, an action, a story of a person, a movement, a change) which
either
a) reflects the main theme of the previous week's session
or
shows God's dream for people coming about (i.e. the Kingdom of God)
or
shows God's dream for people being blocked.

During the next session of *Partners in Faith* the News team:
2. Tells the group who did what to whom, where and how? or something similar – they can use a cutting/photo/cartoon if you like.

3. Tells the group why they chose this piece of news.

Do not model your behaviour on the contemporary world, but let the renewing of your minds transform you, so that you may discern for yourselves what is the will of God – what is good and acceptable and mature. Romans 12:2.

4. Prayer team

Each week a team will lead us in prayer for a period of 7-10 minutes.

Preparation:
Pick a theme based on the previous week's session.
Choose a short piece of scripture that is related to the theme.
Reflect on it together: 'What does this text mean to us?'
Choose a piece of suitable music or a hymn.
Prepare the 10 minute prayer session using this scheme or another suitable one:

Prayer Session

a. A brief Introduction:
e.g. Welcome. Our prayer tonight is based on a reading from ... on the theme of ...

b. A piece of music or a hymn

c. Reading of the short piece of Scripture.

Silence

d. The team gives a brief reflection on the Scripture

e. Sharing thoughts and prayers.
Invite people present to share a brief thought, or a prayer or both.

f. A Blessing.
Make a blessing to round off the prayer.

Do all this in prayer, asking for God's help. Pray on every occasion, as the Spirit leads. For this reason keep alert and never give up: pray always for all God's people. Ephesians 6:18.

5. Tidy Up

This team cares for the space we work in. It means replacing chairs or desks moved during the session, emptying ash trays, collecting posters / papers and making sure nothing is left behind.

6. Team Team

Helping people relax over a cup of tea/coffee is the honour of this team. It entails handing round the tea and coffee collecting the cups and either washing them or stacking them up conveniently.

Continue to love each other as brothers and sisters and remember always to welcome strangers, for by doing this, some people have entertained angels without knowing it. Hebrews 13: 1-2.

Supplementary Material

You may find it helpful to read over this material before the session as helpful background. It is not possible to cover it in detail in the two and a half hour session.

Mystery in Life

The starting point of a relationship with God is wonder – wonder at the mystery of life. Let's look at what happens in people's lives.

Self

At the centre of my being and activity is my 'self', the 'I' . You can say 'I have a body but I am more than my body.' 'I have feelings but I am more than my feelings.' 'I have thoughts but I am more than my thoughts' 'I have desires but I am more than my desires.' The 'I' is the co-ordinator, the one in charge, that always remains the same behind the sensing, touching, feeling, thinking, desiring.

Self interacts with Different Worlds

The self interacts with different surroundings, environments and worlds.

First of all I interact with my own **personal world**. I am aware of the weight of my body. I am aware that I am feeling angry, that I am finding it difficult to sort out my ideas, that I am enjoying what I'm doing, that I'm making choices.

Then there is another world which is that of my **relationships** with people around me. I come into contact with and relate to family, friends, co-workers, neighbours. There is a flow between us. Here we feel either acceptance or rejection, love or loneliness, isolation or closeness. This is the heart of everyday life.

The third world with which I interact is that of the neighbourhood, the **community**, the city, the country, the state. This affects my life – what people do, the laws, customs, opportunities or lack of them for employment, health facilities, taxes levied, welfare available, what the media produce and the slant taken.

Human Experience

Where the self interacts with these worlds, touching, sensing, feeling, thinking and choosing, we speak of human experience, i.e. myself interacting with people and things and my awareness or consciousness of this.

Activity to heighten awareness of the mystery in life

Imagine an island far away: there people grow up, fall in love, get lonely, have children, get sick, feel alienated, etc. just as we do. They haven't been introduced to Christian faith; there are no primary schools, no catechism, no Holy pictures, no mammy saying prayers at the foot of the bed, no church or preaching. But in their ordinary human experience they sense something mysterious. What words would they use to describe the 'something more, beyond...'?

People can buzz about this and give suggestions e.g. 'there is something bigger than us'...'something out there'...)

Then ask people to list what questions the island people might have about this 'being' e.g.

Why are we here?
Is this 'being' the source of life?
Is there a plan?
Is that something for or against us?'
Does it stand in judgement or is it friendly?'
Is it a someONE?'

Then use what they say to make concluding comments such as: There is something/someone greater than me/us which is in some way lovable. I belong to it and it is trying to communicate with me, trying to touch me. The only way it can communicate is through my own experience or through others who write down this kind of experience.

This loving, mysterious thing is capable of speaking to me through all kinds of experience: joy and good times, suffering and pain, hard times. We touch this presence and the presence touches us, in special kinds of high moments but also in ORDINARY moments. What makes the difference is my ability to see beyond the ordinary to the wonderful mysterious loving presence: God seeking me out in love and self-giving.

SESSION THREE

Viewing the Invisible: Our Images of God

Aims
- To highlight faith as God's self-communication perceived and responded to in trust.
- To enable the participants to unearth their images of God.
- To examine the effects of our images of God in our lives.

Materials
Activity Sheets: Handouts 4 & 5.

Time-Table
1. 7.45:   Welcome.
2. 8.10:   Introduction to Images of God.

   9.00:   Break

3. 9.15:   Sharing.
4. 9.55:   Plenary Session.
5. 10.10:   Conclusion.

See Supplementary Material on page 14 before starting.

Suggested Procedure

1. Welcome the people
Refer briefly to the previous session.
Present the time-table for this session.
Ask parish groups to do their respective tasks: news, report, commentary.
Before the prayer, ask people to find someone they don't know and share some thought about last week (no feedback). Use the prayer 'Mystery' (*See Supplementary Material*).

2. Introduction to Images of God
The aim of this input is to explain the basic dynamic of revelation. Use the following as a basis for your presentation.

Introduction
Our theme in the last session was that *religion* is based on *human experience.* There is *ordinary* everyday human experience; then there are special moments or depth experiences which bring us beyond into the invisible but real world of beauty, love and truth. These become *religious* experiences when, through these doorways, we see God as the source of love and truth and beauty. At one and the same time as we experience birth, death, forgiveness, love or beauty, we experience the presence of God as also present *in* and *beyond* it all.

'The *sun* provides *light* in and through which we see; even though we do not see the sun directly we participate in the light of the sun. In a similar though limited way we can say God is present in our deepest experience of existence; even

though we do not see God directly, we participate in the omnipresence of God in such experiences.' (*The Experience of God*, by Dermot Lane)

Another word for what is happening here is *revelation* (act of revealing). In and through these special human experiences the mystery of God at the centre of life is being communicated.

But revelation is *not* simply God's *self-communication*. It is not one-sided. The presence of God must be recognised and accepted and believed by people.

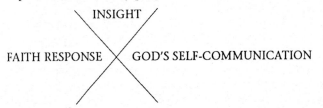

When God's self-communication meets human openness and longing there is the opportunity for faith. Faith is a decision to enter into personal relationship with God. This relationship is one of trust, *confidence, addressed to God as* someONE (Personal). Without faith there is an unrecognised gift, an unaccepted invitation. *Universal revelation* is open to all people. It's about the primary communication of God to persons which takes place in the experience of faith, through contact with creation, human existence and other people. *Basic Faith* is when we accept the invitation to recognise an underlying *ground* for all these special 'bits and pieces' of *meaning* and to accept the universe as in some sense 'friendly' and as being rooted in some *greater being,* power, mystery.

The *act of faith* and the ability to believe is also a *gift* from God. 'No one can come to me unless the Father draws him.'(John 6:44). 'We love because God loved us first.' (John 4:19) 'For by grace you have been saved through faith and this is not your own doing: it is the gift of God.' (Ephesians 2:28). This universal revelation and basic faith is open to all people. Later we will look at Judaeo-Christian revelation and faith. As a result of God's self-communication and our faith response we develop a sense or notion of God, an *image* of God.

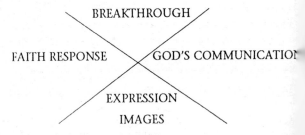

Revelation
All of us here have been born into a faith and raised within the immediate context of a believing family and the larger context of a believing community. So our faith has been nurtured and influenced by parents and grandparents, siblings, priests, sisters, catechists, retreats, but ultimately faith depends upon a mature and conscious decision to believe.

In the course of our life we will have developed some idea, image of God and that image affects the way we relate to God and to others. Now we are going to have a chance to explore and describe our image of God.

Exploration

1. Imagination and our view of God

In order to help the participants get in touch with their present image of God this meditation exercise is used. It gives people the opportunity to freely allow images/concepts to surface. Pace this meditation gently.

I want you to imagine yourself in a place with God.
Where are you? (setting)
What is happening between you and God?
What are you doing? What is God doing?
What are you saying? What is God saying?
What is being expressed between you?
How do you feel in this meeting?
How does God feel about you?

A few minutes to be quiet and let images surface...

Respond in your own way to God in this quiet space...

Now go back and in a reflective way tune into how you picture God and your relationship with God.

2. Describing God

Distribute Handout 4
Introduce it using words like: 'Having meditated on the way you think of God, I invite you to use this sheet to try and describe your sense of God.'

When everyone has had time to finish:
Look over the phrases you chose. Some descriptions may be more accurate for you than others. Circle those which BEST describe your experience of God. Using these words or phrases put together your description of God.

3. Discovering the God behind the Images

In order to further focus our images of God we categorise the phrases we have used under four headings: PERSONAL, DISTANT, AUTHORITATIVE AND LIBERATING, using Handout 5.

After completing the activities, participants are invited to share in twos.

BREAK

3.Sharing

About where our Images of God come from and how they affect us. It is important to emphasise the need for attentive listening to one another.

a) Personal reflection

'You have attempted to describe your sense of God. Now we invite you to ask yourselves quietly where these images come from and how they may affect your life'. Use these questions:
   Q.l. From where did you get your image of God?
   Q.2. How does it affect the way you relate to God?
   Q.3. How does it affect the way you think of yourself?
   Q.4. How does it affect the way you relate to others?

b) Sharing in three mixed groups.

To divide into groups, ask the participants to number themselves off one..two..three; one..two..three.., around the room. Then the ones go together, the twos, etc. Each groups is facilitated by one of the three leaders.

People are encouraged to speak about their image of God and their response to the questions. The leading learners mentally note what is coming up.

4.Plenary Session

The groups re-assemble and the leading learners communicate some of what they have heard.

5. Conclusion

Remind groups of Team Tasks
Use one or other of the following blessings based on people's images of God:

A Blessing
May the good God of everyday life be with you;
The God who is present in the pulse in the neck of a tiny child;
The God whose kindness is present in all fathers who care for their children;
The God of surprises, of new white dresses and pairs of shoes;
The God of faithful friends;
The God who suffers with us in our sickness,
Who walks with us on the beaches by the mighty ocean;
The God who was present in the Phoenix Park when the people were at one;
May this God of life and love and partnership be with us all and always.
Amen

or

A Blessing
May the good God of everyday life be with you;
The God who is present with the boy who walks by the river with his father;
The God who is present in the sense of relief and joy that comes with forgiveness;
The God who is present in the rain on the window with the sun shining through,
The God who is present on the mountains, in the stars and on the snowy boughs;
The God who is present in the birth of a child, and the illness of a husband;
The God who walks with us by the edge of the ocean and helps us across the sea of death;
May this God of life and love and partnership,
this God, as simple as a letter in the post,
be with us all and always.
Amen.

Handout 4

Describing God
(Adapted from 'Creating Small Faith Communities' by A Baranowski, St Anthony Messenger Press)

How we relate to God flows from our images of God.
Tick the phrases below which are close to your own sense of God.

❏ Interested in me
❏ Gives me power to change.
❏ Someone far away
❏ Someone I enjoy being with
❏ Shakes my apathy
❏ Someone who judges me
❏ Source of all things
❏ Someone I can trust
❏ Someone to be careful of
❏ Someone who watches over me
Other:

❏ Someone who saves me
❏ Involved in my life
❏ Someone I have an obligation to
❏ An onlooker
❏ For me – no matter what
❏ Someone to argue with
❏ Someone who sets me free.
❏ A vague presence
❏ Someone who has the answers
❏ A powerful force behind everything
Other:

_____

_____

_____

_____

_____

_____

_____

Handout 5

Discovering the God behind the Images
(Adapted from Praying Alone and Together *by A. Baranowski, St Anthony Messenger Press, Cinncinnati, 1988)*
On Handout 4 you ticked phrases which describe God for you.
Using the categories below, go back to Handout 4 and decide where your images fall.
Place a D for distant, an A for authoritative, a P for present or an L for liberating
after each ticked phrase.

Distant
A powerful force behind everything
Source of all things
Almighty
Someone far away
A vague presence
An onlooker

Authoritative
Someone to be careful of
Someone I have an obligation to
One who has the answers
Someone to bargain with
Someone to argue with
Someone who judges me

Personal
Someone interested in me
Someone who watches over me
Someone I enjoy being with
Someone involved in my life
Someone I can trust
Who is for me ... no matter

Liberating
Someone who saves me
Encourages me to break through
Disturbs apathy
Gives power to change
Sets me free
Gives me a fresh start

Make a sentence or two on:
The God to whom I relate _____

_____

_____

_____

_____

Supplementary Material 1

Mystery
We live in a sea of a dream as it grows,
You hear it if you listen to the wind as it blows,
It's there in a river as it flows into the sea,
It's the song in the soul of the one becoming free.

And it lives in the laughter of children playing,
And in the blazing sun that gives light to the day,
It moves the planets and the stars in the sky,
It's been the mover of mountains since the beginning of time.

O mystery, you are alive, I feel you around.
You are the fire in my heart, you are the holy sound.
You are all of life; it is to you I sing;
O grant that I may feel you always in everything.

And it lives in the waves as they crash upon the beach,
I've seen it in the gods that people have tried to reach.
Oh I feel it in the world, that I know it needs so much,
I know it in your smile, my love, when our hearts do touch.

But when I listen deep inside, I feel best of all,
Like a moon thats glowing bright and I listen to your call,
And I know you will guide me and I feel like the tide
'cause you moved the ocean of my heart that's open wide.

O mystery, you are alive, I feel you around.
You are the fire in my heart, you are the holy sound.
You are all of life; it is to you I sing;
O grant that I may feel you always in everything.

Supplementary Material 2

Additional Notes on Images of God
(accompanied by posters)

1. Experience – Mystery – God
Within our human experience we can identify moments when we become aware of something or someone greater and beyond us. In and through certain events we touch the one we call God. People tell stories about these times: 'One day I...' 'Since then I...' 'I'll never forget when...' because these were occasions when our attitudes, thinking and feelings were changed.

2. Acknowledgement of God and God-Language
The stories we tell recognise and acknowledge that we are in relationship with someone within and beyond our experience whom we call God. We find ourselves using the word 'God' to try and convey that greater reality we have become aware of.

3. Images
No sooner do we speak of that reality we call God than we find ourselves using images to express what we feel and know about our relationship with God. Many different images emerge. Very often the image we use is related to the way God was disclosed to us. If someone becomes aware of God through gazing at the sky, it's quite likely the awareness will be expressed as 'Heavenly God'. The disclosure came through interaction with the sky (heavens) and so sky is used to express God. or if through experience of interpersonal love I become aware of a gracious loving presence, I may express God as love.

Our imagination sees the event as a sign or sacrament of God – so we can speak of sacramental imagination. We can see how this works with parent imagery. Because of our experiences of fatherhood and motherhood we may think of the divine reality as 'generating love' and so it's only natural to speak of God as 'mother' and 'father'.

4. Images from Christian Tradition
We are born into a Christian culture — already shot-through with ready-made images: creator, shepherd, father, mother, king, rock, fire, whirlwind. Sometimes we are using these images before we have had the experience. When we do have a personal experience of God, that experience may influence the traditional image. The traditional gives us a language for the depth of our present experience while the value of the present experience is that it brings the traditional image alive.

5. Limitations
All images have limitations. To call God a father could be taken to mean that ultimate reality, God, is male and that therefore females are second class citizens in relationship to the mystery of human life. Or if our personal history with our father was difficult, the image may convey the sense of God's lack of care and concern, that God is indifferent. If we use the image 'king' does it mean that we are slaves of God? If we call God creator, could we be in danger of having a mechanical perception of God (as clockmaker)?

6. Influence of our Image of God
Our image of God affects the way we relate to God, the way we think of our lives, the way we relate to others and the way we act. Here are examples of the kind of effect our image of God can have on us:

Images of God	Self	Prayer	Action
Tyrant	Battered child	Saying right things	Dominate others
Forgiving Father	Imperfect but free	Open heart relationship	Respect others – instrument of hope
Source of life – Mother	Unconditionally loved	Tender concentration	Nurturing

7. Insights and Values
When we perceive our relationship with God, we express it in images and we tell stories to spell out what it means to relate to God. When we tell stories we develop insights and values. For instance if I perceive God as a loving parent. present to me in many ways in my life, gradually I will begin to see myself as a beloved child – which may help me see the value of others as my brothers and sisters. I will relate to God as a caring, loving father and to others as brothers and sisters.

8. Implications – Actions
How I imagine God and relate to God leads to insight and values and has implications for action. If God is a forgiving God, gradually, as my relationship with God grows, I will become aware of my own prejudice and bitterness and begin to see 'outcasts' in the way God sees them, as valuable persons despite what they may have done or may be like. And I will begin to become a sign of hope to them.

9. God is LIKE all the images we have mentioned and IS MORE THAN what we have said and God is DIFFERENT FROM what we have said.

Final Comments

'If we limit God to our own experience, we miss out on so much richness; on the other hand, if we don't see God in our own experience, then we diminish what God is for us and what we are for God.'

'Are we so attached to our image of God that we have it neatly parcelled up (as friend, protector, etc) and leave no room for surprise? If so, we would be in danger of resting content with an image that is too narrow, and might end up cutting God down to our puny size.'

Supplementary Material 3

Some Stories

In order to bring the discussion on our images of God to a concrete level, we found these stories useful. For each one we asked:

1. What is happening in the story?
2. Why is the person feeling and acting in this way?
3. How might we respond to such a person?
4. How does the God you know speak to this situation?

Margaret

Margaret finds Christianity irrelevant to her life. Her husband left her six years ago. She has three children, the eldest of them just out of school and unemployed. They live in government housing in one of the poorer parts of the city, where she fears for her children because of the violence of the neighbourhood, the gangs that roam the streets and the access to drugs of all kinds. Financial survival is a constant preoccupation and she lives without much hope that life will change for the better. She feels that there is nothing left for her, that she has failed, and she finds herself overwhelmed by bouts of loneliness. Margaret has not abandoned the Church completely but the doctrines and liturgy have little meaning for her. What matters for her is what she experiences each day: the battle to survive, the daily round of work, her hope that her son will find a job, the endurance of loneliness and her hunger for companionship, a hunger that often is met only by the television.

Julia

Julia is a young woman approaching thirty. She finds herself doubting the existence of God. At some times she is inclined to believe in 'something' but at other times she thinks of herself as a non-believer, an atheist. Julia was brought up as a Christian and admits to having picked up from her religious background some important values, including a sense of justice. She is generous and compassionate in the way she lives her life, but the word 'God' and the language of the church mean little to her. The church's idea of God seems far-fetched and alien. It fails to connect with anything which is within the range of her experience. Julia's commitment to social issues is strong, but she finds within herself an emptiness and an obscure hunger for something more. She knows that she has a need for depth and meaning, but she can't be satisfied with superficial answers.

Tom

Tom is a Christian committed to his local parish and to Sunday Eucharist. He has worked hard all his life and he and his wife have watched their children leave home to begin their own families. As he begins his retirement from work he finds life empty. He has high blood pressure and is becoming increasingly conscious that he is in the last stage of life and that his own death must be faced. Tom believes that God exists, that this God has been revealed to us in Jesus Christ, that the church teaches in the name of Jesus and that we are transformed by God's grace. However, he has always believed that grace operates at a level beyond anything he might experience. His faith has always been largely a matter of intellectual assent. Now, as Tom faces the bleak emptiness of his life, his failing health and the possibility of death, his own kind of faith has little to offer him. It makes no connection with his own struggle. He has no access to the richness and joy of a more personal faith that could lead him to wisdom and to peace and the capacity to love more creatively.

Martin

Martin is committed to the church, but his faith has a character entirely different from that of Tom. A family man in his early forties, Martin recently went through a remarkable conversion experience. In his own language he 'found God' and he found Christian community in a charismatic prayer group. All his earlier church life seems nothing compared to his new experience. Martin now speaks easily and often of God and gives the impression of having easy access to God. He believes that God is manifested to those with faith and on different occasions he claims to be directly guided by God in his decisions.

(Taken from 'The Human Experience of God', Denis Edwards, Gill & Macmillan, Dublin, 1983)

SESSION FOUR

The God of Moses

Aims
- To see how the Bible can influence the way we relate to God.
- To situate Moses in his historical context.
- To look at how Moses experienced God and how this experience was expressed.

Materials
Copies of inputs from previous session.
Charts for presentation on Moses.
Chart on key figures and how revelation happens.
Chart with characteristics of the God of Moses (Yahweh)

Time-Table
1. 7.45: Welcome.
2. 8.10: Focusing activity.
3. 8.20: Presentation.
4. 8.40: Buzz Session.

   9.00: Break

5. 9.20: Exploration of the Scriptures
6. 9.50 Open reflection
7. 10.05: Leader's response extempore and reminders re tasks and readings.

Suggested Procedure

1. Welcome
Welcome the people and describe this session and its aims.
Team tasks: news, report, commentary.
Prayer.

2. Focusing Activity
a) In our personal and social history there are KEY FIGURES who influence the way we look at life and the way we act. Their insights, ideas and values influence the way we relate to the world around us, e.g. James Larkin has deeply influenced the way Irish workers think about themselves and the way they organise.

b) Can you name others? Brainstorm and write up names suggested.

c) How have some of these influenced us?

3. Presentation
The God of Moses
Looking at ourselves as members of the people who believe in God we realise we have a common history and in that history there are key figures who influence our way of thinking about God and life. They have had very clear insights into the nature of God and God's plan. They have expressed these experiences of God in images, words and stories to help the rest of us relate to God and motivate us to do God's will. People have considered these so important that they have written them down and communicated them from generation to generation to help us relate more truthfully to God.

The following is material which can be tailored to suit the time and the people with whom you are working. Obviously there is more given than you would use.The accompanying charts will be a good guide for selection of points.

Moses, his country, his people, his God
We have seen that in our lives, there have been *key figures* who have influenced the way we *see* God and the way we *understand* God's will. We have mentioned parents, grandparents, teachers, priests, friends.

Key Figures are those people whose lives, words and actions affect the way we see things and what we do. For instance in Irish History there have been key figures who continue to have an influence on us: Pádraig Pearse, James Connolly, Jim Larkin, King William of Orange, Edel Quinn. On a world level there are other key figures who influence the way people think and act: Mother Teresa, Ghandi, Martin Luther King, Pope John XXIII.

In the history of the people of God there are also *key figures* whose insights and lives affect the way we relate to God. They *expressed* their experiences of God in images, stories and symbols, *to help us relate to God and live out of this relationship.* Others have considered these so important they have written them down to help the rest of us hear God and respond to God. That is how the Bible came about: communities wrote down the stories of Moses and the prophets, to help others find God and do God's will.

Jesus himself was born into the people of God and from early childhood he would have heard the stories of *Moses* and the prophets. These would have helped him know God, know himself, know how to relate to others.

In this session we want to highlight the person of Moses, a key figure in Jesus' education and our own. Let us see how he experienced God, and expressed his experience in stories, symbols, images, and that will shape our own image of God.

Jesus would have read in the Bible:
Yahweh would talk to Moses face to face as a man talks to his friend. (Exodus 33:11)
and
Since then there has never been such a prophet in Israel as Moses, the man whom Yahweh knew face to face. (Deuteronomy 34:10)

In the new Testament Moses is mentioned eighty times. At Jesus' transfiguration Moses is mentioned along with Elijah the prophet.

Situation: Canaan – Egypt
To understand Moses and see how radical his ideas about God were you have to appreciate that he was a real flesh-and- blood person who lived in a land where there was an economy, political power, social classes and a particular culture and religion. Let's turn our minds back to that part of the world called Canaan and Egypt, between the years 1800-1200 B.C.

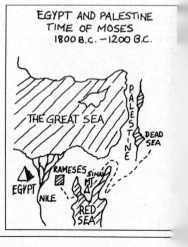

EGYPT AND PALESTINE
TIME OF MOSES
1800 B.C. –1200 B.C.

Our spiritual ancestors were living in that land when it was invaded by a foreign power – the *Hyksos*. These people had an advanced technology (horse-drawn vehicles and cross-bows). They came and dominated the people. They built walled cities and with their armies they forced the people to work for them.

Later, they themselves were dominated by the Pharoah and the Egyptians who played them off, one against the other. So let's look at the situation of the society at that time:

Economy
The kings and Pharoahs had the ownership of the land. The people toiled on the land and had to hand over their surplus crops to their rulers. They had barely enough to survive on.

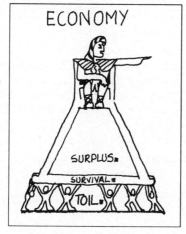

Politics
The people had no say in regard to anything. The power was in the hands of the Pharoah and the Kings. They lived in the palace and in the walled cities. They accumulated wealth in crops and taxes and they had armies to see that work was done. So the people were exploited and powerless. And the Kings were in turn strongly controlled by the Pharoah.

Social Set-up
The social set-up was like this:

Pharoah
Kings
Administration

Tax Collectors
Armies
Artisans
Farming people
Labourers
Armed bandits

Culture
The people were illiterate. The Egyptian alphabet was very difficult.

Religion was set up in such a way that it left the situation just the way it was. The Gods were just a reflection of the status quo (the way things were). The Pharoah had his gods who 'blessed' his situation. The kings had their gods who were with and for them. The priests at that time had land and they liked the way things were, so they told stories of the gods and had celebrations which agreed and confirmed the way things were.

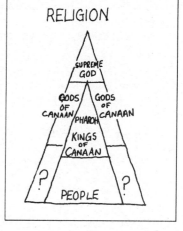

The *people* were a disconnected people, marginalised, oppressed, no traditions, and if they ever thought of god, it was as a non-entity, non-active, non-freeing, who just left them in their misery.

Oppression – death
At one stage when life was unbearable in Canaan, many of the people went down into Egypt where they could find work, labouring for the Pharoah. Gradually they were dominated and enslaved. When they increased in numbers or showed any sign of resistance the Pharoah clamped down on them with force, with cut-backs, even to the extent of killing their male offspring.

On one of these occasions, Moses' mother hid him in the river where he was rescued by the Pharoah's daughter. He was brought up in the palace and received all the privileges of education, nourishment and comfort. He experienced the good life and forgot about his own people.

Oppression – Violence – Moses
The story of Moses is found in chapters 2 and 3 of the Book of Exodus, and in chapter 7 of the Acts of the Apostles.

He defended the interests of the Pharoah. But one day he went along to where his kinspeople were and he witnessed their suffering and he saw an Egyptian punishing a Hebrew. He, in anger, went to defend the Hebrew and ended up killing the Egyptian. Moses, afraid that the Pharoah might hear, ran away into the desert.

This was a very significant experience in the life of Moses. He carried the memories of this sense of failure, of dashed hopes and disappointment into the desert. Gradually there built up in him that need to meet someone to give him hope and meaning. In his pain, anger and disappointment, he seeks God.

First Period of Moses's life
You can see he is blessed. He is saved from death and is given a select education. *He was taught all the wisdom of the Egyptians* – political, economic, technical and cultural. The result is that Moses 'becomes a man with power both in his speech and actions' (Acts 7:22). He had learned much, both from theories and ideas. You might say all the education kept him from seeing reality as it was. He is in minimal contact with his own people's reality.

Second Period
In the second period we see Moses full of *idealism and generosity* come down among the people. He experiences his peo-

ple *suffering* and he receives a great shock. He feels great *anger* when he sees an Egyptian punishing a Hebrew. He goes to defend the Hebrew and ends up killing the Egyptian.

He begins to draw away from the privileged life in the Pharaoh's palace and wants to set about liberating his people: 'I, Moses, have been educated in freedom. I know what freedom means. So I will go to my people and propose this liberty to them. They will acclaim me as their leader and we will all march together...' But all of this was only a plan, an idea.

Moses had no realistic idea of the state of his people – of their possible resistance. (The worst part of their suffering was that they grew used to it). It hadn't entered his mind. But in Acts 7:27-29 we read of the total *collapse of Moses*, a man with immense generosity who had renounced privileges in order to be oppressed with the oppressed. The Bible describes the fiasco that Moses experienced at the hands of his people. They not only refused to recognise him but also reacted: 'Who ever told you to bother about us? We're not interested.' *He was rejected by those he intended to teach.*

He has failed with Pharaoh, severing all connections. He fears Pharoah will look for him. He has failed as a person. He is now a nobody. The courageous Moses has become fearful. He who was ready to risk his own life is now saving his skin. He has lost his head, he wants to get away as soon as possible. He runs away to a strange land where nobody knows him.

He is an *impoverished, frightened* man, startled *by every rustling of leaves* in the night and in the desert. 'I've enough of big ideas, and big undertakings. All my dreams of being a liberator are finished; enough of politics. I too have a right to my own life.' Moses wanted to look for a quiet little place where he could forget the past and these bitter experiences.

Third Period: God breaks into Moses's life

After years of reflecting in *solitude* on his experience, Moses is ripe for something new. In his solitude he realises that nothing has satisfied him; all theories, ideas, experiences have brought little integration. He carries with him disappointment, pain, anger. He is searching, questioning.

Then one day the breakthrough comes. God breaks through into his life. In the Bible the image of the burning bush is used to convey the sense of wonder that the elderly Moses was experiencing.

He sees in the distance a bush burning without being consumed. Moses, *worn out by failure but progressively purified* by solitude and reflection, is ripe for something new.

He wonders, he pays attention, he considers, he reflects, he tries to understand. 'I want to see, to know, to begin again.' He is experiencing a *moment of mystery*.

The Acts of the Apostles puts it in this way: 'When Yahweh saw him going across to look, God called to him from the middle of the bush: "Moses, Moses."' Moses hears his name.

Moses becomes aware that someone who knows him must be there, someone who is interested in him. He had considered himself rejected, unsuccessful, abandoned. Regardless of that, someone is calling his name in the middle of the desert. 'Moses, Moses.' Like as if we were lost in a big city and suddenly someone calls us by name. 'Phyllis, Phyllis.'

This is a decisive moment. Moses is filled with fear: 'What is going to happen to me now?' Presently he hears something he is not expecting. 'Come no nearer ... take off your sandals for the place you are standing on is holy ground.' God is saying: 'Lay aside your ideas of who I am or what I'm like ... I don't fit into your plan.'

Moses thinks: 'This is holy ground, this cursed desert, the abode of jackals, of desolation!'

What does Moses understand?

At this point Moses understands what God's initiative is. It is not Moses who is seeking God and who has therefore to go to purified and holy places to find God. Rather, it is God who seeks Moses and seeks him where he is, in the place where he happens to be, even if it is a miserable, abandoned, accursed place, devoid of resources.

In this encounter he starts to understand that *God is merciful and loving, is concerned about him and about his people*. 'I am the God of your mother, and father, and grandparents and all who have educated you in faith, and of all the key figures who formed you spiritually.'

But to understand how God really is, we continue with Exodus 3:7-9. Notice how carefully worded the text is, all in the first person. 'I have seen', 'I have heard', 'I am well aware', 'I have come down', and God might as well say: 'If there is any compassion in you at all for the people, it comes from me. If you have any sense of freedom, it is I who gives it to you.'

And at this point God says to Moses: 'Now Go. Go and make my dreams come true with my people. I am sending you to Pharaoh, "to let my people go". And if they ask, tell them I have sent you. Tell them I am the one who is among them to free them.' Then Moses realised that he was freed from the bonds of his own presumptions and slowly he yielded to this compassionate, loving, freeing God whose instrument he was called to be. He would communicate this God to the people. The people who had no God would now share this insight and this hope and struggle.

Image of God:
Present, Compassionate, Taking sides, Liberating

Through Moses it is communicated that God is present within and beyond history, that God is compassionate, merciful and is a God of liberation, that God is on the side of the wounded, miserable and oppressed, that God wants us to co-operate with his liberating spirit for a new situation.

This is the God Moses communicates to the people. This is truly a revolutionary statement because, up to now, the people had felt that they had no God or only a useless God but now they are in touch with Yahweh, who wants to be in a covenant, an alliance, with them, so they can be free of misery and oppresssion and move into a new way of life in unity with God and with each other in equality, power-sharing, respect and a living worship.

Moses, of course, does not accept the task without putting up resistance.

Summary:
Image, Action, Story, Passed on
In our history as people of God, we have the key figure of Moses, who experienced the presence of this liberating, loving God in the suffering of his people, who reflected on it in the solitude of the desert. Moses communicated this God, Yahweh, to the people, in words, stories and symbols. Thus the people could relate to God in a new way, could relate to life and society in a new way and could organise a new society in accord with the will of this God. And they kept the remembrance of this God alive by passing the story from generation to generation so that they would never agree with oppression, division, and non-development again.

God of Moses
– One God.
– Present within and beyond life.
– Compassionate and merciful.
– Takes sides with the wounded, hurt, oppressed.
– Liberating God.
– Wants us to co-operate in the building of a better world.

(Much of the above is taken from 'Through Moses to Jesus' by Carlo Martini, Ave Maria Press, 1988)

4. Buzz Session
After the presentation of points, give people time to buzz and take any comments or reactions they have. Note what will have to be dealt with.

BREAK

5. Exploration of the Scriptures
Number off 1,2,3,4, with all the ones going together etc, until you have groups of four.

Distribute the text in Handout 6 with the accompanying questions in Handout 7. Ask that someone in each group be designated to co-ordinate the reflection and sharing. Illustrate with a couple of examples how people may use the material.

6. Open Reflection
Use the following questions to help the group articulate their thoughts about the sessions:
a) What struck you from what you have dealt with tonight?
b) What are your impressions of Moses and the God of Moses?
c) Is that God active in the world today? Where?

7. Leader's Response
The leader responds extempore using the chart with the characteristics of the God of Moses.

8. Conclusion
Remind the groups about the Team tasks. Invite them all to read Exodus chapters 2 and 3 and Acts chapter 7.

Handout 6

Exodus 3: 1-15

The burning bush

MOSES was looking after the flock of Jethro, his father-in-law, priest of Midian. He led his flock to the far side of the wilderness and came to Horeb, the mountain of God. There the angel of Yahweh appeared to him in the shape of a flame of fire, coming from the middle of a bush. Moses looked; there was the bush blazing but it was not being burnt up. 'I must go and look at this strange sight,' Moses said, 'and see why the bush is not burnt.' Now Yahweh saw him go forward to look, and God called to him from the middle of the bush. 'Moses, Moses!' he said. 'Here I am,' he answered. 'Come no nearer,' he said. 'Take off your shoes, for the place on which you stand is holy ground. I am the God of your father,' he said, 'the God of Abraham, the God of Isaac and the God of Jacob.' At this Moses covered his face, afraid to look at God.

The mission of Moses

And Yahweh said, 'I have seen the miserable state of my people in Egypt. I have heard their appeal to be free from their slave-drivers. Yes, I am well aware of their sufferings. I mean to deliver them out of the hands of the Egyptians and bring them out of that land to a land rich and broad, a land where milk and honey flow, the home of the Canaanites, the Hittites, the Amorites, the Perizzites, the Hivites and the Jebusites. And now the cry of the sons of Israel has come to me, and I have witnessed the way in which the Egyptians oppress them, so come, I send you to Pharaoh to bring the sons of Israel, my people, out of Egypt.'

Moses said to God, 'Who am I to go to Pharaoh and bring the sons of Israel out of Egypt?' 'I shall be with you,' was the answer, 'and this is the sign by which you shall know that it is I who have sent you ... After you have led the people out of Egypt, you are to offer worship to God on this mountain.'

The divine name revealed

Then Moses said to God, 'I am to go, then, to the sons of Israel and say to them, "The God of your fathers has sent me to you". But if they ask me what his name is, what am I to tell them?' And God said to Moses, 'I Am who I Am. This,' he added, 'is what you must say to the sons of Israel: "I Am has sent me to you".' And God also said to Moses, 'You are to say to the sons of Israel: "Yahweh, the God of your fathers, the God of Abraham, the God of Isaac and the God of Jacob, has sent me to you.". This is my name for all time; by this name shall be invoked for all generations to come.'

Handout 7

Looking into the Scriptures [25 minutes]
(Taken from NIV Serendipity Bible for Study Groups, Zonderman Bible Publishers, Serendipity House, Littleton, CO 80160)

1. I am more likely to: [place your x along the line to reflect yourself]

take the initiative to meet people   wait for someone to come to me

be easily distracted from my work   never lift my head

make a lot of excuses to avoid getting involved   volunteer for everything

remember a person's name the first time   call everybody 'you'

2. What do you think Moses felt when he saw the burning bush?
(a) Fear
(b) curiosity
(c) awe
(d) confusion

3. What was Moses saying by hiding his face from God?
(a) oh no, what have I done now?
(b) what could God possibly want with me?
(c) God is too holy to look at
(d) I am your humble servant

4. What question was God answering in the first paragraph?
(a) where have you been?
(b) have you any heart?
(c) what happened to your promise to Abraham?
(d) how are you going to solve our problem?

5. What is the 'good news' in the second paragraph?
(a) I have heard my people
(b) I am concerned about their suffering
(c) I will rescue them from the Egyptians
(d) I will bring you into the promised land

6. What is the 'bad news' in the second paragraph?
(a) there's going to be a battle
(b) the land I promised you belongs to someone else right now
(c) I'm sending you to Pharaoh
(d) you are going to lead the people out of Egypt

7. What was God doing by giving Moses his name?
(a) initiating a relationship
(b) revealing his nature
(c) overcoming Moses' latest objection
(d) giving Moses something to hang on to

My Own Story [20 minutes]

1. The 'burning bush' (God's attention-getter) in my life has been:
(a) what God has done in a friend's life
(b) personal crisis
(c) the friendship of other Christians
(d) frustrated plans in my life
(e) unusual successes coming my way
(f) a meaningful worship experience
(g) a particular Bible passage

2. In my life, God's initiative has been:
(a) intermittent
(b) persistent
(c) nonexistent
(d) thunder and lightning

3. If I were in Moses' shoes, I'd share his:
(a) fear of looking God square in the eye
(b) sense of inadequacy to do God's work
(c) concern for what others think of me
(d) wondering if God's plan will work

4. What is God's name for you? I AM ...:
(a) forgiving
(b) loving
(c) patient
(d) tough
(e) all you'll ever need
(f) with you

SESSION FIVE

God's Dream for People

Aims
• To begin to explore the kind of society God wants for people, as revealed in the Old Testament.
• To see the Ten Commandments as the Constitution of a new society.

Materials
Copies of input from previous sessions for distribution.
Copies of report and commentary on the last session.
Charts for a recap of situation in Egypt.
Questionnaire on Vision of Society.
Handout on the Ten Commandments, with questions for the home task.
Six sheets of newsprint, adhesive material and six felt pens.

Time-Table
1.	7.45	Welcome.
2.	8.05	Recap on the situation in Egypt.
3.	8.15	Vision of New Society. Group work.
4.	8.50	Plenary session.
	9.05	BREAK
5.	9.20	Presentation: Vision of a New Society.
6.	9.40	Buzz on the presentation
7.	10.00	Conclusion.
8.	10.15	Final Prayer.

Suggested Procedure

1. Welcome
Welcome the people and describe the sessions's aims and time-table.
Team Tasks: news, report, commentary, prayer.

2. Recap on the situation in Egypt.
Using posters and handout from previous sessions, recap briefly:
> – The social, political and economic situation at the time of Moses, which led to the Exodus.
> – God, as revealed by Moses, is one, unique and liberating.
> – Recall the Exodus of the people, journey across the desert, the emergence of the Covenant. 'You will be my people and I will be your God.'
> – Based on their concept of God, the Israelites struggled to build a society that would embody God's dream for people, i.e. because God is one, all are equal in God's sight.

3. Vision of the New Society
In your minds, recall the situation in which the Hebrews lived and remember how God broke through to them and moved them towards a new kind of society where there would be equality, freedom and participation. Put yourselves in the shoes of the Israelites at this time when they were trying to develop the new society. Each of you will receive an area of life to deal with. Use your imagination and ask yourselves:

'How would we as Israelites arrange this aspect of society in the light of our experience of Egypt and our new insight into God? It's the year 2000 BC; we are in the Promised Land.'

Distribute Handout 8. Assign an area of concern to each local group. Instructions are on the Handout.

4. Plenary Session
Each group shares the results of their imaginative work.

BREAK

5. Presentation
Using the posters and material below as a basis, make a presentation of what the Israelites actually did.

1. God's Dream for People
BEFORE: VARIOUS GODS   AFTER: ONE UNIQUE GOD

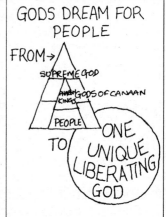

The most basic question for the Israelites and for us today is: 'In what God do I believe?' This is a really key question because the image of God we have influences in a very critical way the way we see others, the way we see life, the way we act towards others and the choices we make.

The people had been used to various gods who had legitimated oppression and exploitation: the Pharaoh and the kings had presented an image of a god who was on their side and backing up their use of power, wealth, etc. This left no hope for the ordinary people.

Yahweh – Liberator God
That's why the new image of God which came to them through Moses was such a breakthrough. Here now was God, the one and only, unique God, communicating that all people are equal and that there is only one God – not one god for Pharaoh and another for the kings. Faith in the One God means that there is no place for inequality or social or racial discrimination.

Covenant
When the Bible talks of 'One' God, it is speaking not only in numerical terms (one: not three or four) but in terms of exclusivity: for the people, God is only this One who presents himself as Yahweh, liberator God. This God is different ... believing in this God we are challenged to organise society in such a way that there will be no domination or exploitation. All are meant to live as brothers and sisters, not some on top and some on the bottom. To love this God is to love your neighbour as you love yourself, not to dominate him or her. This God, who is seen as a faithful spouse, who won't let people down, makes a covenant with the people, an agreement: 'I will be faithful to you,' and the people are called to respond by being faithful to the struggle for a new society in which they can have their basic needs satisfied and experience a fulfilling life.

2. Economics
BEFORE: OWNERSHIP BY FEW (EXPLOITATION)
AFTER: OWNERSHIP BY THE PEOPLE

In Egypt and under the kings the means of production – the land – was centralised in the hands of the kings who accumulated wealth by exploiting people, taking their land and making them work for them.

In the new situation after the covenant, the land is declared God's possession, not the kings' and the people are the stewards of the land. The families or smaller communities are owners of the land and of its production and can dispose of it commercially. Laws were made to ensure that each tribe would have its piece of land on which to plant and survive.

Even though these laws were made, some families still increased their plot of land to a large holding, causing loss and hunger to others: it was to avoid this abuse, and to keep the idea of economic equality, that the law of the Jubilee Year was made. Every 50 years all purchases were dismantled and the land returned to its first owners.
Read Joshua, chapter 24; Numbers 36:1-9; Deuteronomy 6:13-19.

So there was a way of preventing huge differences in income and wealth. This change was possible because the political power was decentralised in an intelligent way.

3. Politics
BEFORE: CENTRALISATION (POWER IN THE HANDS OF THE KING)
AFTER: DECENTRALISATION OF POWER

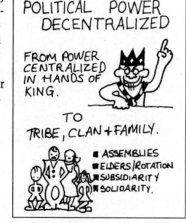

In the tribal system, power was exercised according to the principle of subsidiarity, .i.e. what can be decided on the ground need not be brought to a higher level. The 'family leaders' had autonomy within their respective families or communities.

Apart from the principle of subsidiarity there was the principle of solidarity which prevented groups closing in on just their own interests. The families had obligations with the 'clans' (clusters of families) and the clans had obligations within the tribe. All of this was regulated by the laws.

Joshua 24 indicates how this decentralised power worked. It was more than a right to vote. The people had their 'chiefs' or 'elders' who took part in assemblies of the people where there was free speech and where the directions (priorities) of the people were decided in a communitarian way. This kind of participation in all areas of life freed people from arbitrary power and oppression.

4. Social Set-up
BEFORE: HIERARCHY
AFTER: SOCIAL EQUALITY

They developed a way of organising life in which everyone was respected – there was no great difference in status or prestige. They organised themselves into a tribal system – the twelve tribes of Israel – very different from and opposed to the old system of the city-state and Egyptian imperialism. They attempted to develop a system in which each person would have equal social status (except women!!) and people would relate on the basis of fellow-feeling or community instead of grouping themselves into economic and social pyramids. The organisation was based on mutual solidarity. The smallest unit was the patriarchal family, the intermediate was the clan and the greatest unity was the confederation of tribes. All this organisation was set up so that the smallest unit would have as much control over its affairs as possible. Even a new alphabet was developed with twenty-five letters so that each one could learn to read and write and not be dependent on others to interpret information, etc.

5. Laws
BEFORE: LAWS THAT DEFENDED THE INTERESTS OF THE KING
AFTER: LAWS WHICH DEFEND THE SOCIETY OF EQUALITY

The one God, Yahweh, the liberator, entered into a covenant (alliance/ agreement) with the people. They expressed their faith in Yahweh by organising a society based on equality. This was God's project for humanity and out of it came the Ten Commandments (Decalogue – Ten Words) which were aimed at protecting this new way of living. We are used to interpreting the Ten Commandments in a merely individualistic way, e.g. as sins which people should avoid, commandments that should not be 'broken'. But the people of Israel saw them more as their constitution, safeguarding and defining their new kind of society. Because the people believed in the One God, they accepted God's view of humanity, 'we are all equal and so we must live in such a way as to ensure that equality.' The Ten Commandments are the guidelines for living like that.

> THE TEN COMMANDMENTS ARE THE CONSTITUTION OF A NEW SOCIETY THAT BELIEVES IN GOD WHO IS ONE COMPASSIONATE AND LIBERATING.

The Ten Commandments as the Constitution of a new Society according to God's dream

Here is a way of interpreting the Ten Commandments which keeps close to their original intention: *The text below, which is the content of Handout 9, without the questions added for each commandment, can be used for the presentation.*
Note: Because of the way the commandments have been intepreted in an individualistic way, people often find it hard to think of them from a broader perspective, e.g. of social injustice, and may need to be gently encouraged to move to this level.

The Commandments	
First:	You cannot use the name of our liberating God to legitimate injustice or oppression.
Second:	We cannot limit God to our own narrow, self-centred ideas and plans. (Idols)
Third:	The sabbath is for resting in order to remember the purpose of our work: the building of a world of peace and joy. (A 'trailer' or free sample of God's dream.)
Fourth:	Families in community must be respected and built up. Their rights must be defended. They must have freedom to use power for good.
Fifth:	We must organise a society which promotes life for everybody. Life must be seen as a gift to be nurtured.
Sixth:	Relationships between men and women must be marked by equality and mutual love and faithfulness.
Seventh:	Everyone must have sufficient. Everyone needs comfort and security. No one can have the law allowing them to rob.
Eighth:	The new system will work only if we are all converted to truth in our relationships. Without love of truth, trust and dialogue are impossible.
Ninth and Tenth:	Community and equality are only possible when we get rid of greed and the desire to possess and accumulate.

First : Do not take the name of God in vain
In Egypt under the Pharaohs and in Canaan under the kings, the name of God was used to justify their unjust systems and oppressive actions. The Pharaoh was not relating to the true God, Yahweh, but to an idol – a false god. 'Vain' here means anything connected with a system of inequality and domination which is not God's dream for people. You cannot use the name of God to legitimate oppression, (e.g. in South Africa, some people say that apartheid is God's will and therefore it's all right.)

Second: Do not have false images of God
In Egypt there were people using false images of God to justify oppression. A community that wants to serve the true God must avoid at all costs letting a false image of God creep into their imaginations. We cannot make 'gods' of money, power, exploitation.

Third: Remember to observe the sabbath (seventh) day
In the system under the Pharaohs and the kings, the workers were exploited. If they took rest they were called lazy and punished. The law of the sabbath is to do away with exploitation of people and to guarantee they have rest. Not just to get energy to work harder but to be able to remember why they worked: through work they were co-creating with God, bringing the world to its completion, preparing for a future of peace and joy for all in God's presence. The rest gave them a chance to remember who they were: people loved and freed by God; to celebrate being alive and to gather strength for the journey of life.

Fourth: Honour your father and your mother
In Egypt and Canaan honour was demanded for the kings and Pharaohs. Their will was to be obeyed. In the new system power was to be in the families. At that time, the family was equivalent to a community of families today. That is where decisions were made. This commandment defends the authority of the families in community and of the leaders of these groupings.

Fifth: Do not kill
The system of the Pharaoh did not favour life but rather death to anyone who went against the system. Once freed from the house of slavery the people had to organise themselves in such a way that life was given maximum respect. Do not kill. Everyone must have the right to life. We must build a society where life is valued.

Sixth: Do not commit adultery
The organisation of society in the form of a pyramid, with someone dominating people below, had entered the lifestyle of the people. Families imitated this inequality as men were considered superior to women. Man was the absolute ruler; women and children had no voice or power. A married man could have sexual relations with a single girl (just pay the father). A woman who had a relationship with another man was called an adulterer. So within marriage itself there was inequality and domination. In the new system the pyramid would only be totally destroyed when men and women would live in real equality, complementing one another. Relationships would be equal to equal, in love. Equality must penetrate the intimacy of marriage. Betrayal of one's companion, as much for men as for women, is out.

Seventh: Do not steal
The system of the Pharaohs and kings was based on robbery. The Pharaoh and the kings could take the lands and animals, products, labourers, sons and daughters of the people. They did not pay salaries and robbed the physical force of people. Saying 'Do not rob' is not directed in the first place to the individual but to the people. God wants a new organisation which will not be based on robbery . To stop one part of the people from robbing another part, they knew how to make laws, like the Jubilee Law: after fifty years all sales and purchases of land were undone.

Eighth: Do not say false testimony against your neighbour
The system of the Pharaohs was based on lies. They proclaimed to the people: 'I am the Son of God' and in the name of this lie they oppressed and exploited the people. Pharaoh did what he liked and the poor could not achieve their rights. Judges and lawyers were bought at the courts and no-one defended the rights of the poor, orphans, widows, etc. Love of truth was gone. This commandment is saying, 'do not imitate the example given by the corrupt systems and have the courage to defend your brother/sister, above all the poor, at the courts.'
It also says, 'Struggle for a system in which it may be possible for all to achieve their rights in justice and in which it is impossible to give false testimony against your brother or sister.' Apart from this, the eighth commandment wants to promote love of truth as the basis for relationships between people. Without love of truth, love is destroyed at its roots and life in community is impossible. The new organisation is not just a question of economic and political equality, but a question of sincere conversion of hearts and minds to truth

Ninth & Tenth: Do not covet what belongs to your neighbour
It isn't enough not to rob if one doesn't combat the greed which leads to robbery. It is necessary to eradicate from within oneself the desire to possess, the will to accumulate more and more things. Today the media of different kinds promote the possession of false and artificial necessities. People feel they have to possess more. Very often the bodies of young women are used demeaningly to promote the buying of products. We need a new spirit: simplicity and detachment (not needing many things) in a new society.

6.Buzz Session

Immediately after the presentation allow time for a buzz on the following:
  What struck you what surprised you?
  What puzzled you?
and encourage feedback.

7.Conclusion

Home Task:
Each one receives a copy of the commentary on the Ten Commandments (Handout 9) and each group is asked to make a collage of headlines, photos, or cartoons showing the fulfillment or abuse of a particular commandment, in society today.

8.Final Prayer

Choose a few lines from a suitable Old Testament prayer passage.

Handout 8

Vision of a New Society

We have seen the situation of the people in Egypt.
We have seen that God revealed through Moses, is one, unqiue and against oppression.
God wants freedom and a better situation for people.
Let your imagination flow freely and see what kind of society
the new society in the promised land would be.

Each group has one area to work on.
Use the attached questions to think about the area of life.
Draw up a list of 3-5 recommendations, e.g. 'We would like a situation in which ...'
and put them on newsprint to show to the other groups.

Group 1: Land
1. Who should own the land?
2. How should the land be distributed?
3. What should happen to the produce of the land (livestock, crops, etc)?

Group 2: Political Situation
1. Who should have the power to make decisions about how the country is run?
2. Where should decisions be made?
3. How would you ensure that all had a chance to participate?

Group 3: Housing
1. What should be done to provide adequate housing for everybody?
2. Who should own the houses?
3. Should people be allowed to own their own houses? Just one house? Or as many as they want to?

Group 4: Human Well-being
1. How should the good health of people be promoted?
2. What would ensure that people's lives would be protected and nurtured?
3. What would help people not only to live but to develop their lives?

Group 5: Work and Industry
1. Who should decide what is produced?
2. What should this decision be based on?
3. What should be done to prevent a few people exploiting others?

Group 6: Wages
1. Should there be a minimum wage?
2. Should there be any kind of control limiting the amount of money one person can make?
3. How could we ensure that everybody has the opportunity to save money and to borrow money for worthwhile purposes?

Handout 9a
Instructions

Each one from your group gathers some headlines, photos or cartoons, etc. that show where a commandment is being fulfilled or is being abused. The members of the group come together and pool their contributions. They choose some that make the point clearly and, either at home or at the beginning of the next meeting, stick them on a sheet of newsprint.

First: Do not take the name of God in vain

In Egypt under the Pharaohs and in Canaan under the kings, the name of God was used to justify their unjust systems and oppressive actions. The Pharaoh was not relating to the true God, Yahweh but to an idol – a false god. 'Vain' here means anything connected with a system of inequality and domination which is not God's dream for people. You cannot use the name of God to legitimate oppression, (e.g. in South Africa, some people say that apartheid is God's will and therefore it's all right.)

Choose some cuttings that show:
a) Contradictions between belief in God (Yahweh) and certain actions/situations.
b) Situations/actions which reveal what God really wants.

Second: Do not have false images of God

In Egypt there were people using false images of God to justify oppression. A community that wants to serve the true God must avoid at all costs letting a false image of God creep into their imaginations. We cannot make 'gods' of money, power, exploitation.

Choose some cuttings that show:
a) Situations/actions in which people have a true image of God.
b) Situations/actions which seem to show people following idols such as money, power, etc, rather than God.

Third: Remember To Observe The Sabbath (seventh) Day

In the system under the Pharaohs and the kings the workers were exploited. If they took rest they were called lazy and punished. The law of the sabbath is to do away with exploitation of people and to guarantee they have rest. Not just to get energy to work harder but to be able to remember why they worked: through work they were co-

creating with God, bringing the world to its completion, preparing for a future of peace and joy for all in God's presence. The rest gave them a chance to remember who they were: people loved and freed by God; to celebrate being alive and to gather strength for the journey of life.

Choose cuttings which show:
a) People celebrating the day of rest in a meaningful way,
b) A negative or unfruitful use of the day of rest.

Fourth: Honour your father and your mother

In Egypt and Canaan honour was demanded for the kings and Pharaohs. Their will was to be obeyed. In the new system power was to be in the families. At that time, the family was equivalent to a community of families today. That is where decisions were made. This commandment defends the authority of the families in community and of the leaders of these groupings.

Choose some cuttings that show:
a) Families/communities being supported and built up.
b) Families/communities being weakened or attacked.

Fifth: Do not kill

The system of the Pharaoh did not favour life but rather death to anyone who went against the system. Once freed from the house of slavery the people had to organise themselves in such a way that life was given maximum respect. Do not kill. Everyone must have the right to life. We must build a society where life is valued.

Choose some cuttings which show:
a) Efforts to respect, nurture, develop life.
b) Where life is abused, diminished, taken away.

Handout 9b
Instructions

Each one from your group gathers some headlines, photos or cartoons, etc. that show where a commandment is being fulfilled or is being abused. The members of the group come together and pool their contributions. They choose some that make the point clearly and, either at home or at the beginning of the next meeting, stick them on a sheet of newsprint.

Sixth: Do not commit adultery

The organisation of society in the form of a pyramid with someone dominating people below had entered the lifestyle of the people. Families imitated this inequality as men were considered superior to women. Man was the absolute ruler; women and children had no voice or power. A married man could have sexual relations with a single girl (just pay the father). A woman who had a relationship with another man called an adulterer. So within marriage itself there was inequality and domination. In the new system the pyramid would only be totally destroyed when men and women would live in real equality, complementing one another. Relationships would be equal to equal, in love. Equality must penetrate the intimacy of marriage. Betrayal of one's companion, as much for men as for women, is out.
Choose cuttings which show:
a) Real equality between men and women.
b) Inequality between men and women.

Seventh: Do not steal

The system of the Pharaohs and kings was based on robbery. The Pharaoh and the kings could take the lands and animals, products, labourers, sons and daughters of the people. They did not pay salaries and robbed the physical force of people. Saying 'Do not rob' is nor directed in the first place to the individual but to the people. God wants a new organisation which will not be based on robbery . To stop one part of the people from robbing another part they knew how to make laws, like the Jubilee Law: after fifty years all sales and purchases of land were undone.
Choose some cuttings which show:
a) situations of exploitation or disrespect for means of livelihood and life. b) Situations where there is a fair distribution of goods and the promotion of people's means of life.

Eighth: Do not say false testimony against your neighbour

The system of the Pharaohs was based on lies. They proclaimed to the people:'I am the Son of God' and in the name of this lie they oppressed and exploited the people. Pharaoh did what he liked and the poor could not achieve their rights...judges and lawyers were bought at the courts and no-one defended the rights of the poor, orphans, widows, etc. Love of truth was gone.This commandment is saying, 'do not imitate the example given by the corrupt systems and have the courage to defend your brother/ sister, above all the poor, at the courts.'
It also says: Struggle for a system in which it may be possible for all to achieve their rights in justice and in which it is impossible to give false testimony against your brother or sister. Apart from this, the eighth commandment wants to promote love of truth as the basis for relationships between people. Without love of truth, society is destroyed at its roots and life in community is impossible. The new organization is not just economic and political equality but a question of sincere conversion of hearts and minds to truth.
Choose some cuttings which show:
a) The twisting and distorting of truth.
b) Truth being promoted and proclaimed.

Ninth/Tenth: Do not covet what belongs to your neighbour

It isn't enough not to rob if one doesn't combat the greed which leads to robbery. It is necessary to eradicate from within oneself the desire to possess, the will to accumulate more and more things. Today the media of different kinds promote the possession of false and artificial necessities. People feel they have to possess more Very often the bodies of young women are used demeaningly to promote the buying of products We need a new spirit: simplicity and detachment (not needing many things) in a new society.
Choose some cuttings which show:
a) the promotion of consumerism, greedy accumulation of things and women being used
b) A reasonable, simple attitude to things and persons.

SESSION SIX

The Emergence of the Prophets

Aims
• To reflect on the collages of the Ten Commandments prepared by the groups in which they show God's dream being fulfilled or not.
• To understand why and how the prophets emerged in Israel and what they did.

Materials
Copies of the input from the previous session.
Charts for input with text.
Group collages (scissors, glue, etc, if needed).
Six copies of the prophetic texts, one for each group.
Instruction sheet for home task.

Time-Table
1.	7.45	Welcome and Introduction.
2.		Team tasks.
3.	8.05	Presentation of collages. Comments.
	8.55	Break.
4.	9.10	Presentation on emergence of prophets.
5.	9.25	Buzz Session and feedback.
6.	9.45	Explaining Home Tasks and reminders.
7.	10.10	Final prayer

Suggested Procedure

1. Welcome and Introduction
Welcome the people and describe this session's aims and time-table.

2. Team Tasks
News, report, commentary, prayer, by the respective groups.

3. Presentation of Collages
– Each group first takes time to arrange their collages and decide who will present them.
– Presentation of collages beginning with the First Commandment.
– Leader asks each one to reflect on what has been heard and seen, to buzz about it with another person.
– Leader takes feedback on what has struck, surprised or puzzled people about what the different groups said and also general comments about understanding the Ten Commandments in terms of a Constitution for a new society.

Note: You may find that some have not made sense of this approach; some may be very challenged by it and some may query its usefulness. This can be a good time to encourage critical thinking.

BREAK

4. Presentation on the Emergence of the prophets

The following is a resource text which can serve as a base for a presentation on how and why the prophets emerged. It will help to decide on the main points, and illustrate them with key phrases on a chart.

The Prophets
Exodus and the Conquest of the Land. 1250-1200 B.C.

Liberation and Covenant
It was between the years 1250 and 1200 B.C. that our religion began. It was in the midst of the situation of the oppressed people in Egypt that God revealed God's-self as someone compassionate, who liberates, who is on the side of the downtrodden. This God of the people is revealed through Moses and calls the people into a struggle of liberation. They move out of the situation of oppression and struggle across the desert into a new land. On the way they enter into a Covenant with Yahweh and begin to form themselves as the people of God. With faith in Yahweh they move into the Promised Land.
Texts: Exodus 1-18; Numbers 9-14; Numbers 20-25; Joshua 1-12; Joshua 22-24.

Period of the Judges. 1200–1050 B.C.
From the entry into the land (1200) up to Samuel, the last judge.
In the land the people renew the Covenant and begin to organise themselves into a new kind of society, the opposite to that which they experienced in Egypt. This new society has an economy based on sharing. Politically, power is participated in by all and they worship Yahweh, the God of Freedom. They draw up a new Constitution called the Ten Commandments and many other laws to safeguard this new society. The land is distributed among the families. Socially they re-formed into families, clans and tribes. Power is decentralised and is exercised by the people:

By the Constitution called the Ten Commandments, God indicated the right way for people:
1. Never to return to a life of slavery.
2. To preserve the freedom they won coming out of Egypt.
3. To live in justice and fraternity.
4. To be an organised people that is a Sign of God in the world.
5. To be organised in community as a response to the cry of all the people.
6. To be an announcement and demonstration of that which God wills for all.
7. To practise the love of God and of the neighbour.
Texts: Exodus 19-24; Exodus 32-34; Numbers 31-36; Joshua 13-19; Judges 1-8; Judges 10-18; Deuter. 29-34.

1050 B.C.: Change to a Monarchy

The situation of the Israelites in the land was difficult because they lived surrounded by foreign people, stronger and more advanced then they. There was frequent contact between the tribes and foreigners – and the tribes ended up imitating the customs and religions of these peoples. So, little by little, there were Israelites who oppressed their brothers and sisters as the foreigners did. Social inequality began to increase. Authorities began to act like foreign kings.

This provoked discontent among the tribes (Judges 19:30) and led the people to division and a weakening of the organisation of the Covenant.

Foreigners began to invade the lands and settlements of the Israelites, i.e. the Philistines.

More and more the people began to think that they needed a centralised authority as their form of government. They would prefer a *king* who would direct the whole country and would be the leader of a permanent army. Things came to a head when the Philistines stole the Ark of the Covenant and then returned it. One day those responsible for the tribes and representatives of the people met the Judge Samuel and asked him to give Israel a King like the other people had. The first Kings were Saul, David and Solomon.

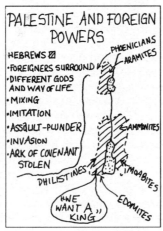

In almost all ancient societies there were groups of artists, poets, singers or seers who were called *prophets*. People sought them out to help resolve their problems by consulting the divinity. Kings often sought the support of these groups of seers. They wanted the support of the divinity to confirm their human power. The same thing happened in the history of the people of God. Samuel, who took on the role of the 'prophet', supported King Saul and King David.

In the beginning the Kings of Israel could count on the support of the prophets. But, after a beginning of great hope, the Kings of Israel began to imitate other Kings (1 Samuel 8:5-20; 1 Kings 11:1-2) and 'their heart was not all for Yahweh as had been the heart of David' (1 Kings 11:4). Basing their behaviour on the 'right of the king' (1 Samuel 8: 18) they introduced enforced labour (1 Kings 5:27; 1 Kings 12:4), they led the people away from the Covenant and to the worship of false gods (1 Kings 11:1-12). They brought back the oppression of Egypt, of which God had said, 'You will never be able to return to Egypt' (Deuteronomy 17:16) and worst of all they did this as if it was the expression of the will of Yahweh who brought them from Egypt (1 Kings 12:28). They imagined Yahweh, the God of the people, to be just like the false gods of other peoples, just like any other idol, without autonomy, reinforcing the exclusive interest of the monarchy.

The Example of Solomon

Solomon is the supreme example of what happened to Israel when monarchy (royalty) became the form of government. He was a King in the style of the great emperors of his time. For instance, all the ancient peoples constructed temples for their gods. To construct a sanctuary was one way of people honouring their god. They also built temples to show the grandeur of the people and the wealth and pride of their city. But there was also another important motivation: the temple being the house of God, they *tied* God to that place. It was a way of guaranteeing the presence of God to them.

Solomon spent twenty years building a temple to show his grandeur and power. He built the temple in accordance with the style and organisation of the Egyptians and foreign kings. He made a construction of stone, lined with cedar wood, in three parts. The most important part was the sanctuary into which he put the Ark of the Covenant which held the stone tablets with the law of God given at Sinai.

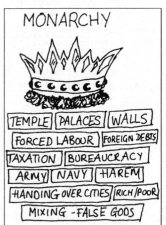

Apart from the temple, he built a huge wall surrounding the city of Jerusalem, a palace for himself and he formed a great army and navy. To build the temple and palace he bought cedar wood from Lebanon and used many foreigners in his country as slave labour. To pay his foreign debts he handed ten areas of Galilee over to the King of Tyre. The great constructions and luxury of the Kingdom of Solomon weighed heavily on the poor people. He made thirty thousand men work months and months in Lebanon. He charged heavy taxes on the peasants. He made a treaty with the King of Egypt and set up a harem which was a means of bringing about political marriages. The Queen of Saba came and was very impressed by the luxury of the Kingdom. These commerical relationships provoked a mixture of religions and life-styles in the country. The covenant with God and the unity of the tribes was no longer respected. So the people of Israel, delivered from foreign enemies at one time, fell into injustice at the hands of the rich and powerful of their own people. The gods of the pagans were adopted.

Summary of what happened

1. Solomon countered the *economics of equality* (Ex 16:18) with the *economics of affluence* (1 Kings 4: 20-23) . Consumer goods had arrived. Satiation of the powerful was in. When there is satiation, it is difficult to maintain a revolution of freedom and justice. Affluence and prosperity is not democratically shared. *Covenanting* which takes brothers and sisters seriously is replaced by *consuming* which regards brothers and sisters as products to be used. In a consuming society it is difficult to keep alive ideas of justice.

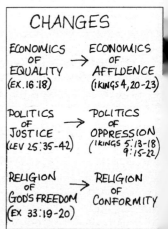

2. He countered the *politics of justice* (Lev 25:35-42) with the *politics of oppression*. (1 Kings 5:13-18, 9:15-22). Fundamental to social policy was the practice of forced labour. It was unmistakably the policy of the regime to mobilise and claim the energies of the people for the sak

of the court and its extravagant needs. No amount of goods, of power, of security was enough. The politics of justice and compassion disappeared to be replaced with the order of the State as the main agenda (the King's order).

3. He countered the *religion of God's freedom* (Ex 33:19-20) with the *religion of conformity*.
The economics of affluence and the politics of oppression could not have endured had the people worshipped the God of freedom and liberation. Instead a controlled static religion was established in which God and his temple became part of the royal landscape, in which the sovereignty of God is fully subordinated to the purpose of the King. Now God is fully accessible to the King who is God's patron and the freedom of God is eliminated. This God justifies Solomon's status quo.

This royal tradition is operative in our world today:

1. How many people find themselves in an economics of affluence in which they are so well off that pain is not noticed and they can eat their way around it?

2. How many find themselves immersed in a politics of oppression in which the cries of the marginal are not heard or are dismissed as the noises of misfits and traitors?

3. How many of us find ourselves with such a comfortable, accessible God that we never experience his abrasiveness, his challenge, his banishment? Every problem is reduced to psychology.

Emergence of the Prophets

When the monarchy fell away from the Covenant to create a system contrary to the one God wanted, then little by little, from the depth of the people, *prophecy* broke forth as a critical, independent force, free in the face of the powers that be. The prophets were an expression of the liberty of God in the face of his lieutenants. Thus began the eternal struggle between prophecy and power. This separation between prophecy and power began for the first time most clearly in the time of Elijah (1 Kings 17-19, 21).

Brueggeman defines the task of the prophet in this way: 'The task of the prophetic ministry is to nurture, nourish and evolve a consciousness and perception, alternative to the consciousness and perception of the dominant culture around it.'

With Elijah, prophecy took on the direction of the defence of the Covenant and of the life of the people against the power of the Kings which they claimed was the power of Yahweh. In this period there emerges the independence of the prophet and the non-conformity of the prophets against the attempts of the King to marginalise him as a heretic against God (1 Kings 18,17; Amos 7:12-13; Jeremiah 18:26,11).

Frame of Reference of the Prophets
A prophet has a double frame of reference:
1. On the one hand a deep experience of God, not of any God, but the God of the people, the liberator God, living and true.
2. On the other hand, a deep experience of the reality of the people in general, but of the people insofar as it is called to be the people of God; an experience of that which the people should be and isn't.

They are like two sides of the same coin. Let's see some aspects of each one:

Experience of Yahweh, God of the People
1. The experience of God brings with itself its own evidence; in it one finds the source of the freedom of the prophets in the face of the powerful.
2. It is an experience of the God of their parents; for this reason it brings with it what God did in the past. The prophet thus becomes in a certain way, the critical memory of the people. He remembers disturbing things others would like to forget.
3. It's the experience of the same God who brought the people out of Egypt, the liberator God, God of the Covenant, called Yahweh. Thus the prophet becomes the one who incarnates the demands of the Covenant and of the law of God.

Experience of the Reality of the People of God
1. The experience of the holiness of God and his demands is, at the same time, an experience of sin, of breaking the Covenant, the faults which exist in the people; an experience of that which the people should be and aren't.
2. When you see *broken glass* on the ground you look around and say, 'some window was broken'. Where the poor appear in the midst of the people, the prophet stops, captures the message and says, 'the Covenant has been broken'. Some people get used to broken glass and ignore it. The prophet does the opposite. He confronts the people with the poor who are left over after the disaster of the breaking and demands change in the name of God and in the name of the origin of the people itself.
3. The broken glass which revealed the breaking of the Covenant in the Old Testament were 'the impoverished', the orphans, the widows, the strangers. The presence of these people in the community revealed that something was wrong. The people were wounded, a living sore (Is 1:6; Jer 30:12-15; 14:17-18; 1:18).

From this double experience thence is born in the prophet the impulse to cry out. It is a denunciation motivated by faith, and at the same time, an announcement of God and the appeal to conversion, to change, to observance of the law and the Covenant, an appeal to return to God and the origin of the people.

The three ways of change and conversion
The call to change and conversion made by the prophet is made in three ways:
1. *The Way of Justice* – seeks to promote the change of structures in society.

2. The Way of Solidarity – seeks the conversion or renewal of the community.

3. The Way of Faith – seeks the renewal or change of consciousness.

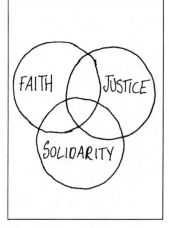

Let's look at the three ways.

1. Way of Justice

Justice exists when everything is in place as God wants, when everything is as it should be. The prophets struggle so that everything and all occupy their place according to the project of the Covenant. They are not theoretical preachers; they denounce clearly the injustices and point out the causes. They aren't afraid to say what is wrong in the organisation of the country, as well as on the part of the persons responsible for the institutions.

The prophets' protests, made on the basis of a re-owning of the Covenant, led to the establishment of new laws so that through them, a new order would be created which would favour the life of the people and bring them to a full observance of the Covenant. One of these, for example, is the law of the Jubilee or Sabbatical Year (Lev 25, Deut 15) which envisages creating a more just agrarian structure in the country.

2. The Way of Solidarity

Not all poverty is the fruit of injustice but all the poor deserve to be welcomed. The community of the people of God should be a demonstration of that which God wants for all. It should be the alliance of God with people against everything which spoils life and marginalises people. It should know how to welcome the victims of impoverishment, caused as much by injustice as by other causes.

There can be no poor among the community of the people of God (Deut 15:4). All should be able to live in the perfect sharing of goods. Even so, ' the poor will always exist' (Deut 14:11; Mt 26:11) for the community, being small, does not control the life of the world nor succeed in eliminating all the economic, political, or social causes which produce poverty. To the extent that the poor of the world come into contact with the community where 'There must, then, be no poor among you,' (Deut 15:4) they should be welcomed in.

3. The Way of Faith

The unjust system makes the poor persons develop a consciousness of inferiority. They experience themselves condemned as persons of no account, even sinners, who do not deserve a better life than they have. Thus the rich can continue tranquilly in their wealth without being worried by the cry of the poor because the poor themselves are to blame for their own poverty.

While this false consciousness of inferiority continues, any work of change, whether in the line of justice or of solidarity, is nothing less than an illusion. It would be like grafting a cutting on to a dead branch, plastering over a cracked wall, or doing plastic surgery on a corpse. So what can be done to take away this basic injustice? Who is able to return to the poor person this robbed consciousness? The rich can return the robbed money. They cannot return the robbed consciousness.

Here enters the basic certainty of the faith of the people of God, i.e. God hears the cry of the poor. The poor do not cry

for the rich but cry to God and God hears the cry and says, 'I am with you'. From this certainty about God is born a new consciousness of personhood and being a daughter or son of God, consciousness of one's basic human dignity.

These are not three separate pathways; they are united. One way is not possible without the others. *Justice* without solidarity and faith, becomes mere political action without humanity and does not touch the depth of the human being. It politicises and toughens the action, wins over reason but does not convince the heart. Solidarity without justice and without faith becomes the mere philanthropy of humanitarian clubs at the service of the system which generates poverty. This type of philanthropy deceives consciousness, neutralises the cry of the poor and impedes the emergence of the critical consciousness of the oppressed. Faith without justice and without solidarity becomes alienated piety, without foundation in reality and without foundation in the tradition of the Bible. It offends God because it transforms God into an idol and deceives the poor because it makes them submissive to injustice.

The prophets of Israel continue the radical movement of Moses in the face of the royal reality (the monarch).

Two examples of prophetic ministry

Jeremiah (a later prophet) practises *radical* criticisms against the royal consciousness. He does this by imagining life as a funeral and bringing the grief of a dying Israel to public expression. He does this to cut through the numbness of the monarchy which pretended that things were alright and must go on forever.

On the other hand, the Second Isaiah practises *radical energising* against the monarchy. He does this by imagining a new beginning, a new rebirth. By using images and poetry he cuts through the weariness of despair to a new hope.

Texts: 2 Samuel 5-24; 2 Kings 17; 1 Kings 1-15; Amos 1-9; 1 Chronic 11-20; Hosea 1-14; 1 Kings 16-22; Jeremiah 1-6; 2 Kings 11-15

5. Buzz Session and Feedback

What struck you?
What puzzled you?
What surprised you?

6. Home Task

A Prophets's Poem for Today
Distribute Handout 9 and explain the procedure:
'Next week you have a Hallowe'en break. You can use the time to do this home-task.
'We invite you to take one of the texts from the Prophets, read it together and compose a poem on what the prophet in question might say in the context of today's world.'

Each team is given one of the following:
1. Hosea chapter 4:1-3; and chapter 2;2-17.
2. Ezekiel chapter 2:1-3; chapter 22, 23;31, chapter 34:1-6 and chapter 37:1-14.
3. Isaiah chapter 6:1-9, chapter 1:2-4; 21-23; chapter 11:1-9; chapter 12:1-2.
4. Amos chapter 3:1-2; 13-15; chapter 4:1-3; chapter 2: 6-7; chapter 8:4-8.
5. Micah chapter 1:1-2; chapter 2: 1-5; 7-11; chapter 3: 1-12; chapter 7:1-7; chapter 6:6-8.
6. Jeremiah chapter 1: 4-5; chapter 2: 2-9; 26-29; chapter 7: 1-11; 11:21-28; chapter 31:1-6; 15-17, 31-34.

Groups get together before they leave to decide where and when to meet and take the texts and instruction with them.

Note: People have much more creativity than they think. Each year people have produced poems of varying standards. The exercise also bonds them together as a group. It is perhaps important to remind them to allow each to have a say in shaping the poems.

7. Final Prayer
Take brief phrases from Joel 3:1-3 and/or Acts 2:14-21.

8. Conclusion
Remind them about team tasks and explain that the leading team will combine the news and prayer tasks for the coming session.

Handout 10

A Prophet's Poem for Today

Working with the Texts

The group gathers in a suitable place. Prior to the meeting the groups may read some of the background to the prophet, for example *Understanding the Old Testament* by F. E. Charpentier or the *Serendipity Old Testament* which give good short summaries of the individual prophets. The Introductions to the Prophetic books in the Jerusalem Bible are also helpful.

Procedure for the meeting:

1. We Invite the Lord
Someone invites the Lord to be with us in reading the Word of God.

2. We read the text.
Will someone please read the text (twice?)

*3. We pick out words and phrases
and meditate on them.*
We pick out words or short phrases that seem to speak to our world today. Read them aloud prayerfully and keep silence in between.

4. We let God speak to us in silence.
We keep silence for two minutes and allow God to speak to us.

5. We share what we have heard in our hearts.
Which words or phrases have touched you personally? (no discussion) and Why?
Someone notes down what people are saying.

6. We discuss how the text relates to society today.
To what would this prophet address himself today? What would he say?
Someone notes down the comments.

7. Putting shape on the poem.

Agree on:
• The main points/topics you want included in the poem.

Then either:
• choose one person to compose it.

or

• delegate individuals to compose a section each.

or

• let everyone have a go and someone edits the final work.

• Decide who will present the poem and how.

SESSION SEVEN

Being Prophets Today

Aims

• To hear the prophetic poems prepared by the groups.
• To explore the implications of the prophetic role for ourselves.
• To identify issues in our situation and possible ways of responding to them.

Materials

Copies of the input, report and commentary from the previous session.
Charts for the presentation. Sets of questions for each mixed group of three.
Text of prayer related to the news.

Time-table

1. 7.45   Introduction
2.   Special prayer/news combination
3. 8.05   Prophetic poems.
   9.05   Break
4. 9.15   Presentation: To be prophetic
5.   Group Discussion.
6.   Plenary Session: response and suggestions.
7. 10.10   Final Prayer.
8.   Conclusion

Suggested Procedure

1. Introduction

Welcome:
'We've been away for a week. To help us mix and get to know each other better, let's use this ice-breaker (Handout 11) called *Finder's Sheet*.'

2. Special prayer/news combination

The report and commentary are presented as usual and the leading team can then introduce the prayer, linking news and prayer together. A sample of how this might work is given in Supplementary Material 1.

3. Prophetic Poems

a) Preparation:
Each group takes a short time to arrange the sharing of their presentations:
- someone to give a brief statement on how the meeting at home went.
- someone to give brief points about the prophet they have studied.
- someone to read a brief passage from the prophet's writing.
- someone to read the group's poem.

b) Group presentations:
A leader asks everyone to listen carefully to the contributions and allows time after each for people to note:
    What did I feel?
    What do I think?
After the final presentation, a few comments are welcomed without breaking the mood of attentive listening.
Some samples of work are included in Supplementary Material 2 & 3.

BREAK

4. Presentation
To be prophetic
What do prophets do?

SEE: Keep their eyes and ears open; are very honest with the reality: see what is happening, especially when people are put down, left out, wounded, hurting, depressed or oppressed. Prophets notice persons, situations, society, environment. Prophets feel deeply about situations, persons, etc.

JUDGE: Prophets are in touch with who God is and what God wants and look at reality in the light of this vision (the scriptures and prayer).
Prophets see the gap between the way things are and the way they could be.

ACT: When the prophets see the gap between the way things are and the way they could be, they feel the call to action and act freely by word and deed.

Partners as prophets:
By Baptism we are called to be prophetic. In the light of our faith we notice that something isn't right or could be better and, rather than sink into *apathy and indifference*, we show our concern.

5. Group Discussion
In mixed groups of three, participants work through these questions:
1. In what ways are we ourselves acting like prophets?
2. Agree on *one* life-situation you know that needs change.
3. In what ways could ordinary people begin to influence that situation?

6. Plenary Session
Each group reports on their findings to the three questions.
Response:
'Already you can see how we, as small christian community groups, could act in a prophetic way. Later on in the course we shall work on this mission more concretely.'
Suggestion:
A possible task for a couple of volunteers could be the writing of a prophetic letter. An outline guide is provided in Handout 12.

7. Final Prayer
Repeat a key line from each poem and pause for reflection.

8. Conclusion
Remind them about the team tasks.

Handout 11
Finder's Sheet

1. Find someone who looks as if he or she enjoys children.

Name..

2. Find someone who looks as if she or he likes to play sports.

Name..

3. Find someone who looks as if he or she loves animals.

Name..

4. Find someone who looks as if he or she is ambitious.

Name..

5. Find someone who looks as if she or he likes traditional music.

Name..

6. Find someone who looks as is she or he likes exciting activities.

Name..

7. Find someone who looks as if he or she is an interesting conversationalist.

Name..

8. Find someone who looks as if she or he enjoys spicy food.

Name..

9. Find someone who looks thoughtful.

Name..

10. Find someone who looks like she or he is all there.

Name..

Handout 12

Writing a Prophetic Letter

1. Choose an issue that needs attention. In a spirit of prayer reflect on it.

2. Ask yourselves
       - what do you see happening in this situation?
       - why is it happening?
       - who is affected by it?
       - what do you think of the situation?
       - what response/action is needed?

Discuss the above.

3. Ask some one or two persons in the group to draft the letter:
       - decide to whom you are sending it:
       - newspaper, T.D., councillor, agency,
        department, health board, corporation.

The letter can follow a pattern such as:
       'We have noticed …
       This is because …
       The effects are …
       We think that …
       We propose/demand/ask/request/suggest …
       Signed …'

Supplementary Material 1

Prayer About The News: A Sample

Prepare:
An open Bible, a newspaper, a lighted candle, tape recorder.

Leader:
Lord, we gather here in your name. We know that poverty remains the central issue of our society. This could hardly be otherwise given that up to one-third of the population in the Republic live in deprived circumstances.

Through Baptism you have called us to be prophets,
Help us to see life around us with your eyes.
Help us to hear cries around us with your ears.
Help us to walk humbly with you.
Help us to love tenderly as you.
Help us to act justly with you.

Lord, in the songs on the radio and in the newspapers we hear your call.

Play the Song of Phil Collins: Another Day in Paradise *or another appropriate song.*

Extract from The Sunday Tribune
Reader (man):
'A person is in poverty,' the ESRI concludes, 'when due to lack of resources, he or she is excluded from the ordinary living patterns, customs and activities in the society.' The ESRI survey indicates the extent to which people are excluded from 'ordinary living standards' in 1980s in Ireland.

'Around 70,000 households – one in 14 of all households – containing almost a quarter of a million people, still have no indoor toilet. One household in ten, or 350,000 people, live in a house without bath or shower. The same number live in damp conditions. 100,000 households, containing 350,000 people, rely on secondhand clothes. Well over half a million people have fewer than two pairs strong shoes. Almost as many again have no warm waterproof overcoat. Close to 600,000 households, which account for over two and quarter million people, do not even have one week's annual holiday away from home.'

Leader:
Lord, we know you hear the cry of the poor,
the cry of your daughter when she says:

Reader (woman): **Off The Wall** *by Cathleen O'Neill*
          The scream started again today
A slow, silent scream of frustrated anger.
Today I wailed at the wall of officialdom.
          smug, smiling, filing-cabinet face,
             Closed to my unspoken entreaty
          Social justice is my right
Don't dole it out like charity!
          Robbed of Independence, dignity in danger
I stood, dead-locked, mind-locked.
Helpless in his sightless one-dimension world I walked away.
          My mind screamed a long sad caoin for the us
          And
          Damned their 'Social Welfare'.

Leader:
Now we listen to the words of your prophet, Lord.
Through these words, you give us strength.

Reader: **Waiting For God**
          Have you not known? Have you not heard?
          The Lord is the everlasting God,
          the Creator of the ends of the earth.
          He does not faint or grow weary,
          his understanding is unsearchable.
          He gives power to the faint,
          And to him who has no might he increases
              strength.
          Even youths shall faint and grow weary,
          and young men shall be exhausted;
          but they who wait for the Lord shall renew
          their strength,
          they shall mount up with wings like eagles,
          they shall run and not be weary,
          they shall walk and not faint.

Pause

Let us pray:
1. For Mary Daly and all involved in the Combat Poverty Agency.
2. For all who work in development projects.
3. For the unemployed action groups in the country
4. For those who run co-operatives and Credit Unions.
5. For newspapers who highlight the existence of poverty.
6. For the Simon Community and Centre Care.
7. For politicians, poets and others who work for justice.
   other petitions.

Psalm 72 paraphrase (alternating sides)
1. Teach us to judge with your righteousness, O God;
   share with us your own justice,
   so we will be able to care for your people with justice.
2. May the land be fruitful,
   may we care for the land
   which we do not own but which you, Lord,
   have given to us to care for.
1. May we help the needy and the poor.
   May we speak out for their cause before their oppressors.
2. May we worship you, Lord, as long as the sun shines,
   as long as the moon gives its light, for all ages to come.
1. In our days, may justice and peace grow
   in our land and hearts.
   Let your justice and peace come down upon us
   like rain on the meadow, the dew on the grass.
2. You, Lord, hear all who are poor who call upon you.
   You have pity on the weak and the poor.
   You save those who are needy and neglected.
1. You, Lord, love the poor, their lives are precious to you.
   You save the lives of those in need.
   Lord, you hear the cries of the poor.
2. We pray there may be plenty of grain in the land;
   Teach us to share your gifts with one another
   and all people.
1. May your name, Lord, be forever blessed!
   May your praise and glory be forever.

(Taken from Women and Poverty, *Combat Poverty, Dublin)*

Supplementary Material 2

Example of a Prophetic Poem

As the crow flies
by Susan Gannon (Rialto Group)

The stark black cry of a Crow
its sudden move to flight
stirs and shifts thick mist
to uncover your world.
Now I will go as the Crow flies
to the silent hidden places.

To labour exchanges crammed tightly with your people
Where shame is invented to make them grateful...
Into ports where the young are torn and taken from
their families, off to strange lands to earn their keep...
Above blocks of flats where a few must fight
for decent homes for all...
Behind walls where the lost inject themselves...
Over beds where they die alone of a dreaded disease...
Among children who most not walk alone,
even your babies are unsafe...
Beyond your border where men and women kill and die
for a cause that changes names...
The innocent imprisoned and ignored
the guilty angered even more
While mothers and widows never stop grieving the loss...
Among your women who struggle daily,
always dragged down
not allowed know their worth.
I stop to look upon the faces of your old
Faces like all those who are forgotten
Their strained expression of powerlessness...
Across the gap that may only be a street
between rich and poor,
the wealthy parade their riches
they tease and chastise those who do not have...
who do not have...
As we fly to other continents
through air choked with filth,
I see over and over the savage rape of nature...
The rape of whole nations,
the slaughter of their Colour,
Language and their Ways...

All the time foolish men stroke each other
play at war and with power
Yet do nothing for the terrorised hungry face of a child...
We rest quietly to hear whispers of protest
and the proud roar of rage
only to see their very throats
ripped from them to keep silent.

The Crow and I land and perch
His squawks ring of doom
But below us among weeds and rubbish
is a small seed,
not seeing what she will become
she sits nervous and unsure.
Recalling for me the smallness of change in your world
that one day will become...
She sits with the poor who see the injustice

and accuse the rich...
With the Unemployed, women, tenants
who find dignity and do for themselves...
She is with the junkies who show you the madness...
With the dying who refuse to be ashamed...
With the carers of young
and who become a voice to fight for their rights...
With the emigrants who won't let you forget
why they left...
With grief when it becomes too much and seeks change...
With the courageous who dare put wrong to right...
With the black, yellow and red faces
who see their beauty and claim what is theirs...
With nature when she refuses to provide until respected...
With the hands that feed and soothe...
With the minds that mock and challenge foolish men...
With the voices that continue to speak out.

The stark black cry of the Crow
It's sudden move to flight
returns a mist to cover your world.
Now like the Crow I will leave
leave the silent, hidden places
with her seeds knowing you must believe the seed can
grow. Stay with her smallness always
for she will break free of her shell,
blossom and become fully alive.

Supplementary Material 3

Everyone seemed to have been deeply moved by the session and some were surprised at the untapped power they had found within themselves. Some felt that they were finding the richness of faith again in their lives, through meeting in small groups. But sadness was also expressed at the fact that there seems to be no vehicle within the church structures which enables people of God to express the richness such as they experienced tonight. The content of the session also made some people feel a little sad, perhaps they were echoing the words of Sheila Cassidy: 'The truth will set you free but first it will make you miserable.'

Commentary
There was obvious a lot of time and effort put into each group's reflection on the prophets. We think this showed openness to the process we are engaged in and a generous commitment to one another. Each group revealed resources and talents, particularly an ability to analyse contemporary economic and social realities in the light of God's word. Did we detect, however, a tendency to talk about these realities as created and maintained solely by others to which we have made no contribution. We wondered if the Word of God would challenge also our values and attitudes.

Commentary
What emerged from the session on the prophets: a breakthrough occured; people realised their own power and creativity and it shocked them.
- the power of poetry over rational stating of statistics was noted and experienced
- a prophetic mood is a poetic mood
- still a 'domesticated' view of reality prevails, with emphasis on the individual: still effort is needed to break through to new angles
- there was great mutual learning: the participants all enjoyed it because it was their work.

Some of the Poems

1.
Material things, property, wealth and lands
We can't get enough; we fill both our hands.
Why think of your neighbour? - he can get by
I'm all right, Jack'; just a blind eye
So sad to see what's happening today -
How can we stop it? Is there a way?
Wake up to see what's happening
in each country and town,
The homeless, itinerants, unemployment all there,
Christians on Sunday and let it end there.
That's not the way he taught us to act .
We must have forgotten, that's a fact.
So speak your mind and use your vote
Change this damn system; give them some hope.

2. Amos speaks in Dublin
Listen, you who crush the young
and rob them of their golden youth
with contracts from your clenched fists wrung
Revenge is mine, Yes, tooth for tooth.
They work in hope till middle age
then unemployed, none re-engaged
Past their prime to emigrate
in silent queues they congregate
How do you propose to compensate?

My old and feeble are a curse
to you who adore the well-filled purse;
My widows and 'wine-os',
My homeless, my poor
Whose very last hope is to tap on your door
are met with stern faces
that front hearts of stone
they return to their hovels
all dignity shorn.

You Shylocks and scrooges
You, bankers, beware
when hell was made
there was still room to spare.

3. Amos and Fr Michael Cleary
He is a man, so very rare,
the people always listen;
because they know he cares,
a priest, a comic, a singer, too
Father Michael Cleary,
we could do with more like you.

You speak the word of God
in a way we understand
To young and old you will lend a hand.

4. Ode to the Lottery
I have an answer to all ills
It does not take too much of our skills
With the Lotto they score
as they go back for more.
But, alas!
as we fail to have any thrill
We are just left to pay all the bills.

5. Hey You!
Hey you who are well-heeled,
who offer second-hand shoes to the poor
you praying in expensive churches
while kids drink cider outside the door;
You who come into our country
to bleed it of riches and power
You who favour achievers
and neglect those without power.

God keeps their tears in a bottle
he hears the cry of the poor;
Repent: look at your lifestlyes
Jesus can offer you more.

If only the world would open up
and we could live as one.
No bickering and comparing,
No greedy or selfish one.
You may not have material gain,
No priceless words to say,
But you have this message for all
to hear today.

Brothers and sisters we are all one.
God is our father
And loves us as one.

6.
Can you not hear my God?
'You have taken the lives of my children
in silent holocausts.
Those you have left you are killing
with drugs, promising ecstasy.
My daughters believing stardom begins on page 3.'

My God says
'Your spiritual famine is almost complete.
Now who will feed you?
My remnant is here.
They are listening right here in this room
They will heal and build and feed you
And all will hear my word.'

7.
You live up here in Ballymun.
You say your life's a mess.
You hadn't much education.
Your presentation's not the best.
But God loves you.

You may not have much fancy clothes,
No fancy house or car.
You know life would be better
if you had a job and pay.

It would bring back your dignity
and take your shame away.

The following excerpts indicate the nature of what went on among the groups:
Report
In some ways any attempt to evaluate last week's session is bound to be inadequate as it would be impossible to cap-

ture the unique atmosphere that prevailed, as the groups shared their reflections on the writings of the prophets and their relevance to the Ireland of today.

The deep insights of the groups were expressed in poetry and both the richness and the honesty were disarming. Jeremiah, Amos. Ezekiel, Micah and Isaiah were metaphorically cast in roles of latter-day interpreters of God's will as they surveyed our island in the late 1980s. The power of people to name their reality was clearly demonstrated through this exercise.

SESSION EIGHT

Spirituality – The Positive Way

Aims
- To highlight the covenant spirituality of biblical faith.
- To focus on the positive pathway of the relationship between ourselves and God.

Materials
Handout for personal reflection.
Handout for collective psalm.
Handout with points on spirituality.
Copies of last week's report and commentary.

Time-Table
1.	7.45	Welcome.
2.		Presentation: Spirituality – The Positive Way
3.	8.20	Guided Meditation.
4.	8.40	Personal reflection.
5.	8.50	Concentric circles.
	9.10	Break
6.	9.25	Open reflection.
7.	9.45	Making a Psalm. Reading the Psalm.
8.	10.10	Reminder of team tasks.

Suggested Procedure

1. Welcome and Introduction
Welcome, time-table, Tasks: news, report, commentary, prayer.

2. Presentation on Spirituality
1. We have seen how God and people related in the Old Testament. Today, we and our God relate in a similar fashion. God still says:
  'I will be your God
  and you will be my people.'
and we are invited to live this covenant with God.

2. There is a basic pattern in the way we relate.

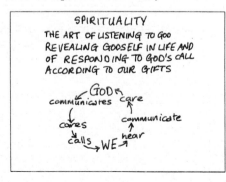

Spirituality is the name we give to the way we relate to God. It is the art of listening to God revealing Godself in life, and of responding to God's call according to our gifts. The hymn, Here I am Lord, conveys the spirit of this relationship.

3. At the core of our relationship is a movement of liberation and development. We are always coming out of Egypt and moving to the promised land.

> COMING OUT OF EGYPT
> AND MOVING TO THE PROMISED LAND

4. This call and response is found at different levels in our lives:

Personal level:
In our personal lives we are called:
From: stressful – meaningless – inactive life
To: free – purposeful – creative life.

Inter-personal level:
In relationships we are called:
From: blindness – distance – hate
To: noticing – nearness – love.

Level of community/society:
We may experience the call:
From: oppression – hopelessness – under development
To: freedom – hopefulness – liberation/development.

Level of creation:
Looking around us, we may see creation needing to move:
From: abused – polluted – uncared-for world
To: respected – clean – minded world.

As we move through life, if we pay attention to ourselves and the world around us, we will experience the call to cooperate in that movement of freedom. It calls for faith on our part that will find the strength/resources to bring about change (God within).

> MOVEMENT
> PERSONAL LEVEL
> FROM: STRESSFUL – MEANINGLESS – INACTIVE LIFE
> TO: FREE – PURPOSEFUL – CREATIVE LIFE
> INTERPERSONAL
> FROM: BLINDNESS – DISTANCE – HATE
> TO: NOTICING – NEARNESS – LOVE
> COMMUNITY/SOCIAL LEVEL
> FROM: OPPRESSION – HOPELESSNESS – UNDER DEVELOPMENT
> TO: FREEDOM – HOPEFULNESS – GROWTH /LIBERATION
> LEVEL OF CREATION
> FROM: ABUSED – POLLUTED – UNCARED FOR WORLD
> TO: RESPECTED – CLEAN – MINDED WORLD

The Positive way:
5. How do we find the strength to believe and to struggle? In history, the people of God gradually realised that the God who freed them was also the God who created them. They noticed how much goodness was communicated in the world, in life, and their reaction was one of thanksgiving, praise and celebration. In the Bible we read many of the Songs of Praise

> GOD WHO FREED US IS THE GOD WHO CREATED US
> "GIVE THANKS TO THE LORD WHO IS GOD WHOSE LOVE ENDURES FOREVER"

(Psalms) they composed, e.g. Psalm 136. When they counted their blessings, the positive feelings of gratitude and joy gave them strength to believe in their own God-given power to overcome all 'Egypt' experiences and bring about the experience of the 'Promised Land.'

6. It might be no harm if you read some of the psalms of praise in your Bible.

In this session, we will focus on the way God communicates goodness to us in life and how this gives us a strong sense of gratitude and faith, so that we can overcome the forces of darkness. In spirituality, this is called *The Positive Pathway to God.*

'Give thanks to the Lord who is good
whose love endures forever.'
– *from a Psalm of praise.*

Tonight we invite you to explore how that same God of Moses, the prophets and the psalmist is present today in the positive pathways of life.

3. Guided Meditation
Use background music, etc.
Either in the meeting room or in a nearby prayer room, invite the participants to join in a guided meditation. The meditation is aimed at helping people become aware of and be sensitive to the presence of our God in our positive experience of life. This gives them a heightened sense of the ways God has communicated positively with them through their positive experiences.

Guided Meditation
(Adapt for your own group)
Where we meet God in our positive experiences

1. Through the physical world – the earth.
Let us use our senses to be lovingly attentive to life, through gazing at, listening to and bonding with the earth. The simplest way to do that is through our imagination and memory, gazing at (contemplating) the wonder of things around us and giving God space to communicate with us through them

Think of clouds – always in different formation and colour, above the flats, tall buildings, fields, hills or over the sea ...

the moon – whose light transforms what is there, as we notice it going back at night from a friends' home, from the pub ...

shifting, changing weather: rain, mist, wind, smog and sunshine breaking through smog ...

Look at the stars twinkling and remember the long years it takes for their light to reach us ...

Remember the smell of clear, fresh air in the hills, the Tallaght hills, over the smooth mountain lakes, over the bog ...

Hear the sea: gently swelling over the sand or pounding the rocks ...

Follow quiet never-ending stretches of water in rivers where we fish ...

Watch slow ripening crops, sheep, cows grazing, hedges dividing, protecting fields ...

Remember sunsets; up along O'Connell Bridge, beyond Guinness, over the canal ...

Follow leaves falling off the branches but, even as they fall, new buds clustering – seeds dying and lying hidden but life cells gathering to burst through again in Spring.

These things are always there, year after year, season after season, day after day. They are all deep abiding signs of God's presence and love and they coax us to wonder, to go beyond the routine and familiar to the Source:
The earth shows forth the glory of God!

It is our privilege to get in tune with the earth and the world around us and meet God there.

2. Civilisation: People co-creating through using their gifts and working with earth's resources:

Through making airplanes, ferries, stadiums, bridges, roads ...

Through inventions that open up ways of communication between people and the world, telephone ... airwaves ...

Through politics and human laws ... the systems by which people market and share the earth's resources: these, when just, can stir our hearts with wonder at God's gift to us of the ability to plan and organise and distribute and protect human resources for living ...

Scientists exploring the laws of nature and adapting materials and plants to serve life: opening up new possibilities for healing, discovering again natural ways of making people well ...

Artists, by word, dance, music, movement, ritual, images, drama, painting, pottery, sculpture, letting us see things and the world differently, freshly; sharing their vision of things and shaping how we see the beauty of God's creation; alerting us to the intricacy of form and the complexity of 'ordinary' created things, recalling the goodness, truth and wisdom of the creator.

3. Contemplating People:
People we come across: faces in the dole queue, in the bus-line, in the shopping centre, in the park, after Mass, at a football game ...

Each face telling a story, some faces lifting your heart, others lined with the struggle to survive, others creased with laughter lines, eyes shining with love, interest or dull with pain and apathy ...

God's face shines through in each, stopping us in our tracks: when I was hungry ... lonely ... in pain ... knowing joy, hope and delight ...

The people you greet each morning, in your own home, in the street, the backyard, in the block: to stand back from the familiar and really look, to see the person ...

New persons, tiny persons just experiencing the world for the first time and opening eyes wide in wonder ...

People where you work each day, turning up each day, each with his/her own story, their own angle on life ... making work lighter with their humour ... helping each other to ease the burden of routine ...

Awkward teenagers, aggressive or apathetic, searching

for truth and meaning and self-esteem...

Those you are closest to, who hold a special place in your heart and with whom you struggle to communicate with reverence and love, and open to surprise ...

A stranger you haven't met before but with whom you feel at home, who sees things as you see them, or who radiates goodness and lights up your heart ...

People who have taken up the struggle to make the world of their local community a better place, who don't give up working for freedom and justice and rights ... in them God again liberating people.

4. Contemplating ourselves:

Shy of doing this: Who are we? Who am I? Wouldn't people find it 'wasting time' to think about me?

The truth that each of us is a loved creation, 'magic' in God's eyes, unique, with a story no one else has in the whole world, with our combination of gifts, called to freedom and self-appreciation, guided by the Spirit ...

We have gifts, and we show them every day: to people with whom we share the hours, with our efforts to speak the truth, our struggle to love one another, or one other or many others ...

In our attempt to be patient, to go through the routine with a sense of purpose ...

To listen, to celebrate, to walk beside ...

To tune into bigger issues beyond me and mine, to them and theirs and to make their issues ours ...

Loving distant people whose lives are full of pain and injustice and exploitation ... wherever ...

As we contemplate in all these areas with loving attention, where we see signs of God's goodness, we say 'Yes', we say 'Thanks', we celebrate, we praise.

Noting what is around us, in things, people, events and responding with praise, thanks, acknowledging the invitation to freedom and growth, asking for help to go on with the struggle, admitting our own apathy, indifference and collaboration with the negative forces: this activity is what prayer is about. It nurtures our relationship with God, the living God of Moses, the prophets, Ruth, Mary and Jesus. And it finds expression in:
  – the humble recognition of what is true.
  – the tenderness of love and solidarity.
  – in the struggle for justice and transformation.

4. Personal Reflection
Each participant is invited to reflect alone and attend to the presence/activity of God in the positive aspects of life, in inter-personal relations, wider society, creation, and personal life. Handout 13 may help people to focus on the positive pathway.

5. Concentric Circles
The chairs are arranged in two concentric circles.
The participants are seated, those on the inside facing those on the outside.
A signal is given and those on the outside tell those on the inside what they thought of at the inter-personal level about the positive aspects of life.(2 mins)
A second signal cues those on the inside to speak of their reflection at the same level.
A third signal indicates that all those on the outside move one place to the right. This means that everyone is facing a different person. The process indicated above is repeated, but now people communicate about their experience at the second level (civilisation).
The process continues until all four levels have been covered. One extra round may be added.

BREAK

6. Open Reflection
Leader:
What did you feel/think about that activity?
What struck you?
Allow people to comment freely about what the experience meant to them.

7. Making a Psalm
When the Israelites became aware of the goodness of God, they communicated their awareness through songs or sung prayers called Psalms (afterwards written down).

Here, on the handout, is an outline of a psalm. Let's try to fill in the blank spaces and make our own psalm. The suggestions will be filled on these sheets and then we shall have expressed the relationship between God and ourselves in this positive pathway which generates a spirit of thanksgiving.

Each parish group fills in a section of the collective psalm.

When each group has completed its section, based on their own reflection, the verses are read aloud.

8. Conclusion
Remind groups about team tasks.

Handout 13
Reflection - The Positive Way

PERSONAL

The nicest thing anyone ever said about me ... ...
Some of the things I'm good at ... ...
Some of the things I like about myself are ... ...
I really feel free when I'm able to ... ...
The best side of me comes out when ... ...
A real treat for me is ... ...

INTERPERSONAL

What I really love about people is ... ...
The nicest people I know are people who ... ...
What I enjoy about working with others is ... ...
My best friend is someone who ... ...
The people I know who care most about others are ... ...

CIVILISATION

The most useful invention in my opinion is ... ...
The industries that most benefit humankind are ... ...
The song that most inspires me is ... ...
The politicians who contribute most are ... ...
The book I enjoyed most was ... ...
The most beneficial services available to people ... ...

NATURE

I love the sky when ... ...
The season I like best is ... ... because ... ...
The most beautiful place I know is ... ...
I love the sea when ... ...
Of all the things that grow I'm most grateful for ... ...
The kind of scenery I love is ... ...

Handout 14
Making a Psalm

Oh God, our God,
    You are the giver of all good gifts.
    You are present in all creation
    In everything that lives and breathes
       and gives life.

We thank you for showing us your goodness through:
(Interpersonal level)

1. _____

2. _____

3. _____

4. _____

All:
Give thanks to the Lord who is good,
whose love endures forever.

We thank you for showing us your goodness through:
(Level of civilisation)

1. _____

2. _____

3. _____

4. _____

All:
Give thanks to the Lord who is good,
whose love endures forever.

We thank you for showing us your goodness through:
(Level of creation/nature)

1. _____

2. _____

3. _____

4. _____

All:
Give thanks to the Lord who is good,
whose love endure forever.

We thank you for showing us your goodness through:
(Personal level)

1. _____

2. _____

3. _____

4. _____

All:
Give thanks to the Lord who is good,
whose love endures forever.

Supplementary Material

Extracts from the 1990 reports on session 8

A.

The heart of the material for the night was what we all wonder about – and maybe change our minds over – many times in our lives: what does it mean to be a 'spiritual person'? We liked C's statement of the process, put in such simple terms: 'the art of listening to God revealing God's self ... through all of life and ... of responding according to our gifts.' With the simple illustration of the circle of God and God's covenant we got a picture of God communicating, caring, and our response in caring and communicating. 'I will be their God and they shall be my people.'

But of course it's not simple, for most of us anyway! To keep 'coming out of Egypt' and getting into 'The Promised Land' of peaceful integration of ourselves and the people and the world around us: we need to have faith in a God who frees, liberates, as being the same God who keeps us in existence. We carry on our battle/liberation on various levels and never feel we have finally got there.

Our group dynamic helped us to share with others something of our personal striving in a positive way. It was nice to be able to pool our visions in this concrete way and to notice the beautiful through the eyes and ears and feelings of others. 'What a wonderful world, I think to myself ...' as the song says.

Finally to give ourselves a chance to 'Sing to the Lord a new song', as St Augustine would encourage us, we composed our own hymns of praise and thanks in sentiments which, while individual, reflected and inspired us all in our striving for this Promised Land.

'O world invisible, we praise you; O world unknowable, we know you,' as the poet Francis Thompson says.

B.

C then did a summary of what we had learned during the previous weeks and spoke about how we could bring this into our lives. We can do this firstly through spirituality. This is the way in which we relate to God and God to us. God is, and has been, present through all of life, from the time of the Israelites to our own time. We can also communicate back with God. God is always calling us out of Egypt and asking us to move to The Promised Land. He does this at the personal level, the interpersonal level, at the level of community/society and at the level of creation. He calls us to leave behind blindness, oppression and hopelessness and to move towards freedom, hopefulness and growth. C ended by speaking about The Positive Pathway. The One who frees us is the One who creates us and gives us life. Our response to him is one of thanksgiving, praise and celebration. This gives us strength for the struggle out of Egypt and into The Promised Land. As a large group, we then went into the chapel and G led us in a meditation which focused on the beautiful things that exist in life. These were divided into four areas: personal, interpersonal, civilisation and nature. After this we divided into two groups and formed two circles in the middle of the room to share our reflections under the same headings. The outer circle moved round the inner circle to make sure that we all had the opportunity to share with a few different people. We then broke into our area groups, to work together in creating a psalm giving thanks to God for all his gifts, for showing us his goodness and for God's presence in each of us, in other people, in civilisation and in nature. Each group worked at a different aspect and, at the end of the evening, we read aloud the psalm which was the creation of the whole group.

Spirituality –
The Negative Way

Aims
• To reflect on how negative human experiences can be gateways to God.

Materials
Guidelines for personal reflection.

Time-Table
1. 7.45   Welcome.
2. 8.05   Leaders' Testimonies.
3. 8.20   Personal reflection.
4. 8.40   Group sharing.
   9.20   Break
5. 9.35   Feedback.
6. 9.50   Response from leaders.
7. 10.10 Final prayer.

Suggested Procedure

1. Welcome
a) Welcome, time-table, team tasks.

b) Introduction
The positive pathway of spirituality means experiencing God in the goodness and beauty of life: in people, events, creation that surrounds us. We find joy and delight in these and fall in love with the One from whom all good things come.

In this session we look at another way of catching glimpses of God through the experience of loss, pain, or darkness. In the Bible we see how key people have been been able to find God in the most difficult situations: e.g. Moses in the wilderness, the prophets in the ill-treatment they received for their unpopular message; people like Job who lost all his family and goods, Ruth who lost her husband and security, etc.

2. Leaders' Testimonies
To set a mood for tonight's session, the we will share with you personal testimonies about times when we questioned God's presence and yet managed to find God through the darkness. *(Examples can touch on illness, personal crisis, death, etc.)*
   1. Testimony on the level of personal life

2. Testimony at the interpersonal level
3. Testimony at the level of wider society.

3. Personal Reflection
Distribute Handout 15 and ask the members to reflect on their own experiences, following the guidelines on the handout.

4. Group Sharing
The situation/mood will determine how to divide the participants into groups, either mixed or according to local area, in 3s 4s or 5s.

Ask someone to co-ordinate each group and near the end of the time, ask the group to decide what they want to say to the question: 'Were people able to find God in the darkness? In what ways?'

Note: It is good to gather the coordinators of the small groups together and ask them to ensure that there is no pressure on people to share, a good quality of listening, no questioning and an atmosphere of support.

BREAK

5. Feedback
First give a prayerful time of quiet to keep the mood. Then ask the groups to share their answers to the question.

6. Response from learning leader
Based on the following:
There are different ways in which people, who have been confronted by the darkness of life, have had a breakthrough into a deeper sense of God, a renewed sense of meaning.

a) Inexplicable suffering
In the face of seemingly inexplicable suffering, such as the untimely death of a loved one, the birth of a deformed child, an accident that leaves someone severely disabled, there is much pain and darkness. It can happen that in people's efforts to respond in that situation, to help or to live with the consequences, they discover levels of love in themselves or others they have never before imagined. And ultimately the Source of this love is God. They may find themselves acknowledging this.

b) The experience of the pain of abandoned children, the plight of people who are old, the pain of the hungry, the distress of the addict, the panic of the homeless: sometimes these experiences, witnessed or gone through, can be occasions when people find energy to heal the world and in that action discover the liberating love of God running through themselves and their actions.

c) People who experience old age creeping up on them, and the tiredness of everyday living or the sadness of being around for a long time while friends and dear ones are already gone, sometimes can develop a sense of solidarity with fragile, vulnerable humanity; can sometimes grow in their expectations about life; can experience a willingness to let go in freedom and find themselves falling into the arms of our faithful sustaining Companion of life.

d) People who have reached rock bottom through their own selfishness and have put their trust is possessing more things, in dominating others, in promiscuity, can wake up to the nothingness of loneliness, boredom and sexual failure and begin to seek new levels of meaning and depth, which they may find in God.

e) The suffering of others, when we let it impinge on our hearts, can generate a movement of compassionate action, which reveals the mysterious depth of love of which we are capable even to the extent of suffering ourselves to do away with suffering. In and through that experience we reach a knowledge of the source of compassionate love.

These are instances of how the negative experiences of our lives can generate an awareness of our God, even through the sense of absence.

7. Final Prayer

Psalm 105 (paraphrase)
How great is my God,
and how I love to sing God's praises!
Whereas I am often frightened
when I think about the future,
and confused and disturbed
by the rapidly changing events about me,
my heart is secured and made glad
when I remember how God has cared for me.

When I was brought forth from my mother's womb,
God's hand was upon me.
Through parents and people who cared,
God loved and sheltered me
and set me on my course for life.
Through illness and accident
my God sustained me.
Around pitfalls and precipices
God has safely led me.
When I became rebellious
And struck out on my own,
God waited patiently for me to return.
When I fell on my face in weakness and failure,
God gently set me upon my feet again.
God did not always prevent me from hurting myself,
but took me back to heal my wounds.
Even out of the broken pieces of my defeats,
God created a vessel of beauty and usefulness.

Through trials and errors, failures and successes,
My God has cared for me.
From infancy to adulthood
God has never let me go.
God's love has led me – or followed me –
through the valleys of sorrow
and the highlands of joy,
through times of want
and years of abundance.
God has bridged impassable rivers
and moved impossible mountains.
Sometimes through me
and sometimes in spite of me,
God seeks to accomplish his purpose in my life.

God has kept me through the stormy past;
He will secure and guide me
through the perilous future.
I need never be afraid,

no matter how uncertain
the months or years ahead of me.
How great is my God
and how I love to sing God's praises!

8. Conclusion
Remind them about the team tasks.

Handout 15
Guidelines for Personal Reflection

The Way of Darkness

1. Can you recall a time or occasion when you experienced pain or darkness because of something that happened in your own life or the lives of other people?

> Remember the details:
> What happened?
> When?
> Where did it happen?
> Who was involved?
> What was it like being in that situation?
> What are the feelings you remember? ...

2. What sense were you able to make of it, if any?

3. Were you able to find God in it
> at the time?
> afterwards?

Supplementary Material 1

This article by Fr Thomas L. Sheridan S.J. was very helpful to us in trying to clarify our thoughts on this complex and ambiguous theme of evil and suffering and how we find God through them.

The Mystery of Suffering and Evil
by Thomas L. Sheridan, S.J.
from Living Faith *by Flynn & Thomas,*
Kansas City, Sheed & Ward, 1989,
and used by permission

Tune in to the news any evening on television, and you can be sure that most of the coverage will be devoted to accounts of human suffering and wickedness. We have become so used to the pain and the evil around us that now we react to only the more sensational cases. But when evil and suffering strike home, as in the untimely death of a loved one, the birth of a deformed child, the cold-blooded murder of someone who lives on my street, then we begin to question.

Why Do Bad Things Happen?
To borrow a phrase from Rabbi Harold S. Kushner, 'when bad things happen to good people,' they instinctively ask, 'Why?' or 'Why me?' or even 'Why me, Lord?"

The fact that we ask these questions means that we expect that there is some meaning to our world, that things do add up, and that somehow there must be a way of fitting suffering and evil into this total context of meaning. To have this expectation that our lives and our world do have some meaning is to believe that there is some Meaning Giver besides ourselves. Otherwise, the simplest answer to the question 'Why?' or 'Why me?' is 'Why not?' Why should there be any meaning to anything at all? This is, of course, the nihilist answer which seems to be gaining ground in our western society, as reflected in the works of certain contemporary playwrights, novelists and poets.

But those who still believe in meaning and a Meaning Giver also sometimes ask, 'Why, Lord?' and we of the Judaeo-Christian tradition ask the question this way because of our fundamental belief in the oneness and goodness of God.

After atheism the simplest solution to the problem of evil is what is called theological dualism. In theological dualism the problem is solved by attributing all that is good to a good Principle, or god(s), and all that is bad to a bad Principle, or god(s).

Actually neither atheism nor theological dualism really solves the problem. Atheism is left with what might be called 'the problem of the good,' viz., how one explains all the goodness and beauty in our world and in human life. Theological dualism ends up with two gods – but what kind of a god would either of them be? If Ultimate Reality, the Ground of Being, the Mind behind it all, is really the Divine, then there can be only one.

We of the Judaeo-Christian tradition believe that God is one and that he is good, all good, all loving in fact. And so when something bad happens we say 'Why, Lord?' and sometimes we say, 'Lord, I know you are all loving; then why didn't you do something to stop the bad thing from happening?' Implicit in this, of course, is the belief that not only is God all-loving, but he is also all-mighty. So many of our prayers are addressed to 'Almighty God' that we presume that he can simply do anything, and therefore he could stop suffering and evil if he really wanted to. Hence the traditional formulation of 'the problem of evil.'

If God is all loving, then he would want to eliminate all suffering and evil.
If he is all-powerful, then he could do so.
The fact that suffering and evil do exist means, therefore, that either:
(a) there is no such God;
or (b) God is not all loving;
or (c) God is not all powerful.
One of these has to go. Which one will it be?

Does God Cause Suffering and Evil?
Oddly enough, we Jews and Christians seem to have been more willing to sacrifice God's goodness than his power. Oh, to be sure, we continue to talk about the goodness and love of God. But the way in which we safeguard his all-powerfulness leaves us with a picture of God which is something less good and less loving than we would like to maintain.

One classic answer to the question why bad things happen to good people was dealt with centuries before Christ in the Book of Job. The author of the Book of Job took an old folk tale about a very good man named Job. One day God was talking with some of his counsellors (this was a very old folk tale), and one of them, 'the Adversary,' says, in effect, 'You're always saying what a great guy this fellow Job is, but why wouldn't he be when he's always had it so good? Let's see how good he is when something bad happens to him.' So God – in the story – says, 'OK, do what you want with him, short of killing him.' And the things the Adversary does to poor old Job! He loses everything, but everything, and ends up on a dung heap cursing the day he was born. And now comes our author's own contribution. He has three friends come to visit Job, and they try to console him by showing him the meaning of his sufferings. It is quite simple: Job must have done something wrong, and he is being punished for it.

Job steadfastly rejects this solution. The bad things that are happening to him are not punishments from God, for the simple reason that he really is a just man and has not done any wrong. At the end of the book Job meets God face to face. The problem is not solved, but he is able to cope with the mystery.

The author of the Book of Job rejected the simple solution to the problem of evil, which says that it is a punishment by God. And yet many still feel this way even in our own day. How often we hear people say, 'He must have been doing something wrong, and now God has punished him for it." But what kind of a God would that be who would be so intent on punishment? Does he have to punish? Why can't he just forgive? And how then are we to explain the suffering of countless innocents? How can we square this with the picture of the God of Love which we have come to learn from Jesus? This punishing God sounds more like a mean old man waiting to get even than the gracious Father of the Prodigal.

Some have thought that this problem could be avoided if we were to keep two points in mind. The first is the distinction made by St Augustine and St Thomas that evil is not a being in itself but a negation or to be precise a privation of being, i.e. the absence of some perfection which should be there. In this way we can say that everything that is, owes its being to God; since evil is not a being, however, but a privation of being, God can in no way be said to cause evil. The second point, which also goes back to some of the classical theologians, is that God does not inflict suffering and evil; he merely permits them. This line of reasoning then continues to maintain that God permits evil since he will not interfere with our freedom, and he permits suffering so that through our sufferings we may grow and develop. Suffering is a kind of divine discipline. Athletic trainers tell us, 'No pain no gain.' And that's the way it is with all human suffering.

The first point is so theoretical that I doubt if it has ever helped anyone cope with the mystery of suffering and evil. Suffering is all too real and evil seems all too powerful a force in our world for us to categorise it as simply the privation of being.

The second point has helped a lot of people who have accepted their trials and sufferings as coming from the hands of a loving God who sends, or better, permits them for some greater spiritual profit. But is this really a solution? What of the many people who aren't able to cope with suffering and are destroyed by it? How could an all-wise and all-loving God permit this kind of suffering? Even in the case of those who do grow through their sufferings, could God not choose some less drastic means for their spiritual discipline? But the real question is: Is it really true that God permits suffering for our greater good? Is this the only way we can deal with the problem?

Why don't we have another look at that other attribute of God, his almighty power? Is it really true that God could prevent suffering and evil if he really wanted to? Could he really?

When I was a very small child, my grand-uncle Louis once asked me, 'Tommy, can God do anything he wants to do?' Proudly I answered with the words I had learned from my Baltimore Catechism, 'Yes, God can do all things, and nothing is hard or impossible for him.' 'Well then,' Uncle Louis asked me, 'Could God make a stone so big he couldn't lift it?' That really stumped me. It wasn't until years later when I was in high school that I remembered this incident. The teacher asked the question, 'Could God square a circle?' This time it didn't take long to figure out the answer. Of course not, since a squared circle is a contradiction in terms, like Uncle Louis' stone.

Theology has always recognised this principle and, with few exceptions, Christian theologians have always maintained that God could do anything as long as this did not involve some contradiction, like 'squaring a circle'. John Macquarrie explains that 'when we talk of the omnipotence of God, we do not mean an irrational force that might break out in any direction, but a power that is ordered and which cannot therefore do some things without disrupting itself.' Why then do we not extend this principle and apply it to the problem of evil?

What I would like to maintain is that God is unable to eliminate all suffering and evil, for to do so would be a contradiction in terms. For God to be able to eliminate all suffering and evil he would have to create an entirely different world from this one. If God were to act to prevent all evil and suffering, this would mean that he would 'simultaneously', so to speak, be creating this world and negating it. Or, to use the theology of creation which we find in the first chapter of Genesis, God would at one and the same time be reducing to chaos that which he was bringing out of chaos.

Suffering and Evil in an Evolving Universe

What kind of a world is this? It is, first of all, a world in which, after billions of years of evolution, there came into existence a planet in which life eventually appeared and then finally human beings, with the power of stepping outside of the stream of evolution, looking around at themselves and their world, seeing what the possibilities were for further development, and then freely choosing to do something about it. In a word, it is a world in which there are beings who can choose to act wisely and well – but who can also choose to act foolishly and do evil. By choosing to create a world in which there would one day be free human beings, God limited his own power. Had he chosen to people the earth with robots, there would have been no possibility for human goodness – or for human evil. But once he chose – and I speak anthropomorphically – to create this world, moral evil was a distinct possibility, and all too soon, alas!, an actuality.

But what about all the suffering that comes from events in our world which happen outside the control of human beings? What about natural disasters like earthquakes, volcanos, droughts, floods, hurricanes, tornados, etc.? What about birth defects? What about pain? What about death?

Let me tackle the easiest one first, pain. Is pain a bad thing or a good? Don't ask me that question when I am suffering from a toothache. But what if we lived in a world without any pain at all? Have you ever been to the dentist and had a novocaine injection which benumbed one whole side of your mouth? Do you remember how careful you had to be afterwards when you chewed? Have you ever picked up a hot pot from a stove thinking it was cool – and immediately dropped it? Why? Because the pain caused your autonomic nervous system to react instantaneously, quicker than you could decide to do, and you were spared a serious burn. Pain is one of the greatest defences the body has. It warns us of disease, of danger, of broken or strained organs. Without it the higher forms of life on this planet would be impossible.

We'll say more about death later on. But what about natural disasters and birth defects? This is where Charles Darwin's evolutionary theory can be a great help to us. For evolutionary theory – especially if we extend it beyond Darwin to include non-life as well – shows us a world constantly in a process of change and in which random events play a very important part. Once again we realise that once God chooses to create this particular world, he limits his own freedom in this respect also. For to create this particular world and not some other world mean that random events and genetic mutations are not only a distinct possibility but a necessity. Could God have created a different kind of world, made of a different kind of matter? Einstein asked this question. I wouldn't presume to try to answer it. But it would seem to be true that if it were a different kind of world, made of a different kind of matter, we would not be a part of it. For it is of the stuff of this world that we are made.

In other words, to speak anthropomorphically again, if you were God you may have had only two choices: to create or not to create. Why did he – or better, does he – choose to create, and to create this particular world? That is the mystery. But as Christians we believe that it must have had something to do with his love.

Finally, human freedom does have an influence on all of these natural causes of suffering, and that both before and after the event. How many birth defects are the result of carelessness, greed, selfishness, culpable ignorance on the part of people – not all, to be sure, but far too many. As far as natural disasters are concerned, the distinction is now being made between the physical event itself (referred to as the 'disaster trigger') and this event plus the human suffering that follows upon it (the 'disaster', without further qualification). A recent study has shown that 'though triggered by natural events such as floods and earthquakes, disasters are increasingly man-made', and it documents the extent to which the human-suffering component is directly related and inversely proportional to the financial and social status of the victims (in other words, the poorer and less influential you are, the more likely you are to suffer from 'natural disasters').

And how much of the human suffering that is the result of such natural causes is compounded after the event by the way in which the victims are treated by their fellow human beings? Or better still, let's put that positively. To what extent cannot such suffering be mitigated and at times transformed into the occasion of great human achievements? Helen Keller was the innocent victim of an event – natural or unnatural, it does not matter – which rendered her blind and deaf. But the courage and tenacity and love of other people, notably of her teacher, Annie Sullivan and of Helen herself, enabled her to lead a much fuller life than many of her contemporaries.

The human sufferings that we have been considering, therefore, are not simply the result of an 'act of God'. We free human beings contribute to them, and we can also ease them.

Having taken another look at God's power and discovered that it is not as literally 'almighty' as we may have thought, let us now have another look at his goodness. Have we really given him credit for being as all loving as we should?

Can God Suffer?
Ask anyone the question, 'What happens when someone you love suffers?' and you will almost inevitably receive the answer, 'You suffer too.' But when you ask, 'Can God suffer?' you almost as inevitably get the answer, 'No.' The reason for this is that our thinking about God, here in the West at least, has been in great part shaped by Greek philosophy. As a result we tend to think of God as (the) Perfect Being. But a Perfect Being cannot change, since that would imply either the loss or the gain of some perfection and it would, therefore, either no longer be perfect, or it would not have been perfect to start with. For God to be affected

by what happens to his creatures, however, would mean some kind of change in him. Suffering was also ruled out for other reasons, for example, the Aristotelian notion that God is substantial act, no potency – but suffering, 'passio' in Latin, is in the category of potency, not act.

In this way we ended up with a notion of God as totally remote from his creation, loving it, to be sure, but not in any way affected by what happens to it. Now what kind of love is that? It is certainly not the kind of love, or the kind of God, that the bible speaks of. There we have a very 'passionate' God indeed, a far cry from the remote God of Greek philosophy, a God who suffers along with his creation, who grieves at evil and suffering, and gets angry at it too.

God helps us when we suffer
He is also a God who does something about it, but not like a fairy-tale god. He usually acts through us.

A friend of mine recently told me a story which fits in very well here. There was a man who lived in a two-story house who found himself stranded in the course of a tremendous flood. The water had reached the first floor when a boat came by and the pilot of the boat urged him to get quickly on board. 'No,' the man replied, 'I believe in Jesus, and I know that he loves me and will save me.' 'Well, I have no time to argue with you,' said the man in the boat, and off he went. An hour later the boat came by again. This time the man had been forced by the rising waters to the second floor of his house, but he made the same protestation of faith and refused once again to be saved. Still a third time the boat came by, and this time the man was sitting on the roof of the house, but he still refused to get into the boat, professing his belief that Jesus would save him. When the boat came by again, there was no sign of either house or man. But up in heaven the man accosted Jesus and said, 'I thought you loved me, and I trusted in you. Why didn't you save me?' Jesus replied, 'What did you expect me to do, pilot that boat myself?'

What does God do about evil and suffering? First of all, he does bring good out of both, and this is what the idea of suffering as a discipline sent or permitted by God seems to be getting at. 'All things work together unto good for those who love God,' said Saint Paul (Rom 8:28). He is the Lord of history, and in his own transcendent fashion, not by manipulating his creation, but by working through it in a truly divine, transcendent manner he brings about the accomplishment of his designs.

He also reveals himself as a God of love and evokes our compassion for our fellow men and women. The Old Testament prophets insisted again and again that God was far more interested in how we treated one another, particulariy the more helpless ones among us like widows and orphans and aliens, than he was in 'burnt offerings and sacrifices.' We see this in other great religions as well. In Gandhi's non-violent principle of ahimsa we can see that the ultimate solution to evil is not punishment but the overcoming of evil by goodness. This is surely a divine solution.

Jesus: God's Definitive Response to Suffering and Evil
But it is especially in the person of Jesus that we see how God deals with the mystery of suffering and evil. In Jesus we see that God is Emmanuel, he is God-with-us. God is not remote from our world. His immanence is the measure

of his transcendence. From its very beginning he has been at work in it, fashioning it according to its own laws. But as Christians we believe that at a certain moment in history, 'in the fullness of time' the Bible says, at just the right moment he entered our history in a unique, though not entirely different fashion in the person of one man, Jesus of Nazareth. And how does Jesus deal with suffering and evil?

First of all, when he encounters human suffering, Jesus does something to relieve it. About one-fifth of the gospel accounts are about his acting to relieve human misery. He is compassionate – he suffers – with anyone who suffers, and he heals. How does he do this? By eliciting the person's faith. Notice how often in the gospels Jesus says, 'your faith has saved you.' Up until very recently theology had become very preoccupied with the business of proving that Jesus really was divine, and it came to look at Jesus' healings and the rest of his miracles almost exclusively for their value as proofs of his divinity. The problem with a lot of this was that we came to look upon Jesus as a wonder worker, a kind of magician out to prove his divine origin by means of these acts of power. But in the gospels Jesus plays down the miraculous aspect of his healing actions and calls attention to the faith of the ones who had requested his aid.

Secondly, when he encounters sinners, Jesus does not punish! Instead he reveals God's own love and compassion for sinners. And what happens? A lot of people who were sinners are completely transformed by this experience of being loved. There are many instances of this in the gospels. My favourite is the one about a very wicked man by the name of Zacchaeus (Luke 19 10). He was a publican, a tax collector for the Roman occupying forces, and publicans were a really bad bunch. Zacchaeus was very short, and he was curious to see Jesus but unable to do so because of the crowds, so he climbed a tree. Imagine his embarrassment – horror, more likely – when Jesus spotted him and called the crowd's attention to him. What looks of contempt and hatred he saw in their eyes, and how he must have feared for his life! But the look in Jesus' eyes changed everything. I like to try to imagine what love and compassion that look of Jesus conveyed. When I recall this story I stop at this point and try to bask in the warmth of that love, for I am a sinner too and I know I can be changed by it. Zacchaeus was totally transformed. Immediately he started to plan how to dispose of his ill-gotten wealth for the benefit of the poor.

But, unfortunately, this approach did not work with a lot of people. Their hearts remained closed even to the power of this love. Some of them had too much to give up, their wealth, their positions of power. Jesus could not make them believe; they were free to refuse his love, and they did. In the end it cost him his life. And in this we see God's supreme tactic for dealing with suffering and evil, the death and resurrection of Jesus.

We sometimes speak of Jesus as 'coming to die for us,' and we isolate his death from the rest of his life and make it an end in itself. But this is a serious misunderstanding, I think.

Did Jesus have to die such a horrible death as the death upon the cross, or could he have lived to a ripe old age and then have died peacefully having accomplished what he set out to do, that is to say, to elicit such a change of heart (metanoia) in his contemporaries that God's love working through them could gradually spread throughout the world

and eliminate selfishness and egoism, greed and exploitation, hatred and envy, and all the evils that make the human lot a vale of tears, and in this way make 'God's reign' a reality on earth?' Theoretically, maybe. But it didn't work out that way, and given the extent to which collective sin had already taken hold in our world, probably couldn't have. But he did try. In fact, he seems to have begun by thinking it really was possible. Perhaps only gradually did it dawn upon him that God's reign was going to come about through his rejection, and his denial, though I dare say that at the time he didn't see clearly how.

It was, therefore, with anguish and dread that he approached his death. 'His sweat became as drops of blood,' so horrible was his agony in the Garden of Gethsemene that night before he died (Luke 22:44). But it was with complete fidelity to the mission entrusted to him by God and with utter trust in God his Father that he went to his death, even to a most horrible death on a Roman cross.

And it was in response to this loving fidelity to the Father's will that God raised Jesus from the dead. In the resurrection of Jesus God set his seal of approval on all that Jesus said and did, transforming his mangled body into a new mode of existence in which he is seen to be truly the Son of God in power (Rom 1-4). In the resurrection of Jesus lies our great basis for hope that evil and suffering and death will not have the last word. Like him, and in him, and with him, we too can triumph over all the ills that do beset us.

But that means that we must be disciples of the Crucified and Risen Lord. This does not mean that we go out of our way to seek suffering. That would be masochism, albeit for the best of motives. It means that, allowing ourselves to be transformed by God's love revealed to us in Jesus, we accept the sufferings that being his disciple is necessarily going to entail.

'And the last enemy to be destroyed is death' (1 Cor 15:26). Death is at one and the same time the most natural and the most unnatural event in the world. It is natural for any multicelled organism to die (only amoebas don't die natural death; they split!). But my death, that's different (as Tolstoy's Ivan Ilych discovered to his horror). My death is horrible to the extent that I cling to my selfhood in a self-protective way that has no room for God or any other person at the center of my being. But if I am able to let go, to 'uncenter,' as Monika Helwig puts it, death can be transformed into a newness of life, a sharing in divinity. The death and resurrection of Jesus makes that possible.

Supplementary Material 2

Extract from the 1990 report on session 9
In the session, precious insights and searching questions
emerged. Most felt that it was after the event of tragedy and
suffering that they were able to find God. Some felt that
their discovery of God was in the form of prayer for help.
Others experienced growth through pain and identified
with the passion of Christ. The point was made that often it
was the person on the periphery of suffering who experienced anger rather than the person who was suffering. For
some, suffering led to a questioning of values. What do you
say to someone who is suffering? Sometimes the person
who responds to a situation finds more love in themselves
than they ever imagined they had. When there are no answers or solutions, it is helpful to know that God is vulnerable in the world and suffers in the world. It is as if God has
to live through the hiccup of nature.

All the sharing was a profound experience and one person
summed it up very well when he said that we were treading
on sacred ground.

The evening ended with Psalm 105.

The God who speaks has revealed himself in darkness.
Sometimes he is covered in pain. Each of us relates to God
from where we are coming from.

SESSION TEN

Spirituality –
The Transformative Way

Aims
• *To enable the participants explore the experience and meaning of compassion as a pathway to God.*

Materials
Handout 13: 'How far would I go?'
Photo Language or video.
Copies of last week's report and commentary.
Activity Sheet.

Time-Table
1.   7.45   Welcome.
2.   7.55   Team tasks.
3.   8.05   Introduction to The Transformative Way.
4.   8.10   Focusing activity.
5.   8.20   Sharing in groups of three.
6.   8.45   Feedback.
      9.05   Break.
7.   9.20   Presentation on The Compassionate Way.
8.   9.40   Reactions.
9.   9.55   Personal reflection.
10. 10.00 Reaction and Snowflake reading.
11. 10.10   Conclusion.

Suggested Procedure

1. Welcome
Welcome the people and describe the time-table and aims for this session.

2. Team tasks

3. Introduction to the Transformative Way
We are looking at the pathways along which we and our God meet. In this session we come to the pathway which best expresses what Partners in Faith is all about. It is our conviction that the God revealed in the Bible is a God of compassion who invites us to be compassionate like God, and in the process we enter into union with God and with all humankind. God has revealed God's-self to us through love and care: we are invited to live in compassionate response to the hurting, the wounded, those in pain, in poverty, in deep need. In this session we want to get in touch with God through the pathway of compassion.

4. Focusing Activity
The team provides some sense-stimulus to the imagination of the participants, e.g. using good clippings and photos, from newspapers, magazines, reviews and agencies, which can be attached to the walls of the meeting-room in readiness. These can feature: elderly people, unemployed people, deprived areas, disabled persons, homeless people, people caught up in drugs, the lonely, fearful, hungry, mentally ill, small farmers, travellers, refugees, the excluded, children of different kinds, young people. Alternatively, you may find a video which will be evocative in the same way.

While a suitable piece of music is being played, participants are asked to move around and silently look at the photo-language and see to which images their hearts are drawn, even in some small way.

Alternatively you may find a video which will be evocative in the same way.

5. Sharing
In groups of three, people share about:
   1. The image that moved me most and why.
   2. When have I experienced compassion in my own or others' lives?
   3. What do I mean when I use the word 'compassion'?

6. Feedback

BREAK

7. Presentation on The Compassionate Way
The following notes are offered as guidelines.

Compassion, the Divine Power in us
We often hear the phrase 'My heart went out to her or to him' and sometimes use it ourselves. What kind of situations would make your heart 'go out to someone'? Last week we focused on some of the situations where we would say our hearts went out to others, e.g. while in the waiting room of a hospital with a parent who has a sick child, or with a parent who has lost a child through a cot death. Other situations would move us, such as seeing someone come home yet again after an interview, rejected and still unemployed. Again, the brutal killing of two women and six Jesuit priests in El Salvador moved us deeply. Our hearts go out – the feeling of grief or horror ignites in us.

When such things happen we ask 'Why'? When we listened to Phil Collins' song about the poor woman in the street our hearts went out after her, but then the song goes on to say 'Think about it, think about it'. When we do think about it, often we get a worrying, negative feeling which says: 'There's nothing I can do about it.' So what is this thing that causes our hearts to go out?

It's known as compassion. It has the popular sense of being soft, nice, listening and gentle, but if it's nice and soft at the centre it also has to be strong and able to endure if it is to achieve anything. Maybe it is double-centred. Look at this word: com-passion, made up of two Latin words, 'Passio' means 'suffer' and 'con' means 'with'. So compassion means to suffer with or stand beside a grieving, sorrowful person. If you really suffer with someone, if your heart really goes out to someone, you will want to do something to change the situation.

The beginning of doing something is to ask why is this suffering happening. What are the causes? Unless we ask why, we are only treating the symptom, rather than getting to the root cause. When we suffer with the unemployed or those killed in El Salvador, we sometimes shy away and say 'Ah, no, that's all to do with politics or economics, not with faith.' But if the root cause of the poverty is political and economic, then the biggest sins being committed in this area are in the political and economic fields. To try to keep God out of politics and economics is to say that there are areas of life where God can't be let in. But God can't be kept out of any part of life: that was clear in the story of Moses, where God led Moses to get involved in political action in Egypt. It's clear, too, in the stories of the prophets: all of them had to take on the political and economic reality which had become unjust. And God is shown, time and again in the Old Testament, working to turn the regime upside down (Psalm 113:7-9). The biggest sins today are being committed, not in the bedrooms, but in board-rooms where political and economic decisions are made that wreck the poor.

Still a nagging doubt can remain: it is all too much, too far away from 'real' compassion. Jesus is often quoted as being compassionate and gentle. He actually told us to be as 'gentle as doves' but he told us to be 'cunning' also. He was perceptive, astute, sharp: he asked awkward questions. Why? He saw and heard the cry of the people, and he spoke about it, called people to work for a change, did something about the situation – and expects us to do likewise.

Let us look at the journey our 'compassion' has to make. It begins in our hearts, but once we have felt it, then we must ask 'Why?'. We need big ears in order to hear the situations that make our heart pain. And our heads have to get into the action, too: we need to analyse with our heads what our hearts have picked up and what our eyes and ears have confirmed to be true. Then we can get tongue-tied, because if we say the unpopular thing, we will be disliked. All that we have FELT, SEEN, HEARD, AND THOUGHT, pushes or compels us to SPEAK. In fact, true compassion makes us speak up about what is wrong.

However, if it only remained at the speaking level, it would remain mere words. Our compassion must transfer to our hands; we must be prepared to work for change in the suffering situation. Armchair compassion is not Christianity - because it is just pity and pity does not transform anything. We are challenged, by our HEART, our EYES, our EARS, our HEADS, to get out of our chairs and get to work with our hands. But again, another form of self pity can bedevil us. We can still say, in the common tradition of the west, 'I can't do much on my own', 'I will sit down again, after all my fine thoughts and insights'. So we cop-out. True, our wish to follow through with compassion can be defeated if we try to be compassionate alone. But we don't have to be alone, we can reach out, hold the hands of others, join hands with those already before us. Together we can work to transform the way things are, through action, through poems, through symbolic gestures.

Compassion is God's power working in us. It is the third way of spirituality, the transformative way. If we allow ourselves to notice with our hearts, eyes, ears, and heads, God, working in our world, calling us to change and transform unjust situations, then we can have enormous effect, joining our hands with other workers for the kingdom in a movement for change, using our feet to walk. This is part of what it means to follow Jesus, as members of the Church. Concrete compassion is the key to the compassionate way.
(Based on a talk by Albert Nolan at Milltown Park, Dublin)

8. Reactions
What struck you, puzzled you, disturbed you?

9. Personal reflection
Give each one a copy of Handout 16, headed:
How Far would I go to change a situation?

10. Reaction
When everyone has finished thinking about the suggestions, ask for some reaction.
Conclude with the following reading:
A Tale For All Seasons
'Tell me the weight of a snowflake,' a small bird asked a wild dove. 'Nothing more than nothing,' was the answer. 'In that case, I must tell you a marvellous story,' the small bird said, 'I sat on the branch of a fir tree, close to its trunk, when it began to snow not heavily, not in a raging blizzard no, just like in a dream, without a wind, without any violence. Since I did not have anything better to do, I counted the snowflakes settling on the twigs and needles of my branch. Their number was exactly 3,741,952. When the 3,741,953rd dropped onto the branch, nothing more than nothing as you say, the branch broke off.'

Having said that, the small bird flew away. The dove, since Noah's time an authority on the matter, thought about the story for a while and finally said to herself, 'Perhaps there is only one person's voice lacking for peace to come to the world.'

*Kurt Kauter from 'New Fables spoke the Carabou.'
quoted in the Gateway Series, St Columban's, Navan.*

11. Conclusion
Remind them about the team tasks.

Handout 16

How far would I go to change a situation?
(Adapted from The Gateway Series, St Columban's, Dalgan Park, Navan, Co Meath)

How ready do you feel about the following:
(Place an X in the appropriate space)

	V.READY	READY	NOT SURE	UNEASY	V. UNEASY
1. Give money to organisations working for peace and development.					
2. get info through magazines or T.V. Programmes					
3. Boycott goods					
4. Sign petitions					
5. Write letters					
6. Attend public meetings,lectures, courses, etc.					
7. Inform family, friends and others of issues.					
8. Organise fund-raising events					
9. Take part in a survey of people's needs					
10 Drop or hand out leaflets					
11 Participate in a march					
12. Steward or organise a march					
13. Speak to groups					
14. Take part in a sit-in					
15. Break the law if you thought it unjust.					

SESSION ELEVEN

Spirituality –
The Creative Way

Aims
• To enable participants to experience afresh what it means to be co-creative with God by expressing their creativity through different media.

Materials
These are itemised under each of the six 'media'.

Time-Table
1. 7.45   Welcome.
2.   Team tasks.
3. 8.05   Exploration of The Creative Way.
4. 8.25   Creative Workshops.

    9.30   Break.
5. 9.45   Presentations.
6. 10.15   Conclusion.

Suggested Procedure

1. Welcome and Introduction
Welcome the people and explain the aim and time-table of this session.

2. Team tasks

3. Exploration of The Creative Way
Some guidelines for the leader:
Tonight we are moving on to looking at how we meet God in reality by co-creating with God. Every day we are creating and co-creating – each time we make something, each time we use the resources around us to bring about something new. Being creative is the opposite of being passive or apathetic. It's about using the energy and power within us to change our surroundings, to link old things together in a new way; it's about taking things and making them stretch:
  • like when we take pieces of wood and make a chair and stool;
  • when we take flour and water and buttermilk and make brown bread;
  • when we find a piece of cloth and make a new dress;
  • when we stretch our weekly allowance with ingenuity and by going from shop to shop, put together a new outfit for the kids.

Being creative gives a sense of achievement to ourselves; we are pleased, satisfied, delighted with what we have done.

Through being creative we overcome despair (the feeling of hopelessness that locks us into believing that things can't be different); we bring joy to others.

In giving expression to our creativity we are giving expression to the gift God gave us when God created humankind, male and female, in the image and likeness of God and gave us the world to develop.

We all know well the moments when we feel dull, unproductive, sluggish, apathetic, heavy, uncreative. What is the way out of this situation? We don't have to wait for a lightning bolt to jolt us out of it. What is within is not dead, only *blocked* and there are ways of unblocking our creative gift.

Take a piece of beautiful music and let it sweep over your senses, let your imagination float free and evoke images of colour, shape, touch, movement, gesture ... and then find a way of holding on to these by using some medium: paint, sound, rhythm, movement, colour, texture, drama, mime, drawing. This is one way we can activate the creative energy and let it transform ourselves and our environment.

Note: The leading learners can illustrate creativity by playing a piece of music or tape and expressing through word, song or gesture what happened when they let that music loose in their consciousness.

4. Creative Workshops

1. Five mixed groups are formed

2. Each group is given a pre-recorded audio-tape and a tape-recorder. On each tape there is a piece of scripture recited by someone with a good voice against a background of suitable music. Here are the texts we used:

a). The Beginning (Genesis 1:1-31)
Medium: Mural Painting
The group is given a twelve-foot length of newsprint, or an old wallpaper roll, paint brushes, pencils and five big containers of primary-colour poster paints; water, brushes and simple plastic containers for the paint.
Music: Dvorak Symphony from *World of Hundred Best Tunes*, Side one, Track Two.

b). Crossing the Sea (Exodus 14:21-31)
Medium: Mime: using movement or dance to express what the listening generates in the group.
Music: Mantovani's Greatest Hits, Exodus Theme, Side One, Track XX.

c). Valley of the Dry Bones (Ezekiel 37:1-14)
Medium: Scuplture (arranging bits and pieces).
The team is provided with a large box containing pieces of cloth, string, odds and ends, bits of wood, toilet roll, branch of a tree, mirror, anything that could be used to construct a creative work.
Alternatively, one could use wet clay in plastic bags.
Music: Evening Falls: verses 1-6 side 2, Track 2.
Edge of Darkness: verses 7-14 Side 2, Track 1.
Orinoco Flow

d). To us a child is Born (Isaiah 9:1-7)
Medium: Collage
This group is provided with pages out of magazines, advertisements, sheets of colour, photos, and asked to make a collage on pieces of newsprint.
Music: Corelli: Side Two, track Two: *Concerto grosso* (Allegro)
.

e). God is Love (Psalm 103) (version from *Psalms Now* recommended)

Medium: Sound and Song:
The group is given a tambourine, bodhrán, boxes with hard peas inside, a whistle, a mouth organ, etc., and is asked to create, through chants or sounds or new lyrics, what comes to them.

Music: Themes from the film 'Brother Sun and Sister Moon', Side B, Second Track.

Each group is given a copy of Handout 17, and the process is explained. The groups go apart to work.

BREAK

5. Presentations
Each group now plays a piece of their tape to give us an idea of the stimulus for their creative work. And then they present the work.

If there is time, a leading learner can comment on the meaning of the night in terms of God's invitation to all to be co-creators by building with what we've got, by linking things in new ways.

6. Conclusion
Remind them about team tasks.
If the next session is a celebration, make sure the groups decide what food and drinks to bring.

Handout 17

Process for Workshop

1. Appoint a co-ordinator

2. Co-ordinator:
> Let's make ourselves comfortable,
> relax and be quiet,
> tune into our breathing.

We are now going to play a short recording of a reading from the Bible with background music.

Our Theme is ... As you listen to the recording let your imagination flow ... see what images, ideas, feelings come to you.

When the recording stops, continue letting your mind free flow, imagining, developing, linking ...

Try to imagine how these images could be expressed in our medium which is ...

Play The Tape

Stop Tape

Keep Silence For One Minute

3. Co-ordinator asks each one to share what has come up in his/her imagination.

If necessary, play the tape again

4. Let us see what we have in common ...
> what is different ...
> *(let each one speak)*

5. Try to link the ideas/images, colours, etc., together.

6. Will someone try to make a start, e.g. shape, movement, words/phrases, outlines.

7. See can we co-operate in making something,
> recognising different gifts
> but letting all contribute in some way.

Go ahead! Make it!

SESSION TWELVE

Review and Celebration

Aims
• To enable the participants to recall and review the sessions so far.
• To celebrate all that has happened and all we have become for one another.

Materials
Posters of each of the sessions
Summary of the Story So Far
Hymns, readings, poem etc for the celebration in Oratory
Questions for the personal review.

Time-Table
1. 7.45   Welcome.
2.   Team tasks.
3. 7.55   Introduction – Review.
4. 8.20   Buzz groups.
5. 8.25   Group Sharing.
6. 8.50   Celebration in Prayer.
7. 9.15   Celebration in food, drink, song, dance.

Suggested Procedure

1. Welcome

2. Team tasks

3. Introduction
Tonight we gather to remember, to review and to celebrate our participation in *Partners in Faith* over the past three months. We'll begin by recalling each session with a poster and a comment and try to get an overall view of what we've been doing.

The story of Partners in Faith *So Far*
Beforehand, make a small poster for each session and prepare a brief summary of what happened. Put up the posters one by one and give the summary. The leaders can alternate the story-telling. Gradually you will build up a mural of Partners in Faith *which serves to help participants recall the sessions and see the links, i.e. the overall flow.*

Supplementary Material 1 includes a summary of all sessions.

Here is a sample poster:

4. Buzz groups
Remembering is a way of owning our experience and insights; secondly, it helps us to get an overall view of what we have been doing, and thirdly, it enables us to appreciate the sessions and enrich others with our different perspectives. For a while, we invite you to reflect back for a few moment ... Now buzz with your neighbour:
    What stands out for you as a good experience?
    Any suggestions?
Distribute Review Sheets (Handout 18) and explain that these individual sheets will be collected.

5. Group Sharing
Appoint a co-ordinator to each group.
-Participants meet in mixed groups of four and share their personal reflections.
At a later stage, leaders put this question to each group:
    'From all you have experienced together, what would you say is at the heart of *Partners in Faith*?'
The co-ordinator gives everyone a chance to speak and then puts together a statement in two or three sentences.

6. Feedback
Leaders ask reporters to communicate the responses to the statements.
Collect the individual sheets.

7. Celebration in Prayer
In the Oratory
A short celebration will put the whole experience on a different plane. Here is a brief outline:

a). Hymn: e.g. Be not Afraid (based on Isaiah 43)

b). Word of Introduction.

c). Reading: Isaiah 9:1-7

d). Sharing of Gifts
Each group is given an envelope containing coloured card stars on which there are quotes from the Scriptures. Each group is asked to choose a quotation suited to each individual in another group. One by one, the members of each group read out the star and present it to the particular person for whom it is intended.
A selection of suitable quotes is given in Supplementary Material 2.

e). Prayers of the Faithful
f). A Christmas Poem, e.g. *Christmas Carol* by Patrick Kavanagh

g). Final Hymn

7. Celebration with food, drink, song and chat
Continue the celebration in the meeting room, with food, drink, music, chat and a song of Partners.

Remind them of the date of the next session in New Year.

Handout 18

Review Sheet

1. What stands out for you as a good experience?

_____

_____

_____

_____

2. What might have been done differently?

_____

_____

_____

_____

3. What do we need to do in the future?

_____

_____

_____

_____

Supplementary Material 1

PARTNERS IN FAITH
THE STORY SO FAR

Session One: PARTNERS IN FAITH
Process: Gathering as groups. Mountjoy Square, New faces, strangers. Marino Waltz. Names. Our own place. Tea. Slide presentation on P.I.F. Prayer. Handouts. Discussion.
Content: Partners in Faith is an adult religious education and training process in and through small faith communities. It's about a renewed religious mentality and new ways of being the church (i.e. small christian community groups). The process involves learning by doing: faith-sharing mutual support, study, prayer and action.

Session Two: MOMENTS OF MYSTERY
Process: Mixed groups to talk of own places. Team-tasks explained. Meditation on journey of life. Picking out special moments of mystery. Explanation. Prayer.
Content: Team-tasks are ways of contributing to the common good – report, prayer etc. We minister to one another. We also slowly build up confidence to prepare, to organize, to present, etc. Human experience is where God breaks into our lives. Moments of mystery are key moments when we experience something bigger than ... a source of wonder, support, meaning at e.g. birth, forgiveness, failure, death, love, nature. All these are gateways to God. Special moments reveal what is there in ordinary moments.

Session Three: IMAGES OF GOD
Process: Teams begin to take responsibility. Meditation on our image of God. Using activity sheet to describe our image. Second Activity Sheet: Is our God more personal, distant, authoritative, liberating? Sharing. Discussing how our image of God affects our lives.
Content: Our image of God is formed through influence of parents, family, teachers, school, and our human experience. This image affects how we relate to God, and others and the world. The kind of God we believe in shows in our attitudes, actions and words.

Session Four: GOD OF MOSES
Process: Handouts and reports and evaluations of previous session. Group a bit more at ease. Input on economic, political, social, cultural situation of Egypt and of life of Moses in that situation. How God communicated through Moses' experience. Reflection on the 'burning bush' as a way of expressing Moses and our moments of mystery. Discussion.
Content: The Bible is the record of the people's experience of God's self-communication. It shows us the kind of God God is and God's dream. The story of Moses and his idea of God is a significant part of the biblical basis of our religion. It helps us check our image of God. Is our God one, personal, compassionate and liberating? Through faith the Bible helps us find God today.

Session Five: GOD'S DREAM FOR PEOPLE
Process: Reminder of situation in Egypt. Groups asked to put selves in shoes of Israelites as they tried to build a new society. Each group given an aspect: distribution of land, political situation, housing, human wellbeing, work in industry. Presentation by groups – newsprint. Input on what the Israelites did. Account of 10 Commandments as Constitution of new society.

Content: The change from Egypt to Promised Land shows what God's dream is: they moved from a situation where the name of God was used to keep wealth and power in the hands of few. Decisions came from top; only those who HAD were worth respecting. They moved to where there was ONE liberating God before whom all are equal. Everyone had fair share. Decisions made based on people's needs. Everyone was equal and deserving of respect. The 10 Commandments were a kind of Constitution to ensure that people continued to work for the kind of society God wanted (The Covenant).
*Each group given a commandment or two to show how they are fulfilled or abused today.

Session Six: EMERGENCE OF PROPHETS
Process: Buzz as groups got their commandment collages together and presented them. They used cuttings, photos, etc. Facts of fulfilment or abuse today. Input on formation of new society. Influence of foreign powers. People ask for a king – development of monarchy.
Content: With coming of the kings – there was again accumulation of wealth and power in the hands of few. This resulted in poverty and oppression. People forgot the kind of God our God is (false religions) and forgot God's dream. Some, who did not forget God and God's dream were the prayerful, poetic prophets who protested. They wanted renewal of faith, living in tender solidarity and action for justice.
*Groups given Prophet texts and asked to compose prophetic poems for today.

Session Seven: BEING PROPHETS TODAY
Process: Icebreaker – asking questions of others. Prayer and news linked, E.S.R.I., and *Another Day in Paradise.* The biggest buzz came when each group summarized their home meeting, read a few Bible texts and then presented their prophetic poems with original insight and creativity . We then reflected on our work.
Content: When we keep alive in our minds and hearts, by prayer and scripture, a true idea of God and search for God's will we look at reality with clear eyes, affirm what is good but challenge what is bad and oppressive. We encourage ourselves and others to wake up to the situation and engage with hope in action for change.

Session Eight: SPIRITUALITY – THE POSITIVE WAY
Process: What does what we have done mean in terms of our relationship with God? Presentation on floor using blue circles of our covenant relationship with God. God communicates and calls. We respond and care. Explanation and meditation on positive way. Personal reflection on positive way in our lives. Sharing in concentric moving circles. Preparation to make psalms of praise.
Content: As people of God we notice and respond to God's communication in our human experience at personal, interpersonal, wider society and nature levels. When we see the good things as God's gifts we respond with thanksgiving and praise. In walking humbly with God we count our blessings and build up our energy.

Session Nine: SPIRITUALITY - THE NEGATIVE WAY
Process: Testimonies by G., M. and C. on how they encountered God in negative experiences at personal, interpersonal and wider levels. Personal reflection on negative experiences which led at some stage to awareness of God. Sharing in groups of four. Open session on how negative experiences

can help us see God.

Content: Bad experiences; self-inflicted, mistreatment, inexplicable suffering or betrayal have for some people been moments of mystery leading to a deeper awareness of God as: support, forgiving, source of purpose or stimulus to action. We see this in the psalms of King David. *God is my rock, my light, my salvation.*

Session Ten: SPIRITUALITY – THE TRANSFORMATIVE WAY

Process: 1) Video on how some Irish people responded in Dublin to suffering in El Salvador. 2) Video on families in El Salvador. Reflection. Input on transformative way as compassionate action. Outline of possible responses to suffering. The Snowflake. Alternatively, use photos and clippings.

Content: In face of situations of suffering some people feel or allow themselves to feel with their hearts, ask why with their heads, and respond in action with hands, and feet and voice. When we respond in compassionate action we know God because we are cooperating with God in transformation as was the case with Yahweh and Moses in face of the suffering of the people of Egypt.

Session Eleven: SPIRITUALITY - THE CREATIVE WAY

Process: Playing of music. Leaders say how it affected their imagination. Each group given a recording of Bible text and music: In the Beginning, Crossing of the Sea, Valley of Dry Bones, A Child is Born and God is Love.

Given also a process by which we listened to tape, let imagination flow and expressed images and ideas in either colour/mural, mime-drama, arranging bits and pieces, collage or sound-song.

Content: We are given the world by God our creator and we are invited to co-create with God: to develop creation, make new things. This session is a sign of how we can all be more creative by use of our imagination and linking things in new and different ways. In the process of co-creating we know we cooperate with God creator.

Supplementary Material 2

Quotes for the Stars:

'I have called you by your name, you are mine.' Is 43:1
'I will make you a light to the nations.' Is 49:6
'The Holy One of Israel has chosen you.' Is 49:7
'Look, I have engraved you on the palm of my hand.' Is 49:16
'I hid you in the shadow of my hand.' Is 51:16
'In great compassion I shall take you back.' Is 54:7
'My faithful love will never leave you.' Is 54: 10
'In saving justice you shall be made firm.' Is 54:13
'Pay attention, come to me, listen and you will live.' Is 55:3
'Seek out Yahweh while he may be found.' Isaiah 55:6
'Yes you will go out in joy and be led away in safety.' Is 55:12
'Your light will rise in the darkness and your darkest hour will be like noon.' Is 58:10
'Yahweh will satisfy your needs.' Is 58:11
'Arise, shine out, for your lgiht has come.' Is 60:1
'I will make you a source of joy from age to age.' Is 60:15
'Yahweh will be your everlasting light.' Is 60:19
'You will be called by a new name which Yahweh will reveal.' Is 62:2
'Yahweh will take delight in you.' Is 62:4
'Be joyful, be glad for ever, at what I am creating.' Is 65:18
'As a mother comforts her child so shall I comfort you.' Is 66:13
'When you search for me you will find me.' Jer 29:11
'I know what plans I have in mind for you, plans of peace.' Jer 29:13.
'When you search whole-heartedly for me, I shall let you find me.' Jer 29:13
'I shall bring you back to the place from which I exiled you.' Jer 29:14
'When you call to me and come and pray to me, I shall listen to you.' Jer 29:12
'I am with you to save you.' Jer 30:11
'I shall restore you to health and heal your wound.' Jer 30:17
'I shall make you honoured, no more to be humbled.' Jer 30:19
'I have loved you with an everlasting love.' Jer 31:3
'I shall guide you to streams of water by a smooth path where you will not stumble.' Jer 31:9
'I shall lead you to the desert and speak to your heart.' Ho 2:14
'How could I part with you, how could I give you up?' Ho 11:8
'I shall pour clean water over you and you shall be cleansed.' Ez. 36:25
'I shall give you a new heart and put a new spirit in you.' Ez 36:26
'I will resettle you on your own soil.' Is 12:2
'Trust in God for ever, a shelter from the storm.' Is 26:4
'Yahweh is waiting to be gracious to you.' Is 30:18
'He who is your teacher will hide no longer.' Is 30:20
'Your God is coming to save you.' Is 35:4.

SESSION THIRTEEN

Scripture & Life in a Small Faith Community

Aims
• To re-affirm the aims of *Partners in Faith*.
• To give participants a chance to experience a way of linking scripture and life in small faith community.

Materials
Texts for each group.
Handout 19 for 'What's in a name?'
Handout 20 on Seven Step Method

Time-table
1. 7.45   Introductions.
2. 8.00   Introduction to this term.
3. 8.10   Introducing Small Faith Community and the Seven-Step Method.
4. 8.25   Bible reflection.
   9.20   Break.
5. 9.35   Reflection on the experience.
6. 10.00   Plenary session.
7.   Conclusion and new task rota.

Suggested Procedure

1. Introductions
Renewing Acquaintance
Form five mixed groups of 6 (by numbering off 1-5). Give each group a copy of Handout 19. Whoever has the Handout answers the questions on it.

2. Introduction to this term
As we begin the New Year, *Partners in Faith* enters a whole new phase. This year we will be doing the following:

1. Building up each parish group as a *Small Faith Community* in which you can experience what it means to support one another in keeping your faith deep, alive and active in the world around you.

2. Deepening our understanding of *what Jesus stood for* in his own country and among his own people so we can be clearer about what we stand for today in our country and among our people.

3. Using a method of *group action*, through which, with step-by-step guidance, each group will identify a concern of the larger group and will design and lead a session for the benefit of all. In this way you will experience how a small group can use power as service.

Through all that has gone before Christmas and the next sessions we hope that you will feel the importance of being a member of a small faith community, in which you are helped to deepen and keep alive your faith in the God of the Bible, and to express it in actions that make God's dream for people come true.

3. Introducing Small Faith Community
A small faith community is a way of being the Church. The essential aspects of such a community are:
- being together and getting to know one another.
- telling one another about our efforts to live our faith.
- reading scripture and linking it with life.
- encouraging one another for action.
- sometimes organising action.
- sometimes organising study.

All the elements are woven into what we do together in each session of *Partners in Faith*. During this term we will emphasise them as well as develop skills related to them. In this session we will concentrate on two of the basic skills:
   a) facilitating a group
   b) linking scripture with life.

The best way to learn any skill is by trying it and then reflecting on what we've done. The basic factors in facilitation of a group are:
- creating a climate of safety.
- encouraging interaction.
- keeping the group to the task.
- directing the group towards achieving its goal.
- intervening when the group progress is being hindered.
- evaluating the progress.
Leader elaborates on each of these points.

The method we're going to use is called *The Seven Step Method*. Its aims are:
- to experience the presence of God.
- to help each member of the group to be touched personally by the Word of God.
- to encourage mutual deepening of the faith by personal sharing.
- to deepen mutual bonds among the members of the group.
- to create trust within the the group.
- to create a spiritual climate for planning action.

The steps involved are as follows:

THE SEVEN-STEP METHOD OF BIBLE REFLECTION

1. We invite the Lord.
Will someone please invite Jesus in a prayer?

2. We read the text.
Let us open chapter ...
Will someone please read verses ...?

3. We pick out words and meditate on them.
We pick out words or short phrases, read them aloud prayerfully and keep silence in between. (This is like 'savouring' the text or lifting out, for everyone to see and hear, the hidden treasure of the text).

4. We let God speak to us in silence.
We keep silence for a few minutes and allow God to speak to us.

5, We share what we have heard in our hearts.
Which words have touched you personally and why?
(No discussion or argument.)

6. We discuss any task which our group is called to do.
Here, if the group has a task in hand, they can report what stage they are at; if not, and they feel there is something they would like to get involved in, they can talk about it and plan. Or simply ask: 'What is being asked of us by this text?

7. We pray together spontaneously.
We end with a prayer/hymn which everyone knows by heart.

These seven steps are on Handout 20, of which you will get a copy.

4. Bible Reflection
We will arrange you in mixed groups. Ask someone to facilitate the first half, and someone else to facilitate the second half of the meeting, if it seems appropriate.

Here are five texts which can be distributed, one to each group:
1. Isaiah 43:1-7
2. Jeremiah 31:31-34
3. Isaiah 42:1-6
4. Ezekiel 34:16
5. Isaiah 49: 1-6.
The Bible Reflection then begins.

BREAK

5. Reflection on the experience
Divide whole group into three (mix by counting off 1,2,3; 1,2,3 ...) Each leading learner takes a group and reflects with them on how the experience went, using these questions:
1. How did the meeting go?
2. How did you feel participating?
3. What was it like facilitating?
4. What strikes you about Bible reflection?

6. Plenary session
Sharing some of what came up in the three groups:
- What was good about it?
- What was difficult?
- What comments have you to make now?

7. Conclusion
Arrange a new rota of team tasks for the new term.

Handout 19

What's in a name?

1. How did you get your name?

2. What does it mean? (if you know)

3. Do you like your name?

4. Who else that you like and admire
has the same name?

5. If you weren't called that name,
what would you like to be called?

6. How important are names in your view?

Handout 20

The Seven-Step Method of Bible Reflection

1. We invite the Lord.
Will someone please invite Jesus in a prayer?

2. We read the text.
Let us open chapter ...
Will someone please read verses?

3. We pick out words and meditate on them.
We pick out words or short phrases,
read them aloud prayerfully
and keep silence in between.
(This is like 'savouring' the text
or lifting out,
for everyone to see and hear,
the hidden treasure of the text).

4. We let God speak to us in silence.
We keep silence for a few minutes
and allow God to speak to us.

5. We share what we have heard in our hearts.
Which words have touched you personally and why?
(No discussion or argument.)

6. We discuss any task which our group is called to do.
Here, if the group has a task in hand,
they can report what stage they are at;
if not,
and they feel there is something they would like to get involved in,
they can talk about it and plan.
Simply ask: 'What is being asked of us by this text?'

7. We pray together spontaneously.
We end with a prayer/hymn which everyone knows by heart.

SESSION FOURTEEN

Palestine at the time of Jesus

Aims
• To set the scene for understanding the nature of Jesus' ministry.
• To present the socio-economic, political and cultural context in which Jesus lived.
• To enable the participants to experience the reality of the different social groupings through role-play.

Materials
Map of Palestine and diagram of a pyramid.
Handouts 21 and 22, role descriptions for each person.

Time-Table
1.	7.45	Welcome and Introduction.
2.	7.55	Team tasks.
3.	8.05	Presentation on Palestine at the time of Jesus.
4.	8.25	Taking on roles.
5.	8.40	Grouping according to roles.
	8.55	Break
6.	9.10	Mixing the groupings.
7.	9.30	Intervention.
8.	9.45	Feedback
9.	10.15	Conclusion.

Suggested Procedure

1. Welcome and Introduction
Welcome the people and describe this session's aims and time-table.

2. Team Tasks
News, report, commentary, prayer.

3. Presentation on Palestine at the time of Jesus
From the point of view of understanding what our God is like and what God wants, the key figure in the Bible is of course Jesus of Nazareth. As members of the Church, baptised and living 'in Christ Jesus', we are growing all the time in knowledge and love of God. To understand more clearly what God wants, the New Testament (the Gospel) is a vital source of light for us, helping us to understand 'the mind and heart of Christ Jesus' who is for us the 'Way, the Truth and the Life'. To know what Jesus stood for it is essential to be aware of the reality in which he lived.

In this session we will:
1. Look at the socio-economic-political reality of Palestine at the time of Jesus.
2. Explore the lives of the different groupings who made up that society.

Palestine at the time of Jesus
From the following, prepare a twenty-minute presentation on Palestine at the time of Jesus. The summary gives the essential points. Other material to fill it out is included in Supplementary Material. The map of Palestine and the pyramidal diagram are very important.

Our approach in *Partners in Faith* is to show how far removed Palestine was from being the fulfilment of God's dream. This will become clear through the outline of the economic, political and social situation and through clarifying the concept of God which influenced the relationships and action of people.

Below is a brief summary of the situation in Palestine. The presenter should fill out the presentation with material from the more extensive treatment given in the Supplementary Material.

Palestine at the Time of Jesus
It was a small country in the Middle-East with a population of 500,000. Jerusalem, the capital, had about 30,000 inhabitants.

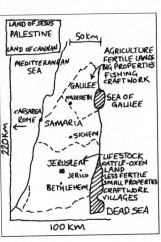

ECONOMY
It was an agricultural country.

Agriculture
(especially in fertile Galilee)
Wheat, barley, olives, vegetables, fruit, wine.

Livestock
(principally in less fertile Judea)
Big animals: oxen and camels.
Small animals: sheep and goats.

Fishing
In the Sea of Galilee. Fish was a popular food.

Craftwork
(towns and villages)
Jars, clothes, oils, foodstuffs, textiles, plates, perfume, leather, luxury items.

Vegetables
Lentils, chick peas, salad, dates.

Means of production
Land, vineyards, olive gardens, wine presses, boats, tools.

Domestic trade
Barter.

Imports
Luxury goods such as cedar (of Lebanon), incense, gold, copper, iron from Arabia (traders and merchants dealt in these).

Exports
Fruit, oil, wine, skins, bitumen (Dead Sea).

TAXES

For the Romans:
- a quarter of the harvest (tributum)
- cash or kind for the army (anona)
- for transport of goods (publicum)
- for moving between regions (custom tax)

For the Jewish People in Jerusalem:
- by virtue of being a Jew (didrachma)
– one tenth of income for the Temple (tithes).
- for the three major Jewish feasts (offering)
- the cost of changing money into Temple coinage.

The Temple

This was the major building where Jewish worship was carried out. It was considered the House of God and here the Jewish religious and political power was centred in the hands of the Jewish High Priests. Here taxes were paid so it was like:

The Central Bank

During the year about 30,000 people came and went to and from the Temple and the crowd swelled to 90,000 for the three great feasts.

GROUPINGS

The Government

Centred in Jerusalem and called the Sanhedrin, with 72 members mostly made up of High Priests, elders and scribes, representing the well-off.

Parties

Sadducees: Jewish aristocracy, large landowners and High Priests.

Pharisees: Artisans and small traders, leaders of the ordinary people.

Zealots: Paramilitaries against Roman occupation, made up of labourers. They wanted a free Israel.

Essenes: Monastic group that withdrew from society.

SOCIETY

Main characteristics of society at Jesus' time

• People were being *exploited* by an unjust system of taxation.

• There was growing *unemployment*, impoverishment and mounting debts.

• Powerful people were unconcerned about the poverty of their brothers and sisters.

• A lot of *sickness* due to malnutrition and poverty: leprosy, blindness, dumbness and deafness.

• Much social tension and conflict:
upper classes collaborating with the Romans, opposition groups to the Romans.

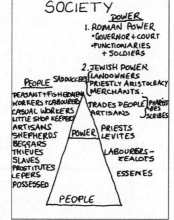

• An *oppressive and ambiguous* official religion; a confused but resistent piety of the people; repression and killing without mercy.

4. Taking on roles

Explain that at that time there were different groupings of people: Pharisees, Sadducees, Samaritans, Zealots, Jewish men and Jewish women. To understand what it was like to belong to one of these groupings it is helpful to role-play.

Let people choose their roles, ensuring that women play the role of Jewish women, if you have a balance of people. Give each one a copy of Handout 21 or 22, where they will find a role description of each category.

5. Grouping according to roles

Form a group with the others who have the same role and answer the following questions:
   a. Who are we? Read the description together and clarify who you are.
   b. What are our concerns about the set-up in our country at this time?
   c. What are our hopes for ourselves, our children, our country?
   d. What is our opinion about the Messiah who is to come?

Get your responses to these questions clear. If necessary or helpful, write down a few words to remind you.

BREAK

6. Mixing the Groupings

At this point new groups are formed in which each grouping is represented by one person, i.e. Pharisee, Sadducee, Jewish man, Zealot, Jewish woman and Samaritan. In the new groups, take it in turns, playing your role, to tell each other:
   Who I am?
   How I see our country at the moment?
   My hopes for ourselves, the chldren, the country.
   My opinion about the Messiah who is to come.

7. Intervention by leaders

'News has come through that there is someone around whom people think might be the Messiah. Staying in your role, work out what advice you would give to him as to how to go about his work.'

8. Feedback

Usually people have continued to play their roles during the feedback and this has proved to be a very good way of raising awareness of the task facing Jesus. Helpful questions to ask are:
   a) What happened?
   b) What did you notice?
   c) What advice was given to the Messiah?
   d) What comes to mind in all of this?

9. Conclusion

Remind them about team tasks.

Handout 21

Role Descriptions A

PHARISEE

I am a Pharisee. I belong to a Jewish religious group; most of us are lay people. We number about 6000. Most of are traders and small business people.

The most important thing in our lives is the Law, handed to us by God. It shows God's purpose and will for the people. We spend a lot of time devoutly studying the Law because we want to be observers and masters of the Law. We have worked out in great detail how the Law applies to each and every situation. And we teach these to the people so they can remain pure and avoid contact with people who do not observe the Law as we do. It's the only way we can achieve salvation. We are nationalists and we want the the Romans out, but at the moment we have to try and live with them.

We organise the synagogues and people respect and look up to us.

We believe that the son of David will come as Messiah to restore the Kingdom of Israel and we prepare for that day by educating the people and by prayer and fasting. You could say we are the conscience of the people and we cannot accept sinners, unbelievers or people without religion. I know God loves those who know and obey the Law, pray frequently, fast regularly, pay taxes, live carefully and avoid contact with sinners.

ZEALOT

I am a Zealot. We are a Jewish resistance group against the Romans. I suppose you could call us a paramilitary group because we engage in guerilla warfare with the occupying forces. We are often called 'Iscariots' because we go around carrying small daggers (*sica*) which we use to assassinate Romans, particularly during the big feasts. For us Israelites only God is Yahweh and this land is his land. The occupation by Romans is a crime against Yahweh. We are nationalists and so we want the Romans out. We are zealous for God, his Temple, his land and our freedom. We oppose all collaboration with foreigners, inter-marriage, contact with gentiles and eating unclean food. Most of us are labouring people. Romans out; no payment of foreign debt; land reform; freedom for slaves: that's what I want. Ours is a holy war against Israel's enemies and God will intervene to bring his work to completion. We want an independent Jewish kingdom. We hate the Romans. In the past they have savagely put us down, crucifying up to 2000 of us at one time.

But the day of vengeance will come when the Messiah will restore at last the Kingdom of Israel.

SAMARITAN

I am a true Jew, although the people who come from the south of Israel despise and reject me. This goes back to a split between the north and south about 700 years ago. We went our own way and have been accused ever since of having 'strayed from the truth'. You see, I don't believe that I am any less of a Jew because I don't accept that everything must be descended from David or that Jerusalem is the only legitimate place where Yahweh is worshipped. We celebrate for ourselves on Mount Garizim.

I think we Samaritans have as much claim on Yahweh/God as the southerners. As a Samaritan, seen as a Jew of mixed origin, and as someone who has taken on Grecian ways, I am an object of disdain. I come last on the social ladder, even behind craftsmen, peasants, unskilled labourers – a total social outcast.

Seven hundred years ago our best people were deported to Nineveh in Assyria. We never saw them again. The Syrians 'planted' our land, intermarried our women – though they kind of followed our religion.

Handout 22

Role descriptions B

JEWISH MAN

I grew up in the north of the country where my father had a small plot of land. In the end he had to sell it to pay the Temple tithes and the Roman taxes. That meant I had to leave home and come to Jersualem to look for work. A trader took me on for a while but he dismissed me when he found a stronger man who could lift the bales of cloth three at a time.

No one else employed me and, by now, if someone did offer me work, I would be too weak to do the job. I make my way to the Temple each day and some of the wealthy Jews throw me a few coins. Sometimes I look for left-over food at the houses of the big landowners who live in town.

So far I have managed to survive but life is pretty miserable. The Temple guards continually harass us beggars. Some religious people, like the Pharisees, abuse us for not keeping all the laws, but since we can't read and nobody takes time to explain them to us, it's impossible. 'Sinners' they call us – they say we are poor and sick because we have displeased the God of our fathers. They also believe that people from the north of the country are scum, not being of pure Jewish stock. They call all of us by one term of contempt, 'the people of the land'.

As far as possible we stick together and keep out of the way of all of them, Pharisees, elders, scribes, the lot. Even God does not seem to have room for us.

JEWISH WOMAN

I am Jewish woman, married, with two sons. I am very glad that I have borne sons: my husband prayed for sons and thanked God when they were born. Every day he still prays in thanksgiving that he himself was not born a woman. Most of my time is occupied with caring for my sons and preparing food, fetching water and cleaning. The eve of the sabbath is a very busy time because there is the special sabbath meal to be prepared and there are special prayers to be said by the mother of the household. I do not go out except to fetch water and I go with the other women. When I go into the street I am always accompanied by my husband and walk a few steps behind him all the way. That indicates to other men that I am a faithful married woman. My husband has the right to divorce me for infidelity. In fact some Jewish husbands have divorced their wives, simply because their behaviour didn't please them. When we go to Jerusalem for the great feasts, I go to the Temple but stay in the outer women's court while my husband takes part in the official ceremonies. When we go to the synagogue at home, I don't take part in the official instructions. You see, according to Jewish law, all women are inferior to men in all things. But we still have our dream: that one day one of us will be chosen to bear the Messiah.

SADDUCEE

I am a member of the party of the priestly aristocracy. Together with other wealthy fellow priests I form the grouping called Sadducees. My power comes from the high status given to priestly families and I am glad to say that the Pharisees, with their strict interpretation of the Law, make sure that a lot of the revenue from the temple is directed my way. I suppose you could say that we Sadducess are very political and that annoys the Pharisees. But I would argue that you have to be political in this day and age. We have to be able to handle the Romans if we want to hold on to our lands and country; in fact if we want to continue to exist at all. I believe in the strict application of the Law and I don't like the way the Pharisees rewrite the Law and try to 'modernise' it, as they claim. On the other hand, I am open to outside influences, especially Greek culture. I have no time for Divine Providence, the resurrection of the body or the existence of such things as 'angels'.

Supplementary Material 1

PALESTINE AT THE TIME OF JESUS

A country 50 kilmetres across, 220 kilometres long; 100 kilometres at its widest.

1. What is produced in the country?
In agriculture the main products were wheat and barley, olives, vegetables, fruit and wine. This was principally in the fertile land of Galilee. Livestock were raised principally in Judea where the land is less fertile. Big animals such as oxen and camels and small animals like sheep and goats were kept. There was also a fishing industry in the Sea of Galilee and fish was a popular food. In the towns and villages there was a lot of craftwork such as jars, plates, vessels for oil, textiles, foodstuffs, clothes, perfume, leather and luxury items. There were craft skilled workers like carpenters, stone masons and weavers.

2. What were the chief means of production?
Obviously there were ploughs and basic tools like hammers and axes. There were tanks for pressing grapes or olives, fishing boats and nets. There were no factories but there were many artisans who were generally self-employed.

Certain public works, like the construction of the Temple, brought together thousands of workers.

3. Who owned the means of production?
In the cities lived the rich landowners. In the country there were small farmers working on properties that got smaller and smaller. Around Lake Tiberius there were poor fishermen, many of whom worked together in simple forms of co-operatives, sharing boats.

4. Who worked for the owners?
On the land there were share-croppers who had to return each year an important part of the harvest in payment for the land rented. There were salaried dwellers on the property of the big landowners. There were agricultural labourers who were hired on a temporary basis and paid daily. There were also salaried shepherds who looked after big flocks, and there were small craft workers and tradespeople.

Then a whole sub-group of under-employed, slaves, unemployed and beggars existed alongside. In the cities there were craft workers of all levels, as well as unemployed, underemployed and beggars.

5. Were there poor people?
Because of the precarious economic situation, there were many poor people such as those who, because of malnutrition, poor hygiene and lack of basic necessities, were sick, blind, lame, hungry, lepers, 'possessed', beggars and prostitutes.

A rural worker earned a silver coin per day, the denarius. A large part of the population of Palestine lived in the countryside and was made up of poor workers surviving from day to day. The rich lived only in cities. Rural workers used to go to the cities looking for work, increasing an urban population that was marginalised and exploited.

6. What different classes emerged?
As has been mentioned, there were rich landowners and property owners and small farmers. Then there were the labourers, workers, crafts people. There were traders and commercial agents, shopkeepers and those involved in administration, like the priests of the Temple and tax collectors (those who organised and those who actually did the collecting). Very often these used corrupt ways of gaining goods.

7. How did distribution of goods and resources happen?
In the settlements there were various taxes:
- a tributum of one quarter of the harvest
- anona: in kind or cash to support the army
- passage money: for transport of goods
- customs taxes between regions and countries.

Great amounts left Jerusalem for Rome. From Judea alone in one year, was collected the equivalent of 600 million days of work in taxes paid to Rome.

In Rome was a whole privileged group who lived at the expense of colonial provinces like Palestine.

For the Temple were collected:
- tithes: 10 % of income harvest (for maintenance of clergy)
- didrachma - by virtue of being a Jew
- 1% for the poor
- offerings, for 3 major feasts
- money-changing; ordinary money into Temple money
- every seven years: products relating to one year of work.

8. Who Benefitted?
Principally the priestly elite and the aristrocracy of Palestine. The labourers who worked on the enlargement of the Temple and on public works were paid from the cashiers of the Temple, as were the clergy and functionaries.

The people, especially in the settlements, had only enough to survive, with so many taxes to pay. The misery got worse when many, who were without resources to satisfy vital needs, got ill.

60% of people's income went on taxes.

9. The Temple – The Central Bank
The temple was in Jerusalem, a badly situated city in an arid region without channels of communication, lacking water and raw material. It lived totally from the Temple.

With a population of 30,000 inhabitants, the city could reach 90,000 during festivals three times a year. The population was made up of employees of the Temple with a great sub-proletariat of beggars and bands of thieves.

10. Principal source of income
All taxes were centralised there. Thanks to pilgrimages three times a year, visitors supported the manufacture and sale of souvenirs, luxury goods, boarding houses and a big trade in animals for sacrifice.

11. Source of employment
At one time, between priests, functionaries, money-changers, sellers and others, about 18,000 people lived from the Temple organisation.

12. Concentration of workforce

A great number of people worked on the enlargement of the Temple in Jerusalem and in quarries. Besides employees and beggars, there were artisans, business people, landowners and priestly and lay aristocracy.

Palestine had a population of 500,000 inhabitants and depended as well on the economic organisation of the Temple. The treasury of the Temple was the same as the treasury of the state.

The adminstration was done by three high priests who were chiefs of finances. With them there lived in Jerusalem a large part of the rich business people (merchants) and landowners. Country people, who were in the vast majority, continued living in a hard situation of exploitation.

When Jesus spoke of the Temple being destroyed, although his objective was deeply religious, he was threatening the economic structure at its foundation, which was the Temple.

... ...

In Galilee, a form of international commerce took place in which various currencies were used:
   Roman: denario (to pay taxes);
   Jewish: siclo (to pay taxes);
   Greek: drachma;
   Phoenician: mina.

Political Dimension

Palestine was divided into two territories:
   a) Judea and Samaria where there was a Roman Procurator who lived in Caesarea and
   b) Galilee where there was a king who lived in Tiberius.

Who had the power to make decisions in the country?

Palestine was occupied by the Romans, so they had the effective power. But they left the Jews a lot of freedom and independence. In Judea and Samaria there was a Roman procurator (Pontius Pilate).

In Jerusalem, the Jewish government was in the hands of a Great Council (the Sanhedrin, composed of 72 members under the presidency of the Supreme High Priest). Needless to say, there were no representatives of the peasants and simple workers.

The Sanhedrin was composed of The High Priests: they were members of the priestly aristocracy belonging to certain families. The Procurator chose the high priests from among four families.

The Elders (senators): laymen chosen from noble families, big landowners or important merchants.

The Scribes (scholars, intellectuals, experts in theology and law): members of the middle class (artisans and traders).

The Sanhedrin depended on the Romans, as the High Priest could be deposed and replaced by the Procurator if he so wished. The elders' land belonged legally to the Romans who could take them over at any moment.

The Sanhedrin functioned like a court deaing with criminal, political and religious affairs. It had power over Judea but its authority extended over the whole of Palestine. It had its base in the Temple which was the political centre. In the villages, problems were resolved by a Council of Elders. In the towns, the Elders of the Council were big landowners and rich merchants. Scribes and Pharisees participated.

Were there political parties? Yes, but very different from today. The parties in Jesus' time were at the same time religious and political. The same law organised the worship of the One God and the political life of the people. It happened that each party defended, in the name of God, a different policy, depending on its wealth, social situation and interests.

Parties

The parties of the dominant class were two: The Sadducees (especially in Judea) and the Herodians (in Galilee).
The opposition parties were three:
   - the Pharisees
   - the Zealots
   - the Essenes

Sadducees

Defended the established order. Conservatives, they collaborated with the Romans because they were realists who accepted the injustice of foreign domination as long as it did not compromise their position. They were from the lay and priestly nobility, chiefs of the Priests and Elders of the Sanhedrin. They had the power in their hands and controlled the religious and political administration and courts of the country.

Herodians (Galilee)

Members of the party of King Herod. Conservatives who favoured the presence of the Romans. Herod Antipas called the city he built 'Tiberius', after a Roman Emperor. They were in civil power and strongly opposed the Zealots. They tried to pick up political agitators in Galilee. They were the people who assassinated John the Baptist. They did not have influence among the people.

Pharisees

They were devout laymen who aimed at observing religious practices to the last detail. They originally came out of the group 'the separate ones' who sustained the armed struggle of Judas Maccabaeus. At the time of Jesus, they came from all strata of society but principally from among artisans and traders. They were nationalistic enemies of the foreign power. In Jesus' time they had no alternative to struggle against the Romans, so they followed the politics of living and working out conciliation with them. They knew how to maintain authority over the people. They appeared as the party of the masses, respected by the people without exercising power directly.

Zealots

An illegal resistance organisation also called 'Iscariots' because they went around armed with a *sica* (dagger). They were nationalists who wanted to expel the pagan Romans who occupied the country. They were persecuted by the Romans. The authorities considered them criminals and terrorists. Their programme in the midlands of Palestine was to abolish debts, bring about land reform and free the slaves. They were recruited from the poorest section of the population of Galilee and had the sympathy of the people. Among them were terrorists who carried out political assassinations, often taking advantage of festivals for this task.

The Essenes
They were like a community of monks who challenged the legal status of the High Priests, did not frequent the Temple, and challenged the Pharisees who declared themselves poor but liked money. They expected liberation from exploitation and national freedom. Persecuted, they abandoned society and went to live in the desert, in the caves of Qumram where they lived together, sharing their goods, studying the scriptures, awaiting the triumphant intervention of the Messiah/Saviour.

The People
Most were unlettered and despised, considered sinful and ignorant. The Zealots had a certain influence with them but the multitudes were afraid, because they didn't accept violence, and because of the oppression. They were disorganised and remained marginalised from political life. Repression was used to keep them down.

The Police
Directly under the command of the Temple and under the orders of the High Priest. They were the ones who arrested Jesus and executed him.

The Roman Soldiers
These were under the orders of the Procurator. They were lodged in barracks in the city of Caesarea (3000 men). They went up to Jerusalem at the time of the festivals to maintain order.

Jesus did not join any party but appeared openly with Zealots (Simon, Judas).

The laws were made by the dominant classes and enforced by them. They were usually made to benefit those in power.

... ...

Cultural Reality

What were the beliefs and values in this society?
What characterised the thought of the whole people was belief in the one God. God leads the people and they should be faithful to God. This idea of God goes right back to Moses and the liberation from Egypt, through the time of monarchy, when kings became corrupt, and the emergence of a society divided into what we would today call 'classes', the prophets called attention to the changed situation.

The hope of another king like David, another Anointed One (in Hebrew, *Messias;* in Greek, *Christ*) began to emerge: one sent by God to do away with divisions and injustices and to unite the divided tribes into one people, free and independent of any domination.

Legalism
In the effort to preserve their identity as a people, the priests developed a legalistic interpretation of the scriptures where every act was governed by a regulation or by some rule defined by the priests. A Jew had to respect more than 600 rules.

Clearly a poor person would be overwhelmed by this. A mother with many children wouldn't be in a condition to keep all these regulations. They were considered impure. The only way of purifying oneself was to go the Temple and offer a sacrifice, an alms, a promise, paying the priest for it.

Scribes
The teaching and interpreting of the scriptures was the task solely of priests, but some lay people also took it on; they were called scribes or Rabbis – doctors of the Law. They translated the scriptures, opened schools and made the synagogues effective. The people had great respect for them because they were specialists in the scriptures, but they were also afraid, because the scribes were linked to the dominant class and controlled the ideas of the people.

The Sadducees
Having all the power in their hands, despite their small number, the Sadducees defended the Temple and took advantage of the religious law to keep the people in ignorance, obliging them to purify themselves for any breaking of the law. In this way, they conserved society as it was. They reduced religious questions to a minimum, did not believe in the Resurrection, and did not hope any longer for the coming of the Messiah.

Herodians
They did not hope for a Messiah and used religion to maintain themselves in power.

Pharisees
In the beginning, they wanted to unite the people against the ideas of the foreigners who could do away with the religion and culture of the Jews. They organised the people in synagogues or houses of prayer. They had moral authority because apparently they lived blameless moral lives themselves. They knew the commandments and ordinances of Moses and were advanced in doctrinal terms. They believed in resurrection and expected a divine intervention – a Messiah who would deliver the people from the yoke of the Romans, and they prepared for this day by prayer and fasting.

But along with the scribes, the pharisees became closed into a sect and became 'owners of the conscience of the people' (cf Matthew 23:13). They centred on individual salvation and the next world. To arrive there, you would need to keep the law (over 600 prescriptions). They disdained the common folk and recommended payment of tithes and taxes to the priests, defending the oppressive structures of the Temple.

Zealots
These wanted a return to ancient religion. They showed a fanatical hurry to see the day of the Lord coming for revenge. Their approach was to use violence to reform worship and priesthood and expel the Romans. They only wanted to purify the temple of corruption, not to change structures.

The Essenes
These lived in sanctity and poverty, with the ideal of purity. They judged themselves to be the true people of God and looked forward to the Messiah, anticipating a Holy War. They contested the Temple system and created a new model of production, disconnecting themselves from the priests. But they ended up closing in on themselves – following an elitist experiment. They had little influence over the people.

The priests, scribes and pharisees, with their religion of precepts and without love, tried to be masters of knowledge, robbing the people of their own historical consciousness. The Zealots, despite arousing a certain interest in the people, emptied the messianic hope because of their fanaticism, their violence and their lack of alternatives.

The Sadducees and Herodians only thought of the present situation which gave them many privileges.

Most people had lost the remembrance of what the prophets had said about the coming of the Kingdom, but there were a few who maintained a vision of a new kingdom (cf Luke 1:46-55).

Some Social Realities

Women
Women did not participate in the life of the society and were considered inferior to men in everything. They were expected to obey men.They normally stayed at home and appeared in public with their faces covered. Daughters did not have the same rights as sons. In the Temple the women's court was separated by a barrier from the men's section. Woman could not read at worship. They could not study to be disciples. Up to the age of twelve and a half, a girl could be sold as a slave. At marriage they became the possession of their husbands.

Sickness
Any unusual kind of infirmity was seen as a punishment from God for something wrong that had been done, and therefore had both a social and religious stigma.

Samaritans
Samaria was set up nine centuries before Jesus. Around 721 BC, Samaria was taken by the Assyrians; the population was mixed with other peoples; there was inter-marriage and mixing of religions. When the people of Judea went into exile, the people in Samaria stayed behind. After the exile, the Jews considered them an impure race, descended from 'foreigners' and 'mixed'. The Samaritans venerated Moses and awaited the Messiah. The Jews held them in contempt and they were marginalized.

Comment:
At the time of Jesus, a theo-cratic state existed: a state in which the religious way of thinking and perceiving reality held it together. There was a dominant view of God which kept the mass of people the way they were, e.g. it was accepted that God loved some people (the 'top' ones), more than others and didn't love some people at all (despised, deformed ...). In such a society, the most politically subversive thing you can do is say that God loves everybody: this is far more radical than any measures taken by the Pharisees or Zealots.

Supplementary Material 2

Excerpt from Report
We first looked at the kind of society Jesus came from. By knowing this it would help us see more clearly why Jesus did what he did. It was a pyramid type of society: at the top of the ladder were big landowners and business men and, closely allied to, them the High Priests, Sadducees; next came Pharisees and scribes, very religious, very strong on the Law – there were 627 laws. They made sure that people paid their taxes to the Temple in Jerusalem. They were very moral people and of pure race. Scribes were very learned and had power through knowing the Law very well. Zealots were very anti-Roman and engaged in guerilla warfare, attacking Romans with daggers. The majority were peasants, shopkeepers, publicans - who were tax collectors for the Romans - lepers, people possessed with evil spirits, the poor and women. Jesus belonged to the artisan or lower middle class.

After this we divided into six groups, each group to study and identify with one class in society in Palestine. Some questions had to be answered ... after tea we regrouped into six groups containing a member from each class. A certain degree of merriment happened as some groups really entered into role-playing. All agreed that society today is very much what it was then. Just before the end of the meeting, a Sadduccee and Pharisee and Jewish woman had to apologise to a Samaritan and a Zealot who were left to do the wash up on their own. This was a genuine mistake and we propose to do it all the next time.

The session began in a congenial and totally relaxed atmosphere. Conciseness and brevity marked the presentation of Palestine at the time of Jesus. The activites (role plays) were entered into with gusto. We were enlivened at the prospect of linking scripture and life in a dramatic manner. Participation was excellent. The members of each group adopted the roles allotted to them with enthusiasm and the 'personal views' expressed were most revealing, especially when news of the advent of the Messiah was revealed. It was an enjoyable exercise. The opinion was voiced that more guidance in the probing of characters might have been helpful.

SESSION FIFTEEN

Jesus reveals God as Abba

Aims
• To contrast Jesus' understanding of God with that of his contemporaries.
• To let a parable confront our relationship with God today.

Materials
6 sheets of newsprint and felt pens.
Copies of the love statements.

Time-Table
1. 7.45 Welcome and Introduction.
2. 7.55 Team tasks.
3. 8.10 Introduction to theme.
4. 8.15 Role groups.
5. 8.30 Plenary Session.
   9.00 Break.
6. 9.15 Background to parable.
        Telling the story.
7. 9.45 Reactions in fish-bowl group.
8. 10.00 Comments.
9. 10.10 Final reflection.

Suggested Procedure

1. Welcome and Introduction
Welcome the people and describe this session's aims and time-table.

2. Team Tasks
News, report, commentary, prayer, by the respective groups.

3. Introduction to theme
In the first sessions of *Partners in Faith* we began to examine our images of God. We began to see that the way we think of God influences the way we live, the way we relate to others and the way we relate to society. Afterwards, in order to check our ways of thinking of God, we looked at God as communicated through key figures and historical actions in the Old Testament.

We now move into the world of the New Testament where we encounter Jesus. He is God made visible and, through what he was and said and did, Jesus communicated a way of understanding and imagining God that was a breakthrough. Particularly, he communicated to us all a way of understanding the one he calls 'Daddy' (*Abba* in Aramaic). To know and accept God as 'Daddy' in the way conveyed to us by Jesus, is to change our lives and world.

4. Role-Groups
Ask the participants to gather into role-groups, i.e. as, in the previous session when they were Sadduccees, Pharisees, Jewish Women, etc.

In each group, appoint an co-ordinator who asks the group to do the following:
    'Recall who you are ...' *Reflect for a few minutes.*
    'As a ... ...(whatever role you have) my idea/image of God is ... ...'
    Let's share what comes to mind.

5. Plenary
Each group tells what it came up with and leader writes up their impressions on newsprint under the six headings:

Sadducee; Pharisee; Zealot; Samaritan; Poor man; Woman

Fill it out with some of the reflections here:

Sadducees: God of the Temple.
Their idea of God was of someone above and beyond, who was to be worshipped in the Temple and through the priests who offered sacrifice. God was someone who wanted to be worshipped by the people on the sabbath and at the great festival times. According to the Sadducees, who benefitted from the trading in the Temple, and who owned land and were wealthy, God favoured the status quo.

Pharisees: God the Law-giver.
God was the one who gave the Law. To be close to God you had to keep all kinds of detailed laws regulating behaviour. If you prayed frequently, fasted regularly, paid religious dues, lived carefully and avoided contact with sinners, you would be close to God. They looked forward to a Messiah who would uphold the laws and be another David.

Zealots: God of the land of Israel.
For them, God was a jealous God who wanted the Jews to be fully in control of the land, with no foreigners occupying it. They, the true people of God, were children of the light; their God was holy and God's will was to rid Israel of foreign rule, customs and presence. The Messiah would be a leader to purge Israel of foreigners in every aspect.

The People: God far away and condemning them.
The people heard the dominant groups say that God loves those who obey the details of the Law and hates those who do not; that God loves the educated more than the illiterate; those who are morally good more than those who are not; those who pray more than those who do not.

Each group, therefore, was saying to the ordinary people: 'If you change and become like us, God will love you.' But the ordinary people were in no condition to change, so they felt guilt and fear and hopelessness. They couldn't come close to God in the ways laid down and so they believed they could not be children of God. God, for the people, was far away, oppressive, distant.

Samaritans: God of creation, law and order.
Despite the Jews' opinion of them, they considered themselves true Israelites. They accepted that there is only one God who has given us the creation and the law of Moses. They accepted the first five books of the Bible. They kept the Sabbath and feast-days very rigidly and they believed

the Messiah would show that their way was the true way.

BREAK

6. Background to Parable

Jesus grew up in among these people, in this country. Through his reflection on the scriptures, his prayer, his daily living, he grew in intimate understanding of God as the most loving parent who cherishes every single person with unconditional love, who is totally and madly 'bonded' to us because we are God's sons and daughters. This God is not distant, or punishing or legalistic but infinitely merciful, and wants each person to share in the goods of creation, to live fully. Jesus' 'daddy' is a new and deeper revelation of the God of Moses and the prophets – a God of love who cherishes all equally and wants us to live a whole new quality of solidarity with one another in tender communion.

How can Jesus communicate this truth about God to the people of his time who have distorted, limited views of God?

Jesus communicated through what he did and said. Let us look for a moment just at what he said. He had to find a way to break through the consciousness of people, of getting people to question their pre-conceived ideas and their ways of behaving. This way he called *parable*. A parable is *not* a nice little story told to make a point to simple people. When you examine a parable, you see that what begins as a familiar story suddenly takes an about-turn, turns things upside down and makes us reconsider our attitudes, our ideas and behaviour. For us today, to appreciate a parable, we have to learn a bit about the background in which it is being told and remember that Jesus wants to help people see familiar things in a new way, wants them to begin to relate in a new way and wants them to organise life in a new way.

Before you listen to the story just appreciate the background:

In Jewish society, a father was a distant authority to be obeyed. He was the head of the family (patriarch). He had authority over his children, regarding whom they should marry, when to divide his property and inheritance with them. He could disown a son who broke the law in a serious way. He could even hand over a rebellious son to death.

A Jewish son was expected to support his father in old age. He could receive a share of the inheritance during his father's life-time but he could not dispose of it before his

father's death. He also had to keep the Jewish law against eating unclean food (e.g. pork), mixing with non-Jews, and he had to practise the laws of worship. Any son breaking any of these laws would be considered 'dead'.

Jesus, in order to show what 'Abba' is like, tells a story of Jewish secular life, something familiar. As you listen, remember your role and your role's image of God.

Tell the story of The Prodigal Son. (Luke 15:11-32)

7. Reactions in fish-bowl group

Form a fish-bowl of six representatives of the six role-groups. One of the leading learners tells the story. Another leading learner now facilitates those in the group in exploring their reactions to the story in the role they are playing:
   What do you feel? What do you think?
   How does the father in the parable fit in with your idea of God?

8. Comment

This material may help complete what the people, in their wisdom, say:

The story of the Prodigal Son was told to shatter and disturb a narrow-based view of God. If there's a grain of truth in the image of God put across by the story, then we will all be in trouble.

We might want to condemn a 'lovey-dovey' kind of religion and say that if the rules were laid down as in the good old days, young people wouldn't be leaving the Church or be so slow in choosing to become priests, etc. But in fact rules don't get you very far and the idea of a punishing God (and the mentality that sees 'Aids' as a punishment from God for your deviance) is not what Jesus proposes.

The people of Jesus' time wanted a packaged, neat kind of God: you'd keep the rules and you'd know that that was what God wanted; God was like a Pharisee, or a Sadducee or a Zealot or a Samaritan, according to what you were yourself.

But Jesus challenged that view because he had experience of a different view: coming out of his own closeness to God – in itself a shocking concept to his own people.

Irishmen today are slow to know their father: they regard their fathers with a mixture of awe, respect; they generally have an awkward relationship. This doesn't mean that there wouldn't be a bonding of some sort.

The younger son in the story didn't seem to have felt that he had an intimate relationship with his father either, and yet the story reveals the very deep bonds existing, the incredible closeness that is real.

Jews wouldn't have understood that Jesus could have such a deep, intimate relationship with God. So, to get across this reality, Jesus chose a non-religious situation of intimacy and affection. Even that shocked the Pharisees and Sadducees: they would have seen him as misusing language in a shocking way: in the patriarchal society of the time, the father was distant, condescending, could expect obedience and love, but not intimacy – and Jesus dares to claim that he has an intimate relationship with God! We have lost the sense of how really shocking it was.

But Jesus claims that this is how God is with people: loving them lavishly and intimately, so that we can have the audacity to address God as 'Abba', following Jesus who was the first person to use that intimate term for speaking to God.

This God is able to love the two sons unconditionally. We tend to think we must earn God's forgiveness (as Jewish people would have thought). But instead, we are invited into the confidence we get if we have an intimate relationship with someone. This relationship causes us to bloom and flower and to become generous to an extraordinary degree.

Jesus could propose all that because he experienced a very intimate relationship with God. We can ask when did it dawn on him? Some say at the Bar Mitzvah (Finding in the Temple) or at Cana, when he had to be about his father's business ...

9. Final Reflection
Meditation
Music: e.g. 'Abba, Father'

Let us gently bring to mind the God of Jesus, Abba, Da, Daddy ... and listen to God's voice.

Quiet music without words.

'I have called you by your name, you are mine.' Is 43:1

'I have loved you with an everlasting love, so I am constant in my affection for you.' Jer 31:3

'You are worth more than many sparrows.' Matt 6:26

'You are sad, now, but I shall see you again and your heart will be full of joy.' John 15:22

'Do not let your heart be troubled or afraid.' John 14:27

'How often have I longed to gather you as a hen gathers her chicks under her wings.' Matt 23:37

'I have come that you may have life.' Matt 28:20

'Courage, it's me, don't be afraid.' Mark 6:31

'Peace be with you.' John 21:19

'Know that I am with you always.' Matt 28:20

'I have loved you just as the Father has loved me.' John 15:9

Let the evening end quietly and reflectively on these statements of God's unconditional love for each one of us.

Supplementary Material 1

The best background reading is from Eamonn Bredin's book *Disturbing the Peace*. Another helpful book is Albert Nolan's *Jesus before Christianity*.

Here we have a few other helpful words about parable:

PARABLE
The parable is essentially a comparison developed in the form of a story. Its primary purpose is not so much to teach as to make its audience reflect on their behaviour, to make them pass judgement on themselves, on their behaviour, so as to make a decision. Perhaps to change their behaviour.

In a modern parable, that would help people re-think their ways of seeing things and acting in Irish society today, remember:
1. Parables are about ordinary people in ordinary situations who are invited to move from one way of acting or seeing things to another.
2. They are about people but the plot is God.
3. The parables all subvert – turn things upside down.
4. They are smooth stories that are interrupted by a sudden new possibility.
5. They all depend upon decisions.
6. There is always the question of urgency in the invitation.
7. You are left without excuses if you don't respond.

Note: Parables contain, in the way they work, the values of Jesus placed in contrast to people's assumptions. They provoke questions and a search for new ways of looking at things or acting.

Supplementary Material 2

Some comments after this session:
The way it is with people, you think you know them, then you see them differently, in a new light. All kinds of things dawn on you about them because you have caught a different aspect of them. They can energise.

Thousands and thousands of people assume that they know what Jesus is like: they are still in touch with the Jesus of their childhood, the baby Jesus, the gentle Jesus meek and mild. Some people have Jesus so locked up (in the tabernacle) that he can't touch their lives.

It might be helpful for us if we could pull down a shutter on all we know and say, 'Maybe we don't know him,' and open the gospels to see what he was really like. We would be surprised at what we would discover about him.

SESSION SIXTEEN

Abba's dream
for people

Aims
To explore Abba's dream for people, using the parable of the Samaritan against its historical context and in relation to divisions in society today.

Materials
Handout 23 on making a parable for today.

Time-table
1. 7.45   Welcome.
2. 8.05   Introduction to theme and focusing activity.
3. 8.20   Background to parable and telling the parable.
4. 8.50   Making a parable for today.
   9.15   Break.
5. 9.45   Presentation of stories and role-play.
6. 10.15   Conclusion.

Suggested Procedure

1. Welcome
Aims, time-table, team tasks.

2. Introduction to theme and focusing activity
If we accept the image of God communicated by Jesus - as a tender, loving compassionate parent who considers each and all of us as offspring equally and unconditionally – this has tremendous implications for our attitudes to other people and the way we choose to relate to them. We are called to live out the fact of our being offspring from the one Source - bonded together in God who calls us to a new quality of relatedness and solidarity expressed in genuine love and care. If we lived out this truth, how different the world would be.

It is amazing how we narrow down our world to a set of closed options, set judgements, predestined conclusions. In some cases the only people we really relate to are immediate family.

Jesus was faced with communicating what God is like and what a world based on this truth would be like - a new quality of human solidarity.

Before we explore this further I invite you to be still for a moment ...

Thinking about our lives, community, society, world, what are the divisions/barriers which you see between people today?
   I see divisions/barriers between ... and ....
Think – Buzz – Feedback.

3. Background to parable and telling the parable

For background material, the best source is Eamonn Bredin's book, Disturbing the Peace, *(Columba Press). Below we give Michael Reidy's personalised version of the background and story, based on the facts. Each learning leader must personalise the account according to their own unique self.*

THE STORY OF THE GOOD SAMARITAN
retold by Michael Reidy

Let's first look at some of the elements that make up a good story-teller: He/she gets to the guts of the community being spoken to; he/she has the accent, which means that he/she is in some way going beyond the head and into their hearts; also he/she keeps the end to the last.

Our problem is (with the stories of Jesus) that as soon as the first word is uttered, we know the end. It's very difficult for us to get into it because we know the end; it's terribly difficult for us to hear that story the way the first people heard it, because the first people who heard the story didn't know the end; the story didn't even have a name until after it was heard for at least thirty years. Long before they were written down, they were told and re-told and heard and re-heard.

Someone like Niall Tóibín has the atmosphere of the place that he's talking about; immediately he's able to tune into the situation, he can get into the skin of the people who are listening. He gets below the skin and, the minute you hear him, you are in the atmosphere through little things, accent, etc.

We have lost touch with some of those seemingly peripheral things and so it's hard to get into the story.

The story we are going to hear again is well known to us and I'd ask you to put the title in brackets. To be able to get into it we need to get in touch with the geography and history; keep in mind the complexity of the roles that you worked through already (Sadducees, Zealots, etc.).

Thinking about the geography: I didn't realise, until about four years ago, that where Jesus lived was such a small country. Now familiarise yourself with where Jerusalem is and where Jericho is, to the south of it; familiarise yourself with where he started his ministry, which was up in the north; and what would that have meant to somebody in the south? The people in the middle were mountainy people, the people who lived in Samaria. Now what do most city-dwellers think of mountainy people? They have a healthy, or unhealthy, disregard for them perhaps.

David, King David, had been the one who decreed that Jerusalem should be the place of importance. However, there had been a very holy place called Shechem in Samaria, equal in importance to Jerusalem. At one time Joshua, one of the Judges (leaders), had said that Shechem should be the place where God would be found. But David decided to have a strong city at Jerusalem. Naturally the people felt a little bit on the fringe of things; then the people in the South decided to re-write history in terms of their pre-eminence; they put themselves at the centre and wrote the others out. And so the Samaritans felt they had been put down, shoved out and that even what God had wanted wasn't being much adhered to.

Solomon succeeded David and he had an extensive building programme and a huge army. He split the country: the south (Jerusalem) was the capital and the north was relegated to non-entity. For two hundred years that was the reality. Then the Assyrians came from the east and they took over the north and so some people were deported from the north and some were left, what we would call a 'plantation'; planters were put in by the Assyrians in order to farm the land and to edge out the others. (Cromwell gave huge tracts of land to some of his soldiers in a similar way). The colonists were viewed with the same suspicion we would view them. But the original people of Samaria inter-married with the colonisers. (We had names for people like that, who would have changed their religion – 'soupers'.)

So there was a huge distancing between the people who lived in Samaria and the people who lived in the south. The people in the south weren't upset: they were confirmed in their low regard for the 'half-breeds' who lived to the north.

In 587 it was the south's turn to experience a fall: a group from Bablyon came in and took all the people into exile: leaders, etc., demolished the Temple and laid everything bare.

What happens to people in exile? Take the experience of our own people in Britain, America and Australia. They stick together, become more Irish and they get a huge sense of their dignity. Huge attempts are made to understand more and more about your background and history and you strive to put yourself on the map. The Jews forced into exile constructed a whole new sense of themselves: at first they had an angry reaction: how come God let this happen to us? Then they wondered whether they couldn't think of themselves as special again: a small, true, faithful group. How did they think of the people in the north? If they thought of them at all, they felt they were the lowest of the low, because they had sold themselves by intermarrying with the 'planters'.

It was while in Exile that they first used synagogues to meet for prayer, to look again at their history and to reshape and rethink it. They began to understand that perhaps they could even write about this. So it is at this time that we get the beginning of their writing down of their history.

After fifty years, a King from Persia, Cyrus, who liked and encouraged their literary attempts to rediscover their sense of their own identity and mission, gave them back their land. They returned from exile. The first thing they decided to do was to build the Temple again, because that was the place where their identity could be seen. Would they want help from those vagabonds in the North? Some of those same vagabonds actually came down and said, 'Can we help?' and they were given short shrift and told, 'Under no circumstances,' because they had betrayed everything the Temple stood for, namely national identity. The Samaritans went back to Samaria and built their own Temple, which was subsequently destroyed by devout and enraged southerners.

Retaliatory action also took place and, in fact at the time of Jesus, a group of Samaritans came down to Jerusalem during Passover and put dead dry bones in the Holy of Holies.

The exile has ended and the people want to study and learn about their tradition. The man who can deliver is the scribe. So we have the emergence of the scribe at this time: he became more popular than the prophet because the scribe knew the five books (Torah) which had told them how they had been and how they should be in the future. The prophet was edged out and the scribe became a very big figure. The people who came back from exile were thirsting for knowledge, wanted to know everything about their history and how they should live. They needed to understand their background. The star of the Samaritan at this time was never lower.

Now to the story – forget that it was eventually named 'The Good Samaritan'.

You're in a culture that loves story and story-telling; usually there are there characters in a story; you also know that it's the first person you're meant to identify with. The story begins: 'A certain man went down from Jerusalem to Jericho' so the first thing you do, listening, is say to yourself, 'I am that man'. When we read it, we think of ourselves as the Good Samaritan. Get that out of your head this time. You are the 'certain person'.

You go from Jerusalem to Jericho; it's a road you know well because you are living in the south and you know that the road from Jerusalem to Jericho is as bad as the worst lane in the next parish, the one you don't go down at night-time especially. This certain man went down that lane. Naturally, you are set upon by thieves and vagabonds; you are the person who is hit and mugged and left bleeding and your possessions taken from you, your Access card, your bag, your hard-earned cash, your keys to the house; you are that person lying on the road; you are fairly desolate really because you know that not too many people use this road. Not too many go from Jerusalem to Jericho.

First you hear a noise and the noise is well-known to you because it is a man's walk, a man's voice, who is, unbelievably, praying. Your mind is completely blown because it is one of your own; it's a priest because he's saying the psalms and you're so thrilled. And you realise that, of all the people who could be going down that road, this man is, incredibly, a priest.

The man approaches you and you look through your barely-opened eyes and you see that he has all the gear on, the little tassles, the cloth over his head. However, to your absolute astonishment, he goes by you. But the minute he goes by you, you say that you were wrong to think like that; it was wrong of you to imagine that that priest would come over to you.

You begin immediately to make excuses for him because you know that if he's a good priest, his biggest job is to keep himself undefiled, in order to be able to offer sacrifice in the Temple. You understand that. He has that sacred job, given to him by the community, and you know that the only reason he didn't come to your aid was because he probably thought you were dead, and if he touched you when you're dead, he would be defiled and would not be able to offer sacrifice purely. In your mind you know he was actually right. That man was a good priest. The very best of priests really, and you were wrong to even think that he would step outside of that and do something else. You were actually full of understanding of the unbelievable act that this man had done, in human terms, in leaving you for dead on the road. This 'understanding' is built into your background, your tradition and especially your religion. You are prepared to understand what cannot and should not be understood, and to do this in the name of religion.

So you settle back and the storyteller tells you that the second person that comes along was a Levi – a functionary of the Temple. Surely this man – you might even know him – but he passes on the other side. And again, at first you're stunned and then immediately you say, 'No, No, he's doing the right thing.' He'd also be ritually impure. So you say, fine, but you are still on the side of the road.

Now're you're listening and you're waiting for the third person, and you know that the person telling the story is a lay person and not a priest, so maybe there's a bit of anti-clericalism going on here. It dawns on you the third person is going to be a Jew, and you're comfortable, and then he tells you the third person to come along is a Samaritan. You are totally astounded and stunned: then you know you're dead for sure, because this guy will stick the boot in surely, kick you and make sure the job in finished. You don't understand this story; you're beginning to feel that this storyteller is a bit weird.

Then he tells you that the Samaritan got off his mount, came down and touched you. And you're horrified at the idea – that this fellow touched you. You don't want to be touched by this person. Then he lifts you up and puts you on his horse and brings you to the Inn. Your whole sense of outrage is risen; you can't accept this happening. This cannot be. This is not true or possible; most people would feel happy if he brought you to the inn and dropped you, but this guy says to the inn-keeper to look after you and gives some money and promises to give more money.

It's only a story and you're wondering what's going to happen. And you remember then that this story was told because some smart alec said, 'Who is my neighbour?' And then the storyteller turns to you and says, 'Who is neighbour to the man who went down?' and you realise that you're caught, you're trapped. He has left you with only one option; you can't say other than that the man acted as neighbour. But it's totally unpalatable, unthinkable and yet it's the way the story is told: that what is unthinkable is thinkable, what is unbelievable is believable, and what is unpalatable must be swallowed. So you know what you have to say. You're forced to choose. He has turned the knife and made you link what you know is unlinkable, at least for seven hundred years. The word neighbour means certain things, but neighbour and Samaritan are being put together; being linked. This is mind-blowing because you know full well that neighbour and Samaritan have been separated for at least seven hundred years.

Is that man saying that everything you have grown to know and accept is being upturned? Surely enemy = Samaritan? This man is behaving like a subversive. He's completely turning on its head everything you've been taught. And furthermore, this is an ordinary story but this man Jesus usually tells stories about the Kingdom of God. Could he possibly be saying something about God, and is he saying that what I thought, and was taught, about God up to now is totally wrong? I was taught, and have always thought, that God could be put into a nice, clearly-defined square, a nice, comfortable picture. Does God act in a way that I cannot fully know? The God of the storyteller lets the neighbour and the Samaritan be linked; does that God want to start something? But I find totally unacceptable a kind of understanding of God that fits into nothing that I know.

Why did Jesus disturb people by parables? It took the reality of the people, lured them in, right up to the end, and, at the end, everything is turned on its head. It was better not to understand because the minute they began to see that his actions and his words and his person were linked, then they began to see that he was parable. Totally life-giving in a way that their own law was not; an extraordinary breakthrough; their old way was totally shattered. They began to feel very threatened and very shook. It would be much easier not to hear the truth at all.

Reactions:
What does the parable tell us about Abba's dream for the people?
Take feedback.

4. Making a parable for today
We'd like to offer you a challenge: to use your imagination in such a way as to be jolted, disturbed out of the closed self-centred world, towards the new world of moving hearts which is the Kingdom of God.

In mixed groups prepare either a story or a role-play to show us new possibilities for relatedness as human beings, offspring of our parent, God.

You must trust that you can do this, and that whatever you come up with will serve to illustrate the struggle to build a new world according to God's dream. The story/role-play need only be three minutes maximum.

Explain and distribute Handout 23.

BREAK

5. Presentation of the stories and role plays
What have we learned from tonight's session?

6. Conclusion
Summary by leader.
No team tasks for the next sssion.

Handout 23
Making a parable for today
Challenging your Imagination

Preparation
1. Choose two sets of people who seem to be at odds with each other.
2. Discuss what are the reasons for the division between them.
3. Reflect on why it seems impossible for them to change the situation between them.
4. Imagine how the situation could be different, and what would make it different.

Task
Using your talents, together make a story or a role-play, based on the two sets of people you have chosen, which is a parable for us today.

Steps
1. Begins with a familiar situation - something we can identify with
2. Let the action unfold. Draw us in. Make sure we can identify with some character in the action.
3. Then, at some point, introduce something unexpected, a twist, which disturbs the way we normally think or act in the situation.
4. Let it turn our world upside down and give us some fresh possibilities to think about.

Note: The effort to do this is what counts. Let loose your imagination. It will put you in touch with Abba's dream for people, the way people are, and the new possibilities. The story or role-play which you present will be about three minutes long.

Supplementary Material 1

PARABLE:
a challenge to disturb our way of thinking or acting.

1. Begins with something ordinary.
2. Invites hearer to enter into the story: This is Your Life.
3. Something unexpected dis-turbs, dis-eases, dis-orientates your life.
4. It digs into your life, remands a response; no easy answers.
5. It is a framework which launches us: we must complete what has begun. We sort out where we stand, what we stand for.
6. World turned upside down
7. New possibilities
8. Always raises new questions/possibilities
9. Always moves to the God question.

Supplementary Material 2

A Parable

Two men went down to Dublin for a job interview.

In appearance they were similar; CVs showed little difference between educational standards or work experience.

But one was from Blackrock, the other from Ballymun.

With the chances of an equal hearing remote, the Blackrock man took his own CV and changed his address to Ballymun.

Composed by the Rivermount Partners in Faith group 1991

General Introduction to Action for the Kingdom

First we want to give an overall view of the Method for Action, the principles behind it and the stages in using it, i.e. the theory. This method is based on the approach of Paolo Freire and is in harmony with the call-response relationship between people and God in the Bible.

A. PRINCIPLES

1. Action is based on concerns relevant to people's lives

To engage in action with people you must get in touch with what they feel are the important concerns and issues. Things that they are interested in and feel worthwhile will attract their involvement and generate energy. To discover these issues demands concentrated listening that gets beneath people's language to what Freire calls 'generative themes'. A theme is a statement about the world (about reality). It is an attempt to understand the world and our relationship to it, at some level of abstraction. A generative theme is a theme, the consideration of which, by a group, leads to the consideration of other themes implicit in it. Themes are real; they exist for people, inside people in their hearts and minds. They cannot be imposed on people. Basing the approach to action on people's themes is, in this sense, different from the tradition of determining the shape and content of an education programme purely in terms of the logic of a specialism. Themes emerge and are named in the dialogue that goes on between people who together are intent on some aspect of reality.

Relating this principle to the Bible, you see for instance how Yahweh and Moses identify what needs to be done, because they have heard the 'cries of the people' in Egypt. The generative theme here is that of domination-liberation. It's on the basis of this theme that God, through Moses, mobilises the people into changing their situation. Similarly, the prophets find their agenda in the poverty and oppression present in society.

In the New Testament, Jesus looks at and listens to the situation of the people with compassion, and soon identifies the legalism, injustice, poverty and sickness that is far removed from God's dream for people. It is in function of these themes that Jesus grounds his action and preaching.

Note: Relevance does not mean never going beyond where people are at the moment.

2. Action involves conversation and dialogue with and between people

Dialogue in love and trust is one of the fundamental characteristics of Freire's approach. Believing in the dignity and equality of people, Freire highlights that you cannot proceed in any action without the free and conscious participation of the people. They are called to be the agents in shaping their destiny. No one is so ignorant that he/she has nothing to contribute; no-one is so knowledgeable that she/he cannot learn from others. Respect for people means working with people, searching together, 'naming the world' together and changing it together.

3. Raising questions about people's experience is basic to the process

Naïve consciousness is characterised by a tendency to simplify problems, to go by appearances and to accept received ideas rather than question them. This is often accompanied by nostalgia for the past and by an argumentative rather than an investigative attitude. It's very passive. There is a tendency to fear the new, or to be into change for change's sake. Naïve consciousness tends to see life history as the deeds of great men and women, and communication as a form of imposition. Tomorrow is expected to be the same pattern as today and yesterday. There is not yet awareness of life as a process in the shaping of which we all have a part to play.

Freire emphasises the concept of critical consciousness. It is not superficial but seeks to go into, to go under, to unveil, to investigate. It is open to revision, tries to avoid preconceptions, accepts responsibility and proceeds through dialogue rather than argument or force. 'But Why?' is the key phrase in this approach. Themes are posed as problems about which people can exercise their active, critical, creative, thinking ability. One can see that this approach is in direct contrast to the so-called 'banking concept', where those 'who know' deposit their ideas into the empty minds of those 'who do not know'.

4. Action is to help people change their situation by acting more freely

In this approach, people are considered to be subjects rather than objects of interest, manipulation or paternalism. The world is not seen as a machine in which each part has a clearly-defined, limited, repetitive role. Rather it is seen as a living organism in which people are agents, who struggle to help create the good society founded on dialogue and respect for each person as a subject; where people take responsibility for themselves and others; where people engage in co-creating what is open to development and in liberating from all that denies life, participation and justice. The world is not static; it is dynamic and all are called continually to change it for the better.

The model for human life is formulated by our Judaeo-Christian tradition, especially through the person of Jesus who shows us that to be human is to be free, critical, creative and responsible members of society as people of God. For Freire, people are conscious beings who, through their work and action, transform the world, creating culture and history. Their vocation is to become more fully human.

5. The process is ongoing involving action/reflection/action

The participants are already engaged in life and action through their daily struggle. This approach calls for reflection about the implicit problems, circumstances, causes, inter-connections and relationships involved in that action, and their own awareness of these. From this conscious consideration emerges new activity. This process is called praxis and involves naming the world, love and work. In praxis you have to hold the two parts together: action without thought is action for action's sake - called activism – and reflection without action is mere talk or verbalism. In other words, the approach calls for love and commitment to people. Put in clearer terms, the approach calls for us to stop, look at the present situation, and think about it, trying to see what change is called for and doing something about it:

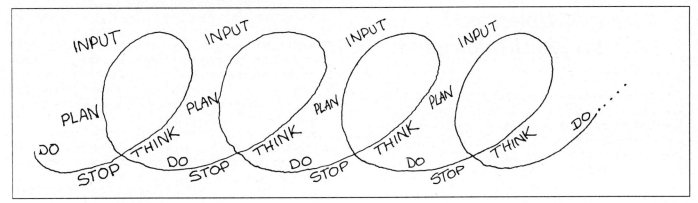

This process is ongoing.

B. STAGES

In presenting the principles, one can place five large posters, with the key phrases on them, across a wall. Underneath these, five more posters with the key phrases of the stages can be added correspondingly.

STAGE ONE
*Listening for people's concerns/issues/problems/needs
'Generative Themes'*

The starting point of this approach is informal or formal listening to people in order to uncover what are their significant problems or issues. Informal listening refers to being alert as one moves among the people, picking up recurring themes in their conversation. Formal listening refers to a conscious arrangement in which people are asked a series of broad-based open questions which will reveal matters of special concern to them. The aim is to name a number of themes as they exist in significant situations or in people's experience.

STAGE TWO
Investigation with people about the emergent theme(s)

In order to enable people to further express how they see the world and live in it, the theme is posed as a problem, in such a way that people can talk about it, describe it, analyse it and deepen their own awareness of what's involved in the theme. They make explicit the consciousness. They become more aware of the constraints on their lives and they begin to tend towards action to change their situation. This process - genuinely talking and thinking on this aspect of their lived reality - is called dialogue. When they have looked beneath the surface of taken-for-granted situations, and begun to see them afresh and in a wider context, they will be able to set aims for further action/reflection.

STAGE THREE
Decision on aims of action and research

Having identified what people want to learn, or do something about, the workers focus on the key statements of the people, on the basis of which they decide what they want to help people achieve, i.e. their aims. They then carry out the research to find resources to achieve these aims.

STAGE FOUR
*Design the learning/action session
Share Leadership*

In designing the session, the leaders must give the participants the first word. Asking a key question, arising out of the previous investigation, will trigger a participative process, where people can again say their own word. This is followed by an input, or activity, adjusted to take into account what group members have just been saying.

Finally, there is dialogue in order to integrate the group's previous knowledge and experience of what has just been presented, or has just taken place.

STAGE FIVE
Do the session(s) and see where it leads

Some kind of action, on the part of the groups or individuals involved, is a hoped-for outcome of the event. It might involve a group action to tackle a specific problem, or action by individuals in their own lives. In the context of using the method in the course, change will be experienced in the lives of those who plan and run the events, in the sense that they become aware of their own ability to act together. However, from one short session, the outcome is likely to be limited to changes in attitudes or an incentive to pursue an action arising from the learning event.

C. USE OF THE METHOD IN *PARTNERS IN FAITH*

Clearly this approach can be used in different settings. The nature of the setting will determine how you proceed. In our case, we are working within the limitations of a course comprised of weekly two-and-a-half-hour sessions. Despite that time constraint, we have managed to enable each group to use the method on the course, at the service of the wider group.

What follows is an account of how we used the method in *Partners in Faith*, followed by the way the stages in the method were distributed in the various sessions.

SESSION SEVENTEEN

Our action for the Kingdom

Aims
- to enable the participating groups to experience their own power to act and to change situations.
- to know the principles and stages of the method for group action
- to listen for each other's concerns
- to identify and list the key themes.

Materials
Posters of principles and stages
Handout 24: Listening sheets
Words for prayer/reflection
Sheets of newsprint and felt pens for lists

Time-Table
1.	2.30	Welcome and introduction, aims and prayer.
2.	2.50	Principles and Stages of the Method.
3.	3.15	The Listening Process (leaders share and listen).
4.	3.30	Personal reflection to identify concerns.
5.	3.45	Listening to one another.
	4.25	Break
6.	4.45	Working in Parish Teams.
7.	5.10	Presenting lists of themes.
8.	5.30	Leading learners comment.
9.	5.45	Final prayer.

Suggested Procedure

1. Welcome and Introduction
You have got to know each other, grown in confidence, got a chance to deepen your understanding of some of the essential biblical message. We will continue to do these things together, but now we want to introduce you to the third aim of Partners in Faith which is:

to enable you to experience your own power to act and change situations for the better.

In other words, how to express your faith in action as a group.

To set the scene, we have a moment of prayer:

Faith in Action
'But someone will say, "One person has faith, another actions." My answer is, "Show me how anyone can have faith without actions. I will show you my faith by my actions." (James 2:18)

The Heart of the Matter
The Lord God said:
I myself will dream a dream within you,
Good dreams come from me you know:
My dream seems impossible, not too practical,
Not for the cautious man or woman:
A little risky sometimes, a trifle brash perhaps.
Some of my friends prefer to rest more comfortably

in sounder sleep with visionless eye.
But for those who dream my dreams I ask
a little patience,
a little humour,
Some small courage
And a listening heart –
I will do the rest.

Then they will risk and wonder at their daring,
Run and marvel at their speed,
Build, and
stand in awe at the beauty of their building:
You will meet them as you work,
In your companions who share your risk,
In your friends who believe in you enough
To lend their own dreams, their own hands,
their own hearts to your building,
in the people who will find your doorway
stay a while and walk away knowing that
they too can find a dream.
And sometimes it will rain - a little variety
Both come from me.

So come now, be content.
It is my dream, your dream
My house you build,
My caring you witness
My love you share
and this is the heart of the matter.
Charles Péguy

2. The Principles and Stages of the Method
The basic material for this presentation is found in the General Introduction to Action for the Kingdom. The presenter needs to express the content in simple, clear terms. We have found it helpful to put the following headings on posters, display the principles round the room first and then display the stages under them.

Principles
1. Action is based on concerns relevant to people's lives.
2. Action involves conversation and dialogue with and between people.
3. Raising questions about people's experience is basic to the process.
4. Action is to help people change their situation by acting more freely.
5. The process is on-going, involving action/reflection/action.

Stages
1. Listening for people's concerns/issues/problems/needs. 'Generative Themes'.
2. Investigation with people about the emerging themes.
3. Decision on aims of action and research.
4. Design the learning/action session(s).
5. Do the session and evaluate.

3. The Listening Process
We want you to reflect on your experience of Partners in Faith so far, using a simple reflection sheet which we will provide. It asks you to look at your experience in order to identify your concerns at four different levels: personal, interpersonal, church/community and society/creation.

The three of us have already reflected on our experience on the course. In order to focus your attention on the task, each of us will share our concerns and model the kind of listening required in this process.

Learning Leader 1 speaks of his/her concerns at the personal level, arising out of *Partners in Faith*.

Learning Leader 2 gives Leader 1 some feedback as to what he/she heard. This is either verified or corrected. Leader 2 makes a note of what was heard.

Learning Leader 2 speaks of her/his concerns at an interpersonal level, to which Leader 1 gives some feedback.

Learning Leader 3 speaks of his/her concerns at the level of Church, etc., and so the modelling continues.

4. Personal reflection to identify my concerns

Using Handout 24, the participants are asked to reflect personally on the issues/concerns/problems which have emerged for them during the course.

5. Listening to one another

We'd like to remind you that it is very important to decide to listen to the other person speaking. At this point, you need to try to discover what are the other person's real concerns/issues.

Ten Tips for Honest Listening

1. Be sure you want to listen; otherwise, all the skills in the world are useless.
2. Be quiet and pay attention. That means that you are not planning your answer while someone is talking.
3. Withold judgement – avoid putting 'shoulds' on a person's feelings. 'I see ...', 'I understand ...'.
4. Respect the other's experience: 'This is my experience ...', or, 'The way I see it is ... tell me what you think.'
5. Don't assume you understand, particularly when the other person's experience is different from or contradicts yours; so ask questions and listen to the response.
6. Test understanding by feeding back what you heard: 'Are you saying ...?' 'Do you mean ...?' 'I hear you saying that ....'
7. Trust in the other's ability to solve his/her own problem.
8. Try to identify, but remain separate from, the other's feelings or ideas. Be aware of your own emotions distorting what you hear.
9. It is impossible to listen and talk at the same time.
10. Different personalities listen and respond in different ways.
(From 'Actions Speak Louder' by Earley & McKenna, Columba Press)

We'd like half of the group to form an inner circle, sitting on chairs facing outwards. The rest can occupy the outside chairs, facing inwards.

To get an even number, a leader may have to join the group. A handy way of getting a mixture is to ask three of the area groups to go on the inside, mixing themselves, and the other three groups to go on the outside, well mixed.

At a signal, the insiders tell the outsiders what their concerns are at the interpersonal level, and the outsiders listen, give feedback and jot down a few words to remember what

what was said. After three minutes, a second signal indicates that the outsiders now tell the insiders about their concerns at the personal level. Another signal is given, whereupon the outside group is asked to move to the right one place, which puts them face to face with new people. This time people are asked to speak about their concerns at the personal level. Then follows movement and conversation and listening about concerns at the community and wider levels. And so on, until all have had a chance to speak about their concerns at the four levels, to have been listened to, and to listen attentively to the concerns of others.

BREAK

6. Working in Parish Teams

Now each parish group meets and the members share with one another the fruits of their listening. It is important to re-iterate that they are being asked to identify other people's concerns, not their own. From pooling their findings, they will have a good idea of what the concerns of the group are, in general terms. They are asked to put down these concerns on a sheet of newsprint. In each group ask someone to co-ordinate and someone to report.

7. Presentation of lists of concerns

The lists are put up on the wall and, using the posters as a basis, the reporter presents the results of the groups' sharing.

8. Leading learners comment

The leading team draw attention to the general themes that are emerging, showing how certain concerns can be clustered together. It is also explained that, before the next session, the leading team will sort out the clusters of concerns into several themes, to help the wider group deal with them.

9. Final Prayer

Hope for a Better World
> It is time we stopped talking of despair
>   and started living in hope.
> It is time we started reading and hearing more
>   of the good that people can do for themselves
>   and for others.
> There are far more good Samaritans in this world
>   than there are destroyers.
> We must not let the public pessimism of a few
>   destroy the optimism of many.
> It is this flame
>   that will illuminate hope
>   for all people.
> It is this hope
>   that will bring about
>   a new and better world.
> Easter is a protest against
>   despair and dejection.
>
> Faith in the resurrection means -
>   not resigning oneself to the 'hard facts',
> it means refusing to accept the status quo
>   and struggling for undreamt-of possibilities.

International Catholic Information, May 1976.

Handout 24
Listening for issues

Look at yourself as a Partner in Faith and, in the light of all you have experienced on the course:

a. At a *personal level* in relation to who I am? What I stand for? What I think? My gifts, limitations, my fears? What are my main concerns?

_____

_____

b. At an *interpersonal* level in relation to interacting with other people, ability to listen and respond ... in relation to taking part in a group, working with or leading a group, what do I feel are my main concerns?

_____

_____

c. At the level of *church/parish* – as someone who belongs to the church/parish, what problems do I have with my own member-ship, my own role? What difficulties do I have with Church in general? How do I see ourselves as a group in relation to the par-ish? What are my main concerns?

_____

_____

d. At the level of *society/environment* what are the issues/problems I feel we as Christians are called to respond to in some way? Choose one or two you'd like this whole group to pay attention to.

_____

_____

SESSION EIGHTEEN

Choosing and Clarifying Themes
Posing Themes as Problems

Aims
To enable each team
• to choose the theme for which they will be responsible.
• to clarify what each team member understands when referring to the theme.
• to learn how to pose the theme as a problem.

Note: Prior to this meeting, the leading team takes all the material and clusters similar concerns together as Themes. This is already visible on the walls of the room when people come in.

Materials
Handout 25 on codification
Handout 26 on decoding questions
Photographs or posters for decoding session
Themes from the last session, clustered together

Time-table
1.	7.45	Welcome, aims, time-table, tasks if any
2.	8.05	Introduction
3.	8.20	Choices
4.	8.35	Clarification in groups
	8.55	Break
5.	9.10	How to pose themes as problems
6.	9.25	Dialogue session as example
7.	10.00	Next steps: schedule for coming weeks

Suggested Procedure

1. Welcome and Introduction
Welcome the people and describe this session's aims and time-table.

2. Introduction
Since our last session, we have sorted out the themes you have identified. These, according to yourselves, are the real concerns of the participants of this course. Is there anything that needs to be clarified?

Allow time for comments and questions.

The task now is for each group to meet and discuss these themes. Choose, in order of preference, the three themes you would like to help the wider group deal with.

N.B. It is not a question of choosing the three themes that are of greatest concern to the team members themselves. The task is still listening for others' concerns and 'serving' them.

3. Choices
Ask for the preferences and write up each group's choices on the board e.g:

> Finglas 1st choice
> 2nd choice
> 3rd choice

and negotiate so that each group will have finally settled on one theme.

In recent times some of the themes which have emerged are:
> Unemployment: its effects on family and community
> Children's needs: children at risk
> Dealing with loneliness
> Building self-confidence
> Putting our faith into action
> Consequences of new awareness
> Building a team
> Working together in groups
> Pastoral planning
> What Partners in Faith is all about
> Choices for the elderly
> Parents-school- community-children
> Scripture and life
> Fear of involvement
> Working in Groups
> Environment
> Responsibility as parents

4. Clarification in Groups
To make sure you are on the same wave-length, use this question in your group:
'When I think of the theme ... I am referring to ... (what) ... (to whom) ... ?'

BREAK

5. How to pose themes as problems
Each group now has a theme of concern to all here. You have a general idea of where people stand in relation to that theme. In order to help the people come to grips with the theme, and to let you know where people want to go in relation to it, you need to investigate the theme further with the people.

The way to go about this is *to pose the theme as a problem* so that people can talk about it, know what they feel about it and analyse it. This will already deepen their own awareness and understanding of the theme, and show you where people want to go with it.

The way to help people to focus on the theme and to discuss it is to prepare a *codification* of the theme:

A Codification is a concrete representation of a significant situation of people's lives, in such a way as to include contrasts, contradictions and relationships and embody themes.

It is used to draw people out, so they can express what they think and feel about the situation.

Drawings, posters, photographs, tape-recordings, stories, role-play, slides, newspaper cuttings, pieces of video, poems, all can be used singly or combined to make a codification.

The task is to find a way of illustrating a theme in its social setting, as a *stimulus* to get people talking about and analysing their reality.

Preparing a codification
In order to prepare a codification, think about and describe:
- A situation in which you saw the theme present
   - What was the setting?
   - What was happening at the time?
   - Who were the actors (people involved) in the situation?
   - How were they relating to one another?
Out of this brainstorm, some ideas for codifications will come.

Qualities of good codification
1. A reasonably familiar or recognisable situation.
2. Not too puzzling, so that those responding to it in a group will be able to find themselves in it and interpret it in the light of their own experience.
3. Neither should it be too explicit, otherwise it appears like propaganda and there is no room for interpretation.
4. The way the parts relate to one another shows contrasts and contradictions.
5. It focuses attention on one theme.
6. It stimulates interest and poses questions.

The best way to understand this is to look at an example. Suppose the theme is 'Schooling'. You want a situation in which the relationships between school, parents, teacher, classroom and community are somehow represented so that people can discuss the theme.

Here is a combination of codifications which have been used:

Taken from Living Adult Education, by G and C Kirkwall

Dialogue: The importance of questions
The next thing is to use the codification with a group of people. It's simply an opportunity to take a closer look at some familiar situation and say what you think. The success of the discussion depends on participants being prepared to share their experiences of the situation with others in the group. The outcome of the discussion will be to prepare learning or action events tackling some of the issues raised.

The first codification is displayed. The co-ordinator asks a series of open questions designed to help people gradually explore and analyse the situation. A standard sequence of questions is used, but others are added as the dialogue in the group develops. Here is the sequence of questions which you will also find in Handout 25:

1. Descriptive
   - What do you see in this situation?
   - What is happening?
   - What is each person feeling?

2. First Analysis
   - Why is this happening?
   - Why are people doing what they are doing?

3. Our Own Experience/Situation
- What similar situations are you aware of in your experience (your own and/or others)?

4. Connected Problems
- What problems are connected with this situation (i.e. your experience - situation)?

5. Second Analysis
- What are the underlying causes of this?

6. Planning Action
- What do you need in order to be able to bring about a change in relation to this concern (i.e. what do you need to be aware of understand, learn or be able to do)?

As you can see there are three different levels of questions:
1. The first level is descriptive. The group is invited to look at the picture and to describe everything they see in it (naming our reality and the different elements in it). This step should never be glossed over or taken-for-granted.

2. The next level: participants are invited to look closely at the people in the situation. You encourage them to read their expressions, postures and gestures and suggest what their relationship to each other and to the situation might be. They also ask why the situation is as it is. (*First Analysis*)

3. At the third level people are asked to relate the situation to their own lives, to place themselves in it. Then they are asked why things are as they are in their lives. This moves people beyond the particular to the wider social, political, cultural and historical factors. (*Our own situation and second analysis*).

The co-ordinator keeps the flow of conversation going. She may draw things together or move things on by further questions.

The observer, at the end of the discussion, outlines the key points of the discussion, quoting from what people actually said. Key words and key phrases are written down. He/she may suggest themes or contradictions that have turned up in the discussion. People agree or disagree.

The co-ordinator checks out whether it is possible to get agreement in the group about what has been the most important theme to emerge in the discussion.

The summary of the discussion will indicate to you what people need to deal with and you can set your aim.

6. Dialogue Session
Demonstrating how groups can go about it.

Leader 1: Can I have six volunteers to engage in a decoding dialogue on the theme of 'Schooling'? Can we have some people who have young children? My companion, Leader 2, will lead the dialogue and Leader 3 and myself will observe.

At this point Leader 2 gathers the people, displays the codification(s) and begins the dialogue. Distribute Handout 26 before the group disperses.

7. Next Steps
In two weeks' time, each group will carry out a decodification session with members of two other groups. So you will need to get together and prepare codifications on your theme, with questions allowing the participants to express what they think and feel about the situation. This will be the investigation session when you will investigate the theme, using decodification.

Work out a schedule such as:
Team A with Teams B and C   Team D with Teams E and F
Team C with Teams A and B   Team F with Teams D and E

Break

Team B with Teams A and C   Team E with Teams D and F.

Each team gets the necessary guidelines and decides:
   • who will introduce the session.
   • who will display the codifications.
   • who will lead the dialogue.
   • who observes and notes what people say.

Note: While the groups are preparing their codifications, we return to another aspect of the course: Jesus' action for the Kingdom.

Handout 25
Questions for Dialogue

1. Descriptive
  - What do you see in this situation?
  - What is happening?
  - What is each person feeling?

2. First Analysis
  - Why is this happening?
  - Why are people doing what they are doing?

3. Our Own Experience/Situation
  - What similar situations are you aware of in your experience (your own and/or others)?

4. Connected Problems
  - What problems are connected with this situation
  (i.e. in your experience – situation)?

5. Second Analysis
  - What are the underlying causes of this?

6. Planning Action
  - What do you need in order to be able to bring about a change in relation to this concern (i.e. what do you need to be aware of understand, learn or be able to do)?

Handout 26
Notes on codification

Codification is a concrete representation of a significant situation of people's lives in such a way as to include contrasts, contradictions, and relationships, and to embody themes.
For example, it may be a photo, a collage, a drawing, role-play, slides, a piece of video, a story, newspaper cuttings, a tape recording.

To prepare a codification
Think about, and describe:
– a situation in which you saw the theme present:
  – What was the setting?
  – What was happening at the time?
  – Who were the people involved?
  – How were they relating to one another?
Brainstorm – and ideas for a codification will come!

Qualities of good codification
1. A reasonably familiar or recognisable situation.

2. Not too puzzling, so that those responding to it in a group will be able to find themselves in it and interpret it in the light of their own experience.

3. Neither should it be too explicit, otherwise it appears like propaganda and there is no room for interpretation.

4. The way the parts relate to one another shows contrasts and contradictions.

5. It focuses attention on one theme.

6. It stimulates interest and poses questions.

SESSION NINETEEN

Decoding

Aim

• To allow each team to carry out a decoding session with others on the course, in order to explore their theme and identify what further, more specific learning/action is required.

Suggested Procedure

1. Introduction and Welcome

Reminder that the schedule is tight if each team is to get enough time.

2. Working in Groups

Put groups A, B, and C in one room, and groups D, E, and F in another room.

Procedure

Group A runs a decoding session with Groups B and C for 35 minutes, with a further 5 minutes for review, etc. Then group B takes over, etc..

Make sure that observers are recording the key points and key words coming up in the dialogue.

Note: In the circumstances of the course, it is only possible to allocate 35 minutes, which is barely sufficient time to achieve the purpose.

A sample time-table is given in Supplementary Material 1. Some examples of codification which came up on our courses are given in Supplementary Material 2.

3. End of Session.

As the participants are leaving, remind them that will need the notes they have taken for the next session.

Supplementary Material 1

Partners in Faith   February 26-27, 1991

Decoding Session

Time-table

1. 7.45 Welcome and explanation of how the night will run.
2. 8.00 Team A works with Teams B and C.
   Team D works with E and F
3. 8.30 Short review
4. 8.40 B works with A and C
   E works with F and D
5. 9.10 Short Review
   9.20 Break
6. 9.35 C works with B and A
   F works with D and E
7. 10.05 Short Review

If time permits, all can gather back in the main room for a short reflection.

Supplementary Material 2

Examples of Codification

a) Theme: Elderly
Sequence of photographs
1. Photo of two nurses guiding an old lady along the corridor of a Nursing Home. The woman is using a walking aid. The home is very shiny and modern.
2. Photo from ALONE of an old woman lying in bed in a very untidy room.
3. An elderly person standing at the door of his/her little house, looking at passers-by.

b) Theme: Unemployment
Song by Christy Moore: Ordinary Man

c) Theme: Faith in Action
Composite picture of people involved in various activities: work, family, church-related, and surrounded by 'issues' needing attention.

d) Theme: Dealing with Loneliness
Playlet of husband and wife together at table and not communicating.

SESSION TWENTY

Setting aims, planning research, task and maintenance

Aims
To enable each group:
- to formulate the aim(s) of their learning events
- to plan the necessary research in order to achieve the aim
- to appreciate the task and maintenance aspects of the group.

Materials
Sheets of newsprint and markers
Handout 27 on Task and Maintenance
Group Task printed out large

Time-table
1. 7.45 Welcome, news, prayer.
2. 8.00 Setting aims.
3. 8.50 Planning Research.
   9.05 Break.
4. 9.20 Task and Maintenance.
6. 10.10 Conclusion

Suggested Procedure

1. Welcome
Settling down, news, prayer.

2. Setting aims
Your task in each group now is to set an aim for your learning event, based on what you've heard informally and especially in the investigation session you held with members of the wider group.

The way to go about this is:
Let the recorder read the summary of the key points, key statements and any agreement reached in the decoding session. Others members confirm, challenge or add to what is reported.
Discuss and formulate an aim for the learning event. Use this formula:
What we want to help the whole group achieve, in this learning session, is ...
In other words, decide whether people need:
- to be more aware of ...
- to understand better ...
- to have more informaiton about ...
- to be able to do ...
- to be able to act in such a way that ... etc.

The leading team members visit the groups to help them resolve difficulties. On this course, the aims need to be specific, limited in scope, and achievable.

Some recent examples of aims:
Unemployment
To help the group become more aware of the effects of unemployment and possible responses to it.

Tensions and Options
To help the group face up to the challenge of Christian living today.

Children at risk
To help the group realise that something can be done at local level to help children at risk and that there is light at the end of the tunnel.

Checkpoints about the aim
1. Is it relevant to the participants?
2. Is it based on the dialogue about the theme?
3. Is it about a) awareness, b) information, c) understanding, d) skills, e) attitude or behaviour change?
4. Is it possible within the time available?
5. Is it clear?
6. Is the problem area too large? Do we need to limit it?
7. Have we access to resources to be able to achieve our aim?

3. Planning Research
Now that your provisional aims have been expressed, the next step is to set about planning any research you need to do. The main resources available to you are:
Ourselves: What do we ourselves know about the problem?
Activists: Whom do we know who is involved in doing something about the problem, whom we can consult?
Specialists: Is there someone who has studied more deeply, whom we can consult?
Literature: Is there any book, pamphlet, newspaper article, report, video or tape that deals with these concerns?

When you've considered the possibilities, you then organise yourselves to carry out research:
What? Who? Where? How? For when?

The time-table for the learning events is as follows:
Negotiate this with the whole group.
e.g. March 12th
      Team A: Unemployment
      Team B: Understanding the Church.

BREAK

4. Task and Maintenance

We want to highlight two aspects of life in groups. The task of leadership in a group is:
- to help the group get its task completed.
- to help maintain a good spirit in the group.

We've arranged an exercise now which will help you become more aware of these two aspects.

Please divide into pairs. One of you will be A and the other B. The A's will form a fishbowl in the centre of the room (i.e. a circle of chairs in the middle of the room) and will do the task below. Meanwhile, each of the B's will observe their A partner as they participate in the discussion.

Handout 26 shows you what to look out for.
Distribute handout.

Here is the task for the A group:
To begin to devise a Way of the Cross suitable for this *Partners in Faith* group.

Remember your goal is to achieve the task, but at the same time maintain a good spirit in the groups.

Right, away you go!

After 8 minutes
Will each A meet your B partner for some personal feedback on your participation in relation to the task and maintenance (2-3 minutes).

Then
Please return to centre and continue the discussion for another 8 minutes.

After another 8 minutes
Return and discuss with your partner for another few minutes.

SHORT BREAK

At this point, we invite the Bs to form the centre group and complete the discussion.

The Bs form the circle and continue the discussion where it left off.

After 8 minutes, recall the Bs to meet with the As for personal feedback on task and Maintenance (2-3 minutes). Then repeat this cycle.

6. Conclusion
Invite comments from the group. Ask people to remember:
 - when they noticed people bring the task ahead.
 – when people assured the participation of others.

Handout 27
Task and Maintenance

Task	Maintenance

Task

1. **Initiating:** Getting the group started on the task. Offering new suggestions, etc.

2. **Asking for information:** Drawing out the resources of the group; identifying information which needs to be found elsewhere.

3. **Giving information** or facts or sharing relevant information

4. **Asking for opinions:** Good decision-making depends on knowing what all the members think and feel about a suggestion.

5. **Giving opinions:** Some do this too much and some too little Sometimes a quick way to get all opinions needs to be found (e.g. straw vote)

6. **Explaining:** Giving practical examples to make a point clear.

7. **Clarifying:** Asking a question or repeating a point in different words to make it clear.

8. **Summarising:** stating briefly the main points made so far.

9. **Checking consensus:** seeing if everyone agrees on a point.

10. **Suggesting a process** for decision-making.

Maintenance

1. **Encouraging:** Being friendly responding to and building on suggestions made by others.

2. **Gate-keeping:** giving a quiet person a chance to join the the discussion.

3. **Setting Standards:** 'Shall we agree that everyone speaks once and nobody speaks more than twice?'

4. **Diagnosing difficulties:** 'I think we cannot make this decision until we get more information.'

5. **Expressing personal feelings** and group feelings: 'I'm getting bored; this is a small point and we have spent half an hour on it.'

6. **Harmonising:** Helping those in conflict to understand one another's views.

7. **Evaluating:** Creating an opportunity for people to express feelings and reactions towards the working of the group.

8. **Relieving tension:** By bringing it out into the open, putting a problem in a wider context, or making a joke.

SESSION TWENTY-ONE

The Learning Events

A most exciting part of the course is when the participants lead the sessions themselves. Most of them base their learning events on this framework:

1. Introduction and Welcome
Our theme tonight is ... etc.

2. Focusing Activity
Just to remind you of our theme, here is a song (poem, short statement) ...
or
Here are the main things you said at the investigation session: ...

3. Say Your Own Word
To give a chance to everyone to say what comes to mind when they think of the theme, ask 'What strikes you on listening to the song (poem, short statement...)?
Let people think, chat and give feedback.
Reminder: this is a chance for the rest of the large group to say their word, not for the team running the event!

4. Main Input/Activity
Some short presentation about the theme, either a talk, illustrated points, or an activity such as using the skill of group work, etc.

5. Dialogue
The key part of the session
Give an opportunity for people to dialogue about what has been presented, dividing them up in whatever way suits your purpose (small groups of 5, 3s, buzz,etc.) Helpful questions are:
   a) What made sense to you in what was presented?
   b) What questions does it raise for you?
   c) Any other comments.
Take feedback.
N.B. Leading team needs to be careful not to get into the role of giving answers: allow people to come to their own insights.

6. Silence
Ask people to be quiet for a while and ask themselves: 'What thought/insight comes to mind now for me?'
Let the people speak.

7. Ask the group to name any action/change/follow-up that
   - each one needs.
   - the group needs.
   - the team might arrange.

8. Conclusion
Review
Do a review of the learning event: It is a good idea to ask the leading team first how they felt about it, whether they achieved their aim, etc. Then ask the participants: 'What would you like to say to the team which led tonight's session?'

Prayer and scripture can be built into the session as appropriate.

Time-Table
It takes three hours for both sessions to be carried through and so it is important to remind people that they will be staying on for an extra half hour. The teams provide their own materials but they may need tape recorder, etc.

Supplementary Material 1

To give some idea of the variety and creativity of the people's work we have included summaries of twelve learning events.

Learning Events 1 and 2 (Monday March 12th)
Team A: Unemployment
The opening song, *Ordinary Man*, helped raise people's feelings about the effects of unemployment and prepared the way for the input on the facts and causes of unemployment in Ireland today. The clear, simple and profound significant facts stirred people's memories and actual experience, and moved the group in various ways: to change in attitude towards the unemployed, to action to find out root causes, to be better informed of the effects of multi-nationals on the economy.

Team B: Understanding the Church
The image of a football team and manager was used to draw out people's experience of Church, both positive and negative. The guest speaker (from another Christian church) responded to these experiences and outlined the essential elements of Christian community in clear, inspiring language. Questions in small groups drew the participants into dialogue as to what needs to happen today to encourage participation.

Learning Events 1 and 2 (Wednesday March 14th)
Team A: Interaction in groups
A brief focusing activity showed two people trying to open a bottle top. Obviously they would have succeeded if they had followed the instructions. There were some guidelines for groups which they helped us work out, after some memorable sharing of their own different personal experiences of being members of groups, starting with the family. The small group meetings on specific questions helped us taste again the value of respectful, challenging listening in groups.

Team B: The Church in Transition - Pastoral Planning
This team had done research in parishes and consulted people involved in parish planning and development. They introduced a taped interview with a member of a local parish planning team explaining what they are involved in and the impact it is having on the person herself and on parishioners. Questions in small groups unearthed people's experiences and feelings related to changes in parishes or blocks to changes. A helpful diagram illustrating what is involved in parish pastoral planning enlightened us as to the complexity of this process.

Learning Events 3 and 4 (Monday March 26th)
Team C: Young People in the Church
This team brought back to us the findings of a listening session they had held with a group of young people in their parish. By the questions they put to us, they led us to see that we could follow on what they had done themselves; they gave us hope about young people and found a way for-

ward in their own parish, after the *Partners in Faith* experience.

Team D: Faith in Action
This team had interviewed groups of people in Dublin who had been through the *Partners in Faith* experience. The positive reports gave us a sense of hope. The sets of questions discussed in small groups helped us look at practical steps we might consider to put our faith into action after this experience in Mountjoy Square.

Learning Events 3 and 4 (Wednesday 28th March)
Team C : Injustice in Society: The Causes of Poverty
This team focused on the theme of poverty and its causes in Ireland, introducing it through the song, *Ordinary Man*. They outlined the cultural, economic and political causes of poverty in a detailed and moving presentation. Through questions in small groups, we were helped to get a hold of the true, shocking facts

Team D: Small groups in Parishes
Using the reality of their own parish, symbolised by a tree with branches, leaves and fruits, they helped us see the multitude of activities that tend to go on in some parishes and led us to imagine the role of a support group nourishing itself with prayer, scripture sharing and going on to decide and plan action within that context. They summed up the role of a support group in a comprehensive circular diagram.

Learning Events 5 and 6 (Monday April 23rd)
Team D: The Elderly
'Memories' from *Cats* was used to arouse feelings surrounding the fact of aging and our experience with older people. The team had carried out personal research with several elderly people and communicated the fruits of this to us in language that caught the actual feelings of older people and showed a keen ability to learn while listening. The positive aspect of the help available to elderly people was stressed but, in the feedback, people's frustrations with caring for elderly people on a daily basis surfaces. Indications of where help for the 'carers' can be had were eagerly welcomed.

Team F: Lack of Self-Confidence
Statements of how we develop our confidence were shared with us, based on sound traditional wisdom. Personal stories of individuals on the team reinforced these and struck a chord in our hearts. Some personal sharing was asked for and this risk paid off, with people sharing the gifts others had noticed in them and the gift they wanted for themselves. The team spoke of how doing the learning event had itself raised their own level of self-confidence.

Learning Event 5: (Wednesday 25th March)
Team E: Education: Relationship between school, home and community
The team helped us look at the relationship between the school, family and community. To gain awareness of this triangle, one of them had attended a seminar on this topic. They also made use of their familiarity with parent-teacher relationships as parents, school staff and in play-groups. The main core of the session revolved around reflecting in small groups on three different sets of questions on three levels: pre-school, secondary and adult. The ensuing dialogue surfaced valuable insights on how the school system operates and the areas of self-potential and development it

doesn't reach and doesn't claim to reach.

Team F: Children at Risk
This team had invited two persons who are currently working with children at risk in an inner-city parish. After reminding us of what children get up to (burning cars and school building, robbing, etc) by showing us again the pictures they had used of their decoding, they invited the guests to share with us their stories. The obvious love and dedication with which these two men spoke of the children they work with, despite all the odds, served to raise our own hopes that something can be done: there is light at the end of the tunnel.

Supplementary Material 2

Here is the outline of the learning event about *Children at Risk:*

Welcome
1 Reminder of some points kept by the observer during the investigation session.
2. Focusing Activity: A collage of many of the bad things happening in the area and testimonies about it.
3. Say Your Own Word
Ask people to speak of their experience of young people at risk in their local area.
4. Input
a) A twenty-year-old describes his experience of growing up in the area.
b) Poster indicating amenities for youth in area.
c) Youth worker who works with joy-riders, vandals and trouble-makers.
5. Dialogue:
'What does this presentation say to your own experience?'
6. Silence, followed by ideas, insights, from people.
7. Action:
'Is there anything we can do in our area on behalf of youth?'

Supplementary Material 4

Method for Group Action: The Faith Dimension

The first step in this method is that the team set out to *notice* what the people are concerned about in their life-situation. This means making a real effort to listen to what is going on in their lives. As the team moves among the people, it makes the effort to be deliberately attentive to the things they refer to and talk about: their worries, concerns, problems, interests, i.e. the issues *they feel an interest in.*

This demands an effort to go out of ourselves and put ourselves *in their shoes* or feel things *from underneath their skin.* As you listen, you begin to become aware that, underneath the talk, there are certain *themes* which generate or would generate interest in people if they were brought up for discussion. These themes trigger off some energy in the people. That is why they are called *generative themes.* You have to be pretty sensitive to get in touch with what's really of interest to people. From your contact with them in groups, streets, shops, meetings, outside the church, the pub, the hairdresser, homes, school, you learn to get in touch with whatever may be a key concern for them at the level of personal life, family, community, work, leisure, etc..

Having listened, you choose one theme you would like to help the people do something about.

The next step is to bring that *theme* to the notice of some of the people, as a concrete topic of conversation, in order to listen more deeply, so as to find out what they think or feel about it now, what they know or don't know about it, what they would like to learn or do about it. This means arranging a serious conversation about the theme with the people, after which you will be more aware of what needs to be done about it. (Objectives or aim.)

You will then be able to say, 'In relation to this theme, the people would like to look at, learn more about, or do something about, this aspect ...' i.e. you now have the aim of your co-operative action with the people. Then, after some research, you arrange a session or sessions to enable the people to fulfil their need for awareness, knowledge, action.

The key to the whole process is the ability to really listen to what the others are genuinely concerned about or interested in.

Faith dimension of this approach

Faith means being able to find and commit ourselves to God in life. For someone without faith using the method above, we are simply listening to people and their concerns. For someone with faith, the people are our brothers and sisters before Abba, and their concerns and issues are the voice of God calling us and inviting us to respond and co-operate in bringing about more life and life in abundance (John 10:10) or, in other words, co-operating with God in the building of the Kingdom of justice, life, peace and compassion.

When we identify generative themes, in faith we can interpret them as signs of God's call and it is by faith that we engage in the mission of acting to bring about growth, freedom or, simply, more life.

Let us take an example. Our team tunes in to the experience of the people; in that *human experience* we notice that something really *significant* is what is happening to some children; they are at risk or are being neglected. To the person of faith, this is not just a *significant human experience*. It is also a *religious experience*. By faith, the voice of God is heard saying, 'I am Abba and you are my sons and daughters. Your little brothers and sisters are in danger and I want you to care for them with me. Together let us protect and nurture them. Whatever you do to the least of your brothers, that you do unto me.'

It all depends on how we see things. Our faith through God revealed through Jesus, gives us a new way of seeing ourselves, others, and the world around us and, through that faith, we hear God's calls in the concerns of the people and we mobilise to respond in action. We do this in little ways and big ways.

But for those who have Gospel faith, we will hear God's call especially in those who are excluded, marginalised, exploited, hurting, or down-trodden, and we will feel the call to announce, by presence, action and word, *Good News* of bringing about growth, freedom and justice.

Like Jesus, we find out what God wants by listening to the people in the light of God's project for humanity.

God's project:
– is liberation, growth and development for all, especially those who are oppressed;
– was first fulfilled in the history of the Hebrews in Egypt;
– was fulfilled completely in the person of Jesus of Nazareth, the Christ;
– is being realised continually by the power of the Spirit when people respond to the cries, concerns and serious needs of others today.

In short, when we hear God's voice in reality, and commit ourselves in hope to bringing about new life, then we are signs and agents of the Kingdom of God – God's project for humanity.

Prayer, scripture, study, the Eucharist, and encouraging partnership are the ways we fit ourselves to seriously engage in this mission.

Supplementary Material 5

Comment after the learning events.
These sessions were the highlight of the year. The participants experienced their own growth and giftedness in a practical way. The 'gap' between leading learners and the local teams faded, to give place to genuine dialogue. Our own insight after the events is that here is a key place where people do their own 'theology': reflect on their reality, dialogue about it, look at it in the light of faith and commit themselves to go beyond for the sake of the Kingdom. Following the learning events with the session 'Discovering the Spirit in our midst' helps us capture the 'revelation' that has happened among us through the graciousness of the Source, Son and Spirit, whose joy is to be among people.

SESSION TWENTY-TWO

Jesus' action for the Kingdom

This session fits into the course while the groups are preparing sessions at home.

Aims
• To see what Jesus stood for in the context of the society in which he lived.
• To examine the implications for our lives as Christians today.

Materials
Outline of the diagram below.
Diagram of synagogue.
Handout 28: Luke 13:10-17.

Time-table
1. 7.45   Welcome, aims, time-table, team tasks.
            Introduction to theme.
2. 8.10   Palestine at time of Jesus: structures
            - build-up and explanation.
3.   Buzz, and comments
   9.00   Break
4. 9.15   Reflection on Freed woman
5. 10.05 Other comments, reminder of tasks.

Suggested Procedure

1. Welcome
Aims, time-Table, team tasks.

Introduction to the theme
In the parables, we see how Jesus struggled to find the most adequate, most satisfactory, most impact-filled image to reveal the mystery that he calls by the familiar name of 'Abba'. He is never satisfied with any of them and he begins to search again, because each image can only show facets of this profound mystery. God, he says, is like a doting father, he is like a foolish shepherd who risks all to save one, or a foolish housekeeper who, with amazing singlemindedness, spends her time for what others regard as worthless and then spends forty-worths of it celebrating when she has found it, or the employer who pays workers according to calculations based, not on what they deserve, but on his own prodigal generosity ... Jesus announces to us this gracious, loving, merciful, compassionate God who wants all people united with God and with each other. Jesus tries to inflame our imaginations so that we will realise that abundance of love within us and let it expand towards others.

Eamonn Bredin, *Disturbing the Peace*, pp 94ff

His mission, which he took from God, is to proclaim the Kingdom of God, that is, the communicating to us of God's love and graciousness and companionship with all.

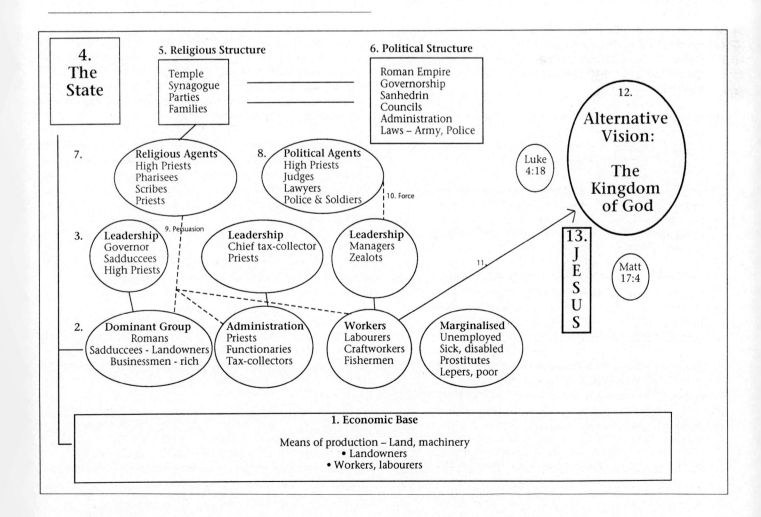

When we speak of the 'Kingdom of God' what do we mean? The following words are based on the writings of Fr Enda Lyons:

'God reigns when we recognize the eternal value of ourselves and our fellow human beings, when we show genuine love and care, especially to those in pain, poverty, in deep need; and when we struggle to create a situation in which all can fulfill their God-given potential.'

When this is happening, God's dream is being fulfilled: the world that God wants is coming about. Jesus sets out to announce this Good News of the Kingdom in his own country.

To whom is the coming of the Kingdom most relevant? To those who are most needy. The heart of the loving, compassionate God will go out most to those who are excluded, put down, hurting, in pain, deprived, under-developed. As Jesus is in intimate union with God, he sees the world from the perspective of the poor, the most needy, the least fulfilled.

Let's look, in this session, at how Jesus worked to make God's dream come true.

2. Palestine at the Time of Jesus

This presentation is made by building up the diagram step by step. Outline the diagram lightly in pencil before the session. Then, as you explain each point in turn, go over the relevant part of the diagram with a felt marker.

Explanation of the diagram

1. In any society, people have certain needs: food, goods and services.
To meet these basic needs, people need to produce.
They have land and raw materials.
They have energy and skills.
They have means of production: tools, equipment, machinery.

One can ask:
Who owns the land?
Who owns the means of production?
Who works for whom?
How are things produced?
Who controls distribution?
How do these affect social relations between people?

2. How food and goods are produced, distributed and used, forms the economic base of society.

The way people are related to the economic base causes the emergence of different groups in society:
a) *Dominant group*: The owners of land and machinery, i.e. Romans, Sadduccees, landowners, business people.
b) *Administration*: Priests, functionaries, tax collectors.
c) *Workers*: Labourers, craft workers, fishermen ...
But a fourth group emerges, due to unemployment, poverty, malnutrition and lack of access to resources:
d) *Marginalised*: Beggars, unemployed, prostitutes, lepers, sick, disabled, poor.

3. Each of these groupings produces a group of leaders, who express and communicate the interests of their group and organise to ensure that their interests are met. This happens in all the groups except the fourth:
a) Governor, Sadduccees, High Priests, merchants.
b) Chief tax collectors, priests ...
c) Managers.
d) No one.

4. The state of Israel was created and held in place by the dominant groups. The state includes:
   – the religious/education structure.
   – the political structure.

5. The religious/education structure propagated the values and beliefs of the dominant groups, mainly through the Temple, the synagogues, the parties and the families.

6. The political structure ensured that these values were expressed in law and that the laws were kept, i.e.:
   the governership (Romans)
   the Sanhedrin
   Councils
   law courts
   military
   police
   prisons

7. The religious/education structure had its agents to communicate its values and beliefs. They were:
   the High Priests
   the scribes
   the priests
   the Pharisees

8. The political structure had its agents to exercise its power:
   the judges
   the lawyers
   the police
   the military

9. The dominant groups tried as much as possible to spread their values and beliefs through persuasion (education) rather than by force. They wanted to keep 'peace and stability', i.e. things the way they were.

10. However, when life becomes unbearable, and people realise the injustices, they begin to protest and rebel (e.g. Zealots). Then the State applies force. The State uses power to control: it passes tougher laws and makes use of the police, prisons and army. When the situation is under control, the State returns to the use of persuasion.

11. Of course, the destitute and poor are never taken into consideration. They are the broken glass, the marginalised, the outcasts of no importance.

12. People who are in groups a) and b) acquire certain privileges through education and ability. They can be strongly drawn to support the status quo, or they can make an option to identify with the situation of those who have least money, power, status or health, and work with them for a new situation, a new society.

13. Jesus was born into the third group, the workers. He saw people exploited by an unjust system.
He saw growing unemployment and crippling taxation.
He saw powerful people unconcerned by the extreme pov-

erty of their brothers and sisters.
He saw social tensions and conflicts.
He saw repression – force used to put down those who objected.
He saw upper classes collaborate with the empire.
He saw religious ambiguity.
He saw the people confused but hoping.
He reflected on the scriptures, Moses, Isaiah the prophet.
He reflected on Yahweh.
He developed a personal relationship with Abba – an intimate relationship with the loving source of all life.
He saw all as offspring from the one source, sharing the same life.
He asked himself: 'Is this Abba's dream for people?'
He sensed his mission.

Dialogue with the group
The leader asks, with reference to the wall presentation:
'What would God's dream be for this situation?'
Buzz and feedback.

Leader places the poster about God's reign on display and asks:
'Does this affirm, challenge or go beyond what you said, or vice versa?'
Take responses.

Leader asks: 'For whom would this be "Good News"?'
Buzz and feedback.

Leaders then place posters, with the following quotations, on the wall, saying, 'This is how Jesus describes how he went about doing his mission.'

The Spirit of the Lord is upon me, because he has anointed me to preach good news to the poor. He has sent me to proclaim freedom for the prisoners and recovery of sight for the blind, to release the oppressed, to proclaim the year of the Lord's favour.

Luke 4:18

Jesus replied: 'Go back and report to John what you hear and see: the blind receive sight, the lame walk, those who have leprosy are cured, the deaf hear, the dead are raised, and the good news is preached to the poor.

Matthew 11:4-5

Jesus sets out:
'The time has come,' he said, 'The Kingdom of God is near. Repent and believe the good news'

Mark 1:15.

The presentation is concluded with the following:

The Action of Jesus
Jesus became aware of his mission to proclaim God as Abba who loves all people equally and to bring about God's dream for people - the Kingdom. Jesus looked at the situation and decided to ACT so that God would reign in the world.

a) *Involvement*: Jesus was very sensitive to and deeply involved with people and situations which least reflected God's dream. He felt the hurt and painful injustice of the sick, the poor, the old, the marginalised.

b) *Compassion*: He suffered with people in their wounded-

ness and oppression. His heart went out in tender, vulnerable love.

c) *Healing*: His compassion expressed itself in tender care as he showed real solidarity with the afflicted, the downtrodden, the excluded and the put down, through his healing.

d) *Criticism*: His compassion led him to be critical, harshly critical of anyone or any system which caused people to be oppressed and wounded and prolonged their hurt. He acted for justice by criticism of the rich and powerful.

e) *Forgiveness*: He freed people from the shame that was attached to illness in that society. He enabled them to stand upright before Abba and others.

f) *Message of Faith and Hope*: At the same time as he showed the love and care of God, he proclaimed the coming of this Kingdom through preaching and parables, so that people could change their mind-set.

Summary
Jesus' action was broad and down to earth. The salvation he stood for was wholeness of body, mind and spirit. Untying all human bonds, enabling people to 'stand upright' in every sense was what he was about. He stood for and worked towards bringing about a situation in which people can achieve this true wholeness. Since such a situation can exist only where there is love, he stood for a deep change of heart in people, from selfishness to love. He again fulfilled the request of Yahweh in Micah:
- *to walk humbly*: he gave people a new way of looking at God and life. He asked people to believe in God as a loving Parent who wants all treated as brothers and sisters. He gave a new sense of hope, that oppression can be overcome.
- *to love tenderly*: he saw the hurt, pain and woundedness and oppression of people and reached out in compassionate, tender and vulnerable, healing love.
- *to act justly*: he publicly criticised the system and its leadership who maintained an unjust system where people were down-trodden and hurt. He wanted a different system – not based on inequality and domination and greed, but a community of equals where resources were shared and all had a part to play.

**JESUS' ACTION WAS TOWARDS
THE POOR, THE WOUNDED,
THE HURT, THE MARGINALISED
FOR A NEW SITUATION
OF COMMUNION AND PARTICIPATION.**

BREAK

4. Reflection on the Freed Woman
Distribute Handout 28, Luke 13:10-17. Read the text slowly and invite 5 or 6 people to help you reflect on the text.
Place the diagram of a synagogue on the wall. Interview the 5 or 6 about the story, e.g:

Part I
1. Where did the action take place?
2. What is a synagogue for?
3. What was Jesus doing there?
4. What else did he do?

6. what did he do for the woman?
7. What was her response?
8. What was the ruler's response?
9. How does Jesus react to the ruler?
10. How does Jesus describe the woman?
10. What are the feelings of the ruler and adversaries?
11. What are the feelings of the people and the woman?
12. Who is making proper use of the synagogue?
13. What names are used for Jesus?

Part Two
1. Has anyone ever been Jesus to you like this?
2. Have you ever been Jesus to others in this way?
3. In your area/community who has been Jesus in this sense? in Ireland? in the world?
4. What is happening when people act like this?
5 Why did Jesus act like this?
6. How does this fit in with our lives today?

Open Forum
What comes to mind now?

5. Conclusion
Reminder of team tasks.
If there is time, give each group a text and ask them to make up questions about it for an interview.

Handout 28

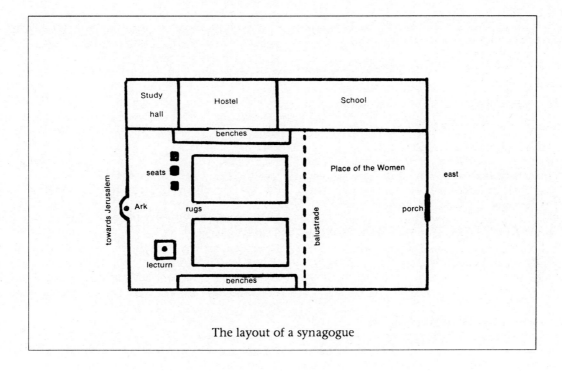

The layout of a synagogue

One Sabbath day he was teaching in one of the synagogues, and a woman was there who, for eighteen years, had been possessed by a spirit that left her enfeebled; she was bent double and quite unable to stand upright. When Jesus saw her he called her over and said, 'Woman, you are rid of your infirmity,' and he laid his hands on her. At once she straightened up and she glorified God.

But the synagogue official was indignant because Jesus had healed on the sabbath, and he addressed the people present: 'There are six days,' he said, 'when work is to be done. Come and be healed on one of those days and not on the sabbath.' But the Lord answered him, 'Hypocrites!' he said, 'Is there one of you who does not untie his ox or his donkey from the manger on the sabbath and take it out for watering? And this woman, a daughter of Abraham whom Satan has held bound these eighteen years – was it not right to untie her bonds on the sabbath?' When he said this, all his adverseries were covered with confusion, and all the people were overjoyed at all the wonders he worked. (Luke 13:10-17)

Supplementary Material

This material is good background for the idea of the Kingdom, a key idea in the whole course.

In the situation of Palestine, Jesus announced Good News. He says: 'I have come to bring good news to the poor.' (Lk 4:18, 7:22)

What is good news?

Something that makes us rejoice because this news, when heard, eliminates something that we feared, something dangerous, something we do not like, something bad or evil and it promises us, in some way or other, a better future. Good News is promising news. It makes us happy because it makes us hopeful about the future. It energises us. It's the kind of news that generates hope.

Who was Jesus' Good News for? - The poor

Who was going to feel excitement at the message? There can be no doubt that what Jesus said and did was good news for the poor, and bad news for the rich and powerful, even though, in the long run, it will ultimately benefit every-body. 'Blessed are you who are poor, for yours is the Kingdom of God.' The poor knew that the rule or Kingdom of God embodied all their hopes and aspirations. To hear that the time had come to fulfil these hopes and aspirations was *real good news.*

What was the Good News?

The Good News was about the Reign (Kingdom) of God in the lives of people - God's rule among people. It could be described as power that had been displayed in the wonderful works of God in the past, in Exodus and the Promised Land. For the poor the Kingdom would mean liberation from their sufferings.

In the experience of the Reign of God there are four basic ideas:

1. *The liberation of the poor from hunger, sickness, and guilt is the work of God*, an act of salvation and a sign that God is beginning to reign. (Luke 11:20; Mt 11:2-5; Mk 5:34; Lk 17:19; 18:42.)

2. *The Reign of God is a project for which God and human beings are responsible.* (Mt 13:409; 24-30; 31-32; Mk 4:26-29; Lk 9:62.)
Ploughing, sowing, planting and harvesting is the work of the farmer. But the actual growth of the plants or trees is the quiet and invisible work of God. (cf. Mk 4:26-29.)
Jesus is the great example of this human work. He took the initiative by his words and deeds, and taught the poor who followed him to do the same.

3. *The Reign of God demands total commitment.*
(Mt 6:33; 13:44-46)
The human work involved in the coming of God's kingdom does not admit of compromise or hesitation. It is a matter of life and death.
The gospels give us a glimpse of this new practice. We are introduced to a man who began the process of liberating the poor from their sufferings, by healing the sick, dispelling the fear of demons, encouraging the weak and powerless, teaching people to share what they had, and doing so himself. Moreover, he confronted the system, ignored its purity regulations, argued with the upholders of the sys-tem, led a demonstration by riding into Jerusalem on a donkey, staged a sit-in in the Temple courtyard, and drove out the traders and money-changers with a whip, was confronted by the authorities, went into hiding, was betrayed, mocked, put on trial, sentenced to death and, finally, tortured to death on a Roman instrument of repression.

4. *The Reign of God is about a whole quality of human solidarity between people.*
What transforms communities or societies into the reign of God and the work of salvation, is the way people in them relate to one another and to others. They are joyful, happy and celebrating communities of brothers and sisters who love one another, share with one another and are even willing to die for one another. In other words, they live together in solidarity and yet they remain open to others and are without any thought of taking revenge upon their enemies. (e.g. Lk 14:7-24; Mt 12:36-50; Lk 6:27-38; Mt 5:38-48; Acts 2:42-47; 4:32-35.) They are communities with a purpose, with a goal, communities that are part of the divine project that Jesus called the reign of God.
(Based on ideas by Albert Nolan, *God in Africa.*)

What would God's Reign look like?

1. Basic Needs

Every person has the right to the satisfaction of his or her basic needs. It is wrong for some to live in luxury while others face utter deprivation. Beyond this, it is a society in which everyone has not just a bearable, but a satisfying, fulfilling life.

2. Equal Respect

All forms of degrading treatment and circumstances are opposed. The snobbery and patronising attitudes of the privileged are rejected, as well as the feelings of deference and inferiority they foster. In other words, the situation where people are appreciated for their social position, not for their personal qualities, is rejected.
It is a society in which everyone has an equal social status and in which people relate to one another on the basis of fellow feeling or community, instead of grouping themselves into economic pyramids.

3. Economic Equality

There are no huge differences in income and wealth found both within countries and between them. It's not that everyone should have exactly the same income, since people have different needs and aspirations. But much more equality of income is certainly called for.
As for equality of opportunity, it shouldn't be a case of an equal start in the rat-race, but the provision to everyone of ways to develop their individual talents in a satisfying and fulfilling way.

4. Political Equality

There are ways by which people can exercise a much greater power over the shape of their lives. Not just a vote but structures that enable people to participate in decision-making about government, industry, education, family life, social services.

5. Sexual, racial ethnic and religious equality

No-one is treated worse than others because of their sex or sexual preferences, their culture or colour, their religion or lack of it. Blatant discrimination is condemned, as in racial segregation and religious persecution, and also rejected are

sexism, racism and intolerance which lead to systematic differences of wealth, power and status. Also opposed are any
discrimination or irrelevant differences against anyone who
is old or disabled.

(See John Baker, *Arguments for Equality*, Verso Books.)

Another way of saying it
Being in such intimate communion with God, Jesus knew
what kind of ruler God is. God is compassionate: 'Jesus
speaks and acts in the name of a king who is compassionate, who does not make distinction ... He acts in the name
of a father who loves all children equally, without excep-
tion ... who makes his rain fall and his sun shine on the
just and the unjust.' (Eamonn Bredin, *Disturbing the Peace*,
page 124). Jesus also was deeply in tune with, and sensitive
to, God's vision for human life: to the type of situation
which God wants for our world, to the form which God's
Reign or Kingdom takes. We can see, from the gospel accounts of his ministry, how Jesus understood this.
The kingdom of God, or the situation for which Jesus
worked and which he served, is really one in which human
community in its fullest reality exists. It is one of real companionship - companionship among people together and
with God. It is that 'original' situation in which people felt
no shame in front of each other, with God walking among
them 'in the cool of the day'. It is the situation which Vatican II speaks of when talking about the Church - one in
which there exists 'intimate union with God and ... the unity of humankind.' (Lumen Gentium, art 1).

It is the situation which is very beautifully described in the
Mass of Christ the Universal King:
   an eternal and universal kingdom
   a kingdom of truth and life,
   a kingdom of holiness and grace
   a kingdom of justice, love and peace.
It is for the coming of such a kingdom that Jesus taught his
disciples to pray and for which we do pray when we say,
'Thy Kingdom Come.'

Enda Lyons, *Partnership in Parish*.

The Kingdom of God
is the goodness of God IN us
accepted and lived.
It is therefore the power to love and be free.
It is this dynamic possibility we all have
of living in communion with one another
and so with God.
It exists in people who recognise the power of God
(the Spirit of God)
by living the Beatitudes and the Law of the Gospels in
which
- love, not law, is the essence,
- others are my brothers and sisters,
- God is Abba
- the earth is ours to steward.

It is the struggling to live the values of love, justice, communion and creativity. It is the struggling for a situation
which enables people to live in love, justice, communion
and creativity. The world into which we are born is not a
perfect world. While the basic goodness of God is reflected
in people's lives, it is also the case that there is self-
centredness, an atmosphere of bad will, unjust structures,
divisions, sickness and woundedness.

SESSION TWENTY-THREE

The meaning of the cross

Aims
• To enable the participants to respond to the question: If Jesus was so good, why did they kill him?
• To identify how living the Cross is witnessing and acting for God's dream.

Materials
Large cross
Handout 29
Handout 30 with phrases about 'Living the Cross'
Posters for the presentation
Video: 'A Passion'
Music

Time-Table
1.	7.45	Welcome, aims, time-table, team tasks.
2.	8.00	Introduction to night: video. Reactions.
3.	8.25	Presentation on 'Living the Cross'.
4.	8.40	Dialogue.
5.	9.00	Reflection on 'Living the Cross'.
	9.20	Break
6.	9.35	Celebration of the Cross (Way of the Cross).
7.	10.00	Conclusion.

Suggested Procedure

1. Welcome and Introduction
Welcome the people and describe this session's aims and time-table. Team tasks.

2. Introduction to theme
Central to the whole Christian way of life is the cross. 'Take up your cross and follow me.' In this week, a whole day, Good Friday, is dedicated to the memory and meaning of the cross. We have looked at Jesus in the context of his country and his people. We have seen what he stood for and the option he lived. He met with criticism, persecution, torture and death. In this session, we wish to explore the meaning of the cross for Jesus and for us.

Focusing activity
This short video, *A Passion**, takes nine minutes. We invite you to look at it.
* *Distributed by Mennonite Board of Missions, 1251 Virginia Avenue, Harrisburg, VA 22801-2497.*

Say Your Own Word:
    1) What feelings does it evoke in you about Jesus? (just register the feelings; no comment)
    2) What thoughts come to mind?
    3) Why was Jesus killed?

3. Presentation
The Meaning of the Cross
The four posters and material below, repeated on Handout 28 can form the basis of a presentation on the central symbol of our faith.

1. Source, Offspring, Life
Through Jesus, it was revealed that we all come from the same *source*. We are all *offspring* of the same source in Jesus, and we all share the same Spirit of *Life*. We are called to live in communion and love with the Trinity and each other. We have the same *dignity* and are called to recognise and live in *equality*. We are called to *wholeness* of body, mind and spirit and to live in *unity*.

When there is hurt, we are moved to *compassion, solidarity* and the promotion of *freedom*. We work for *justice* and, when there is failure, we are moved to *forgiveness*. This is the *vision* and these are the *values* of God's dream for people.

2. Mixed Situation
Neither Jesus nor ourselves were born into a world where these values and vision were totally in operation. Our world is also characterised by the *humiliation* of many people, by gross *inequality* in wealth, power and status, by *illness, division* and *indifference* rather than compassion. Instead of freedom, often there is *oppression* at different levels. There is much *injustice* and *bitterness* mixed up with the positive values as outlined above.

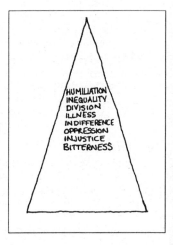

3. The Cross = Way of Liberation
The cross means trying to live out the gospel values, despite the obstacles in ourselves, in others and in society. It means *suffering to do away with suffering*. It is the *painful living of the truth*. It is co-operating with Abba's activity in life.
When we promote freedom where there is oppression, there will be pain, maybe conflict, but something new will be born. The way of liberation is the way of the cross.

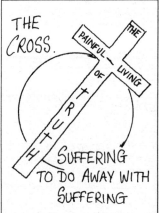

4. Communion - Resurrection

When we show genuine love and care for those in poverty, in pain or in deep need, overcoming our own fear and apathy, overcoming resistance or hostility, we are bringing about new life. When we are in communion with our fellow human beings we are in communion with our Source (Abba), we are truly offspring of that Source in Jesus and we are living by the Spirit. This was shown when God raised Jesus from the dead.

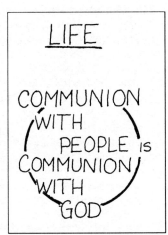

Our mission is to spread this Good News by who we are, by what we do and by what we say. The cross is living this truth despite the difficulties.

Two sets of values: the second set is the opposite of the first:

dignity	humiliation
equality	inequality
wholeness	illness
unity	division
compassion	indifference
freedom	oppression
justice	injustice
forgiveness	bitterness

This provides a basis for comment.

The central message of Christianity is found within this session on the cross.

4. Dialogue

a) What strikes you hearing this presentation?
b) What do you think of this way of looking at the cross?
c) What questions does it raise?

5. Reflection on Living the Cross

For all of us there are *values* we live out of spontaneously, values we have to stop and choose, and others we aspire to. On Handout 30 there is a series of phrases which, in one way or another, reflect the meaning of the cross. Use this Handout to help you reflect on your own living of the cross.

Buzz with one other person on the phrases you ticked.

BREAK

6. Celebration of the Cross
(In oratory or quiet place)

Bring in the large cross. Play some quiet background music, e.g. 'Once Upon a Time in the West', by Ennio Morricone.

THE WAY OF THE CROSS

First Section: **Living the Cross at the personal level**

'If any of you wants to come with me, you must forget yourself, carry your cross and follow me. For the man who wants to save his life will lose it; but anyone who loses his life for my sake will find it.' Matt 16:24-25

God speaks to me in the situations, events and happenings of everyday life – in my home, the neighbourhood, the group, the community. I listen and hear God's call. Often my feelings stop me from responding. I find it too difficult to say 'Yes'.
 I feel afraid to choose, speak, act;
 I feel embarrassed;
 I feel awkward;
 I feel indifferent;
 I feel discouraged.

And this happened to Jesus:
 'My Father, if it is possible,
 let this cup pass,
 let this cup pass,
 let this cup pass ...
 Nevertheless, if this cup cannot pass by,
 but I must drink it,
 your will be done.
 Matt 26:36 ff.

And Jesus chose to overcome his fear.
This is the Way of the Cross in one's personal level.

The words of Psalm 40 express Jesus' faithfulness to Abba, despite fear and anguish. Let us say them with him:
All:
I proclaimed the saving justice of God in the great assembly.
See, I will not hold my tongue, as you well know.
I have not kept your saving justice
locked in the depths of my heart
But have spoken of your constancy and your saving help.
I have made no secret of your faithful and steadfast love,
in the great assembly.

Let us pray:
For light to see our own worth and that of others,
 Let us pray to the Lord.
For courage to choose life,
 Let us pray to the Lord.
For the power to stand up for the values of the Kingdom,
 Let us pray to the Lord.
For those who have helped to keep us going,
 Let us pray to the Lord.

Quiet moment ...

Second Section: **Living the Cross at the Interpersonal Level**

This is my commandment: love one another as I have loved you. No one can have greater love than to lay down his life for his friends.
Jn 15:12-13

God calls us in our relationships with other people and we are free to respond; but often we find it difficult to give ourselves. We cannot bear the pain of loving for it means:
    overcoming our tiredness when someone needs attention;
    being patient with the distressed and depressed;
    spending time with the lonely;
    listening deeply to our friend;
    forgiving the one who has hurt us;
    going out to the one who has lost self esteem;
    giving our time, energy and talents to those in need;
    trusting ourselves to be able to bring healing,
    even when we feel inadequate.

Very often we are reluctant to give, like Simon of Cyrene:
'As they were leading him away, they seized on a man, Simon of Cyrene, who was coming in from the country, and made him shoulder the cross and carry it after Jesus.' *Luke 23:26*

And sometimes Jesus felt this reluctance:
'At once, a woman whose little daughter had an unclean spirit, heard about him and came and fell at his feet. Now this woman was a gentile, by birth a Syrophoenician, and she begged him to drive the devil out of her daughter. And he said to her: "The children should be fed first, because it's not fair to take the children's food and give it to the little dogs." But she spoke up: "Ah, yes, Sir," she replied, "but little dogs under the table eat the scraps from the children." And he said to her, "For saying this, you may go home happy; the devil is gone out of your daughter." So she went off home and found the child lying on the bed and the devil gone.' *Mk 7:25-29*

The words of Isaiah remind us of what it means to live the cross at the interpersonal level:
All:
The Lord has taught me what to say
So that I can strengthen the weary.
The Lord has given me understanding
and I have not rebelled or turned away from him.
Can a woman forget her baby at the breast?
Feel no pity for the child she has borne?
Even if these were to forget
I shall not forget you.
Isaiah 49: 15

Let us pray:
For the gift to appreciate everyone we meet,
    Let us pray to the Lord.
For the gift of compasssion for those in pain,
    Let us pray to the Lord.
For the gift of energy to go to those in need,
    Let us pray to the Lord.
For the wisdom, patience and understanding to love our neighbours,
    Let us pray to the Lord.
For the tenderness of heart to forgive,
    Let us pray to the Lord.

Third section: Living the Cross at the Wider level

'When he saw the crowds, he felt sorry for them because they were harassed and dejected, like sheep without a shepherd.' *Matt 9:36*

When we look honestly at the reality which surrounds us, and see situations where people have no access to opportunities, to resources, to growth or development, to participation and decision-making, we live the cross here through:
    a voice raised in protest;
    a pen put to paper;
    a meeting called to discuss;
    information collected;
    plans made;
    an action done;
    and going on, keeping on going,
        despite blocks,
        despite criticisms,
        despite refusals,
        despite discouragement,
        despite opposition.
For in this way, new life is brought.

'Be prepared for people to hand you over to the Sanhedrins and scourge you in their synagogues. You will be brought before governors and kings for my sake, as evidence to them and to the gentiles. But when you are handed over, do not worry about how to speak or what to say; what you are to say will be given to you when the time comes, because it is not you who will be speaking: the Spirit of your Father will be speaking in you.' *Matt 10:17-20*

Let us recite, with Jesus, Psalm 22:
For he has not despised
nor disregarded the poverty of the poor,
has not turned away his face,
but has listened to the cry for help.

Of you is my praise in the thronged assembly,
I will perform my vows before all who fear him.
The poor will eat and be filled,
Those who seek Yahweh will praise him,
'May your heart live forever.'

Let us pray:
For the eyes to see injustice,
    Let us pray to the Lord.
For the heart to feel the pain,
    Let us pray to the Lord.
For the hands to heal,
    Let us pray to the Lord.
For the feet to march,
    Let us pray to the Lord.
For the ability to organise,
    Let us pray to the Lord.
For the power to transform,
    Let us pray to the Lord.

Fourth Section: Living the Cross at the Level of Creation

'To the Lord belong the earth and its fulness
the world and all that dwell in it.
He has founded it on the ocean
and set it firmly on the waters.' *Psalm 24:1-3*

In and through nature and all creation, God speaks to us. Through the skies, atmosphere, grass, trees, lakes and rivers, the mountains and seas, clouds and rainbows and stars.

In our world, we know that the waters and land are being

abused and polluted, that our skies are smothered. We see the resources of the earth exploited, especially by nations who have plenty. We see herbs and plants used as lethal drugs; forests and green spaces destroyed, with no thought for the future,

How graciously Jesus appreciated the world, given to all by the Father, the source of all being. In Jesus we are brothers and sisters of one another and of all the earth. The same Spirit of life breathes in and through all of us. How graciously Jesus apreciated the world:
     the harvest, fields, the vineyards,
     the lilies of the field, the birds of the air,
     the fig tree, even the foxes:
all were woven into his teaching and preaching.

With Jesus we can praise God, the source of being, who gives us the earth to care for:
All:
O Lord, our Lord
How great is your name throughout the world!
I look up at the heaven, shaped by your fingers,
At the moon and the stars you set firm.

What are human beings that you spare a thought for them or the children of Adam that you care for them?

You have made us a little less than a god;
You have crowned us with glory and beauty,

Made us stewards of the works of your hand,
put all things into our care.

Sheep and cattle, all of them
and even the wild beasts, birds in the sky
and fish in the sea, as they make their way
across the ocean.

Let us pray:
For the gift to appreciate earth, and sky, air and water,
     Let us pray to the Lord.
For the gift to be able to protect and care for all your creation,
     Let us pray to the Lord.
For the gift to be active in co-operating with the restoration and healing of life,
     Let us pray to the Lord.
For the gift to co-create, set free, for the glory of your name,
     Let us pray to the Lord.

Let us conclude with the prayer of the Cross:

Leader:	The Cross
All:	we shall take it;
Leader:	The bread
All:	we shall break it;
Leader:	The pain
All:	we shall bear it;
Leader:	The joy
All:	we shall share it;
Leader:	The gospel
All:	we shall live it;
Leader:	The love
All:	we shall give it;
Leader:	The light
All:	we shall cherish it;
Leader:	The darkness
All:	God shall perish it.

(The Iona Community Worship Book, Wildgoose Pubs, Glasgow, 1988)

7. Conclusion
Remind about the date after Easter.

Handout 29

The Meaning of the Cross

1. Source, Offspring, Life

Through Jesus, it was revealed that we all come from the same *source*. We are all *offspring* of the same source in Jesus, and we all share the same Spirit of *Life*. We are called to live in communion and love with the Trinity and each other. We have the same *dignity* and are called to recognise and live in *equality*. We are called to *wholeness* of body, mind and spirit and to live in *unity*.

When there is hurt, we are moved to *compassion, solidarity* and the promotion of *freedom*. We work for *justice* and, when there is failure, we are moved to *forgiveness*. This is the *vision* and these are the *values* of God's dream for people.

2. Mixed Situation

Neither Jesus nor ourselves were born into a world where these values and vision were totally in operation. Our world is also characterised by the *humiliation* of many people, by gross *inequality* in wealth, power and status, by *illness, division* and *indifference* rather than compassion. Instead of freedom, often there is *oppression* at different levels. There is much *injustice* and *bitterness* mixed up with the positive values as outlined above.

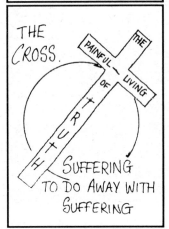

3. The Cross – Way of Liberation

The cross means trying to live out the gospel values, despite the obstacles in ourselves, in others and in society. It means *suffering to do away with suffering*. It is *the painful living of the truth*. It is co-operating with Abba's activity in life.

When we promote freedom where there is oppression, there will be pain, maybe conflict, but something new will be born. The way of liberation is the way of the cross.

4. Communion - Resurrection

When we show genuine love and care for those in poverty, in pain or in deep need, overcoming our own fear and apathy, overcoming resistance or hostility, we are *bringing about new life*. When we are in communion with our fellow human beings we are in communion with our Source (Abba), we are truly offspring of that Source in Jesus and we are living by the Spirit. This was shown when God raised Jesus from the dead.

Our mission is to spread this Good News by who we are, by what we do and by what we say. *The cross is living this truth despite the difficulties.*

Handout 30

Living the Cross

The cross is choosing to live the values of the kingdom in difficult circumstances.

It is: Yes   No

1. Speaking out what has to be said, despite being afraid.   ☐   ☐

2. Standing up for yourself, despite feeling you're a nobody.   ☐   ☐

3. Being in despair but choosing to try and live.   ☐   ☐

4. Overcoming apathy or the tendency to 'sit on the fence' and

   committing yourself to make an effort.   ☐   ☐

5. Deciding to take a risk, despite fear of failure.   ☐   ☐

6. When your heart is hardened against someone and you take the step of forgiving.   ☐   ☐

7. Staying with someone very down-hearted.   ☐   ☐

8. Choosing to side with people who are being unfairly treated.   ☐   ☐

9. Taking an interest in someone who is not realizing his/her potential.   ☐   ☐

10. Noticing someone very hurt and wounded and offering a healing presence.   ☐   ☐

11. Putting yourself out for someone in pain or poverty.   ☐   ☐

12. Fighting for the rights of victims, outcasts or excluded people.   ☐   ☐

13. Challenging someone who is spoiling his/her life.   ☐   ☐

14. Getting involved in community action and taking the flack.   ☐   ☐

15. Working to change structures so that all people can have a voice and participate in life.   ☐   ☐

16. Joining others who are working to change a bad situation.   ☐   ☐

17. Taking part in a protest walk which is highlighting an unjust situation.   ☐   ☐

18. Making representations to authorities about the way our environment is being abused.   ☐   ☐

19. Criticising authority for what they are doing to people.   ☐   ☐

20. Campaigning to have clean air or to stop manufacture of arms.   ☐   ☐

21. Supporting efforts to obtain better health facilities.   ☐   ☐

22. Doing something against the grain,

   e.g. speaking out because you see life being exploited or destroyed.   ☐   ☐

23. Refusing to stand down from the truth, despite persecution.   ☐   ☐

24. Struggling so that people can have green areas, trees, water, space.   ☐   ☐

Supplementary Material 1

The cross is:
- trying to live the truth when it's hard.
- trying to love people when it's painful.
- going against sin in myself and in the environment.
- bringing about new life.

We saw Jesus, in his own environment, living the truth and suffering.
- he overcome his own fear and the temptation not to get involved.
- he overcame the abuse of law by healing on the sabbath.
- he risked persecution by defending the downtrodden, the sinner.
- he showed the way of forgiveness when authority wanted punishment.
- he spoke the truth when the powers did not want to hear it.
- his was the way of the cross,
   the painful living of the truth,
   suffering to do away with suffering.

To love is to know pain.

Supplementary Material 2

These notes were useful to us to get a comprehensive angle on the cross.

Reflection on the Cross

1. Jesus discovered himself in an environment where the forces of evil were ruling: abuse of religious law, sickness, divisions, exploitation of the poor by the rich, pride and hypocrisy, abuse of sex.

2. He experienced the call of God and allowed the Spirit to rule and guide his heart and behaviour. He accepted letting God rule his heart and working to allow God to rule in society, to change society so that it would be according to the Beatitudes.

3. He was tempted not to do his mission. In this course, we had a meditation in which we realised that both Jesus and ourselves are tempted not to love and not to make the effort.

4. We saw Jesus in his life.
- He declared by word and deed that the person is more important than the law. (Mt 3:1-6)
- He showed that love and pardon are the essential elements of our relationships with God and with our neighbour _ not law and punishment. (Jn 8:1)
- He brought captives, poor, blind, dumb, lame and sinners to a new life. (Jn 9:1-4)
- He made it very clear that the other person is my brother or sister. (Lk 10:25-27)
- He struggled to help the authorities overcome their own blindness. (Mt 23)

This is the way of salvation or liberation, but it is also the way of the cross.

Supplementary Material 3

Questions and Answers
(From The Kerygma Course, Seville Place, Dublin.)

1. If Jesus lived in our area today, would he get the same hassle as he got in his own time?
Yes, because he would be aware of what's wrong, especially injustice, and try to do do something about it. People might think he was mad.

2. In our community is it possible to live by the values of the Kingdom?
Not impossible but difficult because:
- the kingdom can be compromised by money.
- service may be difficult because of the struggle for survival. Then again, maybe the struggle for survival is service.
- fellowship can be thwarted by fear and mistrust.
- participation can be difficult because of work pressures, e.g. overtime, or lack of work.
- we have become apathetic.
- if church were separated from the state we would have greater scope for criticism and change.

3. Is the cross (suffering) necessary for making God's kingdom come?
The cross is everyday life. In other words the cross is:
- making the effort (dying to yourself) to listen and understand why your partner in marriage is speaking or acting in a certain way (to bring new life).
- swallowing your hurt pride (dying to your self) in order to resolve a problem peacefully and constructively at a meeting (bring new life).
- burying the law of the least effort to help bring the gospel law of service and love into society (new creation).

Observation:
This group brought up two kinds of suffering:
a). Inevitable: cancer, accidents, flood, sickness, pain, which can either embitter a person or purify a person. (We touch here on the mystery of evil.)
b). Liberating, i.e. suffering to do away with suffering, try to live and promote kingdom values in difficult situations.

4. Is love possible without suffering?
True, faithful love always involves suffering.
a) Personal level: communication means leaving yourself open to getting hurt.
b) Family level: effort to be tolerant, make peace, forgive.
c) community/society: leave yourself open to conflict, criticism, misunderstanding.

5. 'You must avoid suffering at all costs.' Is that true?
a) You can't avoid it because of environment, sickness, money and misunderstanding or confusion.
b) If you ignored the values of the kingdom, apparently you could avoid a lot of suffering, but would you feel happy or authentic?
In short, we see that the cross is:
- love for people.
- testimony against sin.
- abandonment to the Father.
- the way to new life.
'If anyone wants to be a follower of mine, let him renounce himself and take up his cross and follow me.' Mt 16:24-25

The cross is living the Beatitudes in the power of the Spirit, in spite of outside obstacles (e.g. injustice) and inside obstacles (e.g. fear).

Observation:
In the face of a difficult situation, one can take either of three attitudes:
  - *aggression.*
  - *withdrawal.*
  - *positive confrontation.*
Which one do you think is the way of living the cross?

Supplementary Material 4

Another reflection which represents what is behind this session.

What was Jesus struggling for?
Three words come to me: conversion, cross, creation.

Conversion
If we're to understand what Jesus wanted, it involves conversion, which is about changing from one thing to another, like changing from oil-fired heating to solid-fuel heating. It's the same thing (source of heat) but different. When we think we have grasped something and understood it, that's the very time we lose the sense of it. It becomes predictable, familiar, no longer 'new' or challenging. So conversion is a necessary part of the life process.

a) Intellectual conversion
This means stopping one way of thinking and learning another.

b) Moral conversion
Concerned with action, with what I do and my reason for doing it. One kind of behaviour is based on satisfying what I think I need; another is based on living out justice, compassion, etc.

c) Religious Conversion
This is to do with being in love with God, getting beyond our own needs and loving people I like anyway, moving to a love that is growing all the time, towards unrestricted love.

Of course we never achieve these three levels of conversion. We're always in need of repenting, getting a change of mind, but it's important to realise that we can't grasp what Jesus is on about unless we're being converted.

Cross
This means having the mind of Jesus who invites us to carry the cross. Often we use the term 'cross' to talk about the suffering that happens to us, but the cross is also what happens to us when we try to live as Jesus lived, trying to be on the side of life, dealing with that struggle, true to something very deep, very truthful, that is alive in ourselves.

Jesus speaks of 'taking up' the cross. The cross isn't just something that hangs around us: the invitation is to a positive choice to accept the consequences of living as Jesus lived.

Creation
This is what we refer to by terms such as 'turning things upside-down', 'topsy-turvy', 'reversing values', etc. God's design in creating the world is only a dream until Jesus lives his life. It is only when we see Jesus, and his willingness to live out God's dream, that we see God's will (what God wants for the world) happening. Then, for ourselves, as co-creators, we help to make happen on earth what God wanted from long ago.
(Based on a talk by John O'Brien C.S.Sp.)

SESSION TWENTY-FOUR

Resurrection

Aims
• To enable the participants to get in touch with the experience of Resurrection in the Gospel and in their own lives.

Materials
Newsprint and markers for group symbol.
Handouts 31 and 32.
Copies of Resurrection prayer.
Copies of new rota of team tasks.
Flowers, candles, music.

Time-table
1.	7.45	Welcome, aims, time table.
2.	8.05	Introduction to theme.
		Two songs and feelings listed.
		Comment by leader.
3.	8.30	Our experience of Resurrection.
4.	8.40	Sharing in groups of four.
		Making a poster.
		BREAK
5.	9.15	Presentation of symbols.
6.		Resurrection Prayer
7.		Conclusion, New Rotas.

Suggested Procedure

1. Welcome and Introduction
Welcome the people and describe this session's aims and time-table.

2. Introduction to theme
There is a pattern in all our lives, a pattern in the shape of movement from death to life, from darkness to brightness, from despair to hope. The source of this movement is found in the death and resurrection of Jesus. Because of him, all of us can participate in the passage from death to life. In this session, we are going to look at the experience of Resurrection in the lives of the apostles, and in our own lives, in order to promote *hope* among us all.

Imagine the scene: the one who had proclaimed a God who is our friend, close to us, knowing all our needs, is there hanging on a tree, crucified. Imagine the shock to his followers. In the Old Testament there are these words: 'Anyone hanged on a tree is cursed by God.' How could this creature dying on a tree be blessed by God? Mustn't it be the case that this shameful death was a sign for all that he had nothing to do with God? He must have been completely wrong in his message and behaviour. Jesus appears God-forsaken and his cause (his dream), which was so much identified with his person, is abandoned. How could anyone believe in him in face of such a humiliating death? Imagine the effect on those who had given up everything to follow him. It looked like the end – but the end it was not.

It was only after his death that the movement invoking his name began and spread. How could a new beginning come from such a disastrous end?

Let's explore this experience by listening to two songs:
1. Ordinary Man by Christy Moore
The words of this song are on Handout 31.
Play the song.
What feelings are expressed in this song?

And now another song:
2. Joe Hill sung by Luke Kelly
The words of this song are on Handout 32.
Play the song.
What feelings are expressed by this song?

Here are some feelings people have identified in these songs:

Ordinary Man	Joe Hill
anger	admiration
	a Willie Bermingham feeling
bitterness	courage
bewilderment	continuity
disappointment	can't be put down
despair	death – life
depression	defiance
energy-sapped	fighting oppression
frustration	hope
fear	inspiration
hopelessness	joy
hurt	living on
humiliation	strength
ingratitude	spirit lives on
injustice	solidarity
let down	support
rejection	struggle
loss, oppressed,	resurrection
revenge powerlessness	spirit can't be killed
resentment	spirit of life
sadness	triumph
trapped	spirit can't be killed
unappreciated loyalty	unity
unhappiness	victory
worthlessness	willing to keep alive
weariness	

Comment
Let's say the feelings in column A are like those of the disciples after the crucifixion, and that the feelings in B are like those of the disciples when they took on the world.

Something happened which moved the disciples from dejection, despair, hopelessness, to hope, energy and certain victory. What happened is called *Resurrection*.

By God's power, Jesus passed from death to life and his followers were allowed to have this irrefutable experience of Jesus in his new life with God.

Our God is indeed a faithful God. In raising Jesus from the dead, God concretised his goodwill for people, expressed the irresistible power of his saving will, and showed us how much we can trust God, to the extent of being able to attempt the impossible, to the point of being able to hope that life can be born from death. To live in communion with people like Jesus is to be in communion with the Source of all life.

Here is a statement we might dwell on:

To believe in resurrection
is to believe in someone who acts in us
and for us
with immense power,
capable of bringing life from death
and of making old become new,
orientating us to a future
of huge dimensions.
To believe in the resurrection
is to believe that no limit,
no barrier,
no difficulty,
nothing in this world,
will be able to kill the life and hope
which were born in the heart of God's people.

3. Our Experience of Resurrection

Let us look at the extent to which this resurrection is
present in our experience.

Personal reflection
Leader reads slowly.

Life is going along fairly purposefully.
There is a worthwhile goal or set of goals in view.
You and others are feeling
fairly optimistic and hopeful.

Something happens to dash your hopes,
things fall apart,
and there is a sense of failure, pain, loss or hurt.

A strange period follows.
Is there anything worthwhile?
Are we always to be disappointed?
How can we possibly continue?

In some way,
a new strength, energy, emerges,
the strength to begin again.
Our hope is more grounded and mature.
We move forward with a new sense of purpose,
even joy.

1. Can you recall an incident in your own life, or of others,
when you experienced resurrection?

2. What colours/images/symbols would you use to express
what happened?

3. What are the ways by which we keep a sense of hope
alive in us?

4. Sharing in groups of four

After you have shared, make one symbol or image of hope
and put in on a piece of newsprint. Underneath, fill in
some of the ways we keep hope alive in ourselves.

BREAK

5. Presentation of Symbols
Place the posters on the wall or the floor.

6. Resurrection Prayer
Begin with a hymn of hope and trust, e.g. 'Be Not Afraid.'

Leader
Let us celebrate the Resurrection and the Life.
We participate in the Resurrection:

All
When we overcome fear and struggle to make things better.

Reader
The Spirit you received is not the spirit of slaves, bringing
fear into your lives again;
it is the spirit of sons,
and it makes us cry out, 'Abba, Father'.
Rom 8:14

Leader
We participate in the Resurrection:

All
When we continue to believe and act for change despite
depression or resistance.

Reader
If we have died with him, then we shall live with him,
If we hold firm, then we shall reign with him.
2 Tim 2:11-12

Leader
We participate in the Resurrection:

All
When chains are broken and people are liberated.

Reader
When Christ freed us, he meant us to remain free.
Stand firm, therefore, and do not submit again
to the yoke of slavery.
Gal 5:1

Leader
We participate in the Resurrection:

All
When enmity melts into reconciliation.

Reader
For he is the peace between us,
and has made the two into one
and broken down the barrier which used to keep them
apart, actually destroying in his own person
the hostility caused by the rules and decrees of the Law.
Eph 2:14

Next verse of the hymn.

Leader
We participate in the Resurrection:

All
When we move from self-centredness to solidarity.

Reader
It was by faith that, when he grew to manhood,
Moses refused to be known
as the son of Pharaoh's daughter
and chose to be ill-treated
in company with God's people,
rather than to enjoy for a time the pleasures of sin.
Heb 11:23

Don't ask me to leave you.
For I will go where you go
and stay where you stay.
Your people will be my people
and your God my God.
Ruth 1:16—17

Leader
We participate in the Resurrection:

All
When barriers and obstacles are overcome for community.

Reader
And there are no more distinctions between Jew and Greek,
slave and free, male and female,
but all of you are one in Christ Jesus.
Gal 3:28

Leader
We participate in the Resurrection:

All
When fear and despair are transformed into courage.

Reader
In the world you will have trouble but be brave:
I have conquered the world.
Jn 16:33

Leader
We participate in the Resurrection:

All
When organised greed shatters into sharing.

Reader
If a man, who was rich enough in this world's goods,
saw that one of his brothers was in need,
but closed his heart to him,
how could the love of God be living in him?
Jn 3:17

Another verse of hymn.

Leader
We participate in the Resurrection:

All
When apathy is changed into passion

Reader
My children, our love is not to be just words or mere talk,
but something real and active;
only by that can we be certain
that we are children of the truth.
1 Jn 3:18-19

Leader
We participate in the Resurrection:

All
When people who feel powerless begin to choose new life.

Reader
And how infinitely great is the power
that he has exercised for us believers.
This you can tell by the strength of his power
at work in Christ,
when he used it to raise him from the dead
and make him sit at his right hand in heaven.
Eph 1:19-20

Leader
We participate in the Resurrection:

All
When the voiceless make their truth heard.

Reader
But you will receive power
when the Holy Spirit comes on you
and then you will be my witnesses ...
to the ends of the earth.
Acts 1:8

Leader
We participate in the Resurrection:

All
When the forces of death give way to the forces of life.

Reader
For I am certain of this:
neither death nor life,
no angel, no prince, nothing that exists,
nothing still to come,
not any power or height or depth,
nor any created thing
can ever come between us
and the love of God
made visible in Christ Jesus our Lord.
Rom 8:38-39

Final hymn: He is Lord, He is Lord.

7. Conclusion
New task rota.

Handout 31

Ordinary Man
by Christy Moore

I'm an ordinary man,
nothin' special, nothin' grand,
I've had to work for everything I own.
Well I never asked for a lot,
I was happy with what I got,
Enough to keep my family and my home.

Now they say that times are hard
and they've handed me my card,
They say there's not the work to go around.
When the whistle blows the gates will finally close,
Tonight they're going to shut this factory down,
Then they'll tear it down.

I never missed a day
nor went on strike for better pay.
For twenty years I served them best I could.
With a handshake and a cheque
it seems so easy to forget
loyalty through the bad times and the good.

The owner says he's sad
to see that things have got so bad
But the Captains of Industry won't let him lose,
He still drives a car and smokes a cigar,
And still he takes his family on a cruise.
He'll never lose.

Now it seems to me
such a cruel irony,
He's richer now then he ever was before.
Now my cheque is all spent
and I can't afford the rent,
There's one law for the rich, one for the poor.

Every day I've tried
to salvage some of my pride,
To find some work so's I might pay my way,
But everywhere I go
the answer is always no,
there's no work for anyone here today.
No work today.

And so condemned I stand,
just an ordinary man,
Like thousands beside me in the queue,
I watch my darlin' wife
tryin' to make the best of life,
God knows what the kids are goin' to do.

Now that we are faced
with this human waste,
A generation cast aside,
For as long as I live, I never will forgive,
You've stripped me of my dignity and pride
You've stripped me bare.

Handout 32

Joe Hill
Sung by Luke Kelly

'I dreamed I saw Joe Hill last night
Alive as you and me.
Says I, 'But Joe, you're ten years dead.'
'I never died,' says he.
'I never died.' says he.

'In Salt Lake City, Joe, by God,' says I,
Him standing by my bed,
'They framed you on a murder charge.'
Says Joe, 'But I ain't dead.'
Says Joe, 'But I ain't dead.'

'The copper bosses killed you Joe,
They shot you, Joe,' says I.
'Takes more than guns to kill a man,'
Says Joe,'I didn't die,'
Says Joe, 'I didn't die.'

And standing there as big as life
and smiling with his eyes,
Joe says, 'What they forgot to kill
Went on to organise,
Went on to organise.'

'Joe Hill ain't dead,' he says to me,
'Joe Hill ain't never died.
Where working men are out on strike
Joe Hill is at their side,
Joe Hill is at their side.'

'From San Diego up to Maine.
In every mine and mill,
Where workers strike and organise,'
Says he, 'You'll find Joe Hill,'
Says he,'You'll find Joe Hill.'

I dreamed I saw Joe Hill last night
Alive as you and me.
Says I, 'But Joe, you're ten years dead.'
'I never died,' says he,
'I never died,' says he.

Supplementary Material 1

Some useful points as background:

There are three things to be asked about the Resurrection:
1. What really happened?
2. What was its significance then?
3. What is its meaning for us today?

1. What really happened
a) The crucifixion was the end of the disciples' faith in Jesus. They were disillusioned, depressed, disappointed, despiring, fearful, hopeless, angry, resigned, bitter. 'But we had hoped that he would be the one to set Israel free.' *Lk 24:21*. When Jesus was around, everything seemed possible; he spoke with such conviction, he acted with such effect, people gathered, people were healed, new possibilities were felt. But with the Jewish and Roman authorities uniting against Jesus, ending in his trial, death and burial, the situation seemed hopeless. They went into hiding; the men went back to being fishers of fish.

b) However, within a short time, these people were standing up courageously going out and preaching and witnessing to Jesus as risen, confronting the authorities, putting up with criticism, persecution and imprisonment, with a whole new understanding of life based on Jesus, and prepared to *risk* their lives for the truth they stood for. A whole new spirit was among them. Listen to Peter (Acts 2: 22ff):
> 'Fellow Israelites, listen to what I shall tell you about Jesus of Nazareth. God accredited him and through him did powerful deeds and wonders and signs in our midst. You delivered him to sinners to be crucified and killed, and in this way the purpose of God from all times was fulfilled. But God raised him to life and released him from the pain of death, because it was impossible for him to be held in the power of death.'

c) What had happened? Something extraordinary happened between these two historical situations. The disciples had experienced the crucified one alive, even though the crucifixion had shattered their earlier faith in him. They express this in different ways. The oldest account of how they expressed their new experience is in Paul's letter to the Corinthians 15:3-8:
> 'In the first place, I have passed on to you what I myself received: that Christ died for our sins, as Scripture says: that he was buried, that he was raised on the third day, according to the Scriptures; that he appeared to Cephas and then to the twelve. Afterwards he appeared to more than five hundred together; most of them are still alive, although some have already gone to rest ... Well, then, if Christ is raised form the dead, how can some of you say there is no resurrection? If there is no resurrection of the dead, then Christ has not been raised. And if Christ has not been raised, our preaching is empty and our belief comes to nothing ...'

There are also many stories of how they saw, and eventually believed, the women's strong conviction that he was alive.

The New Testament makes it clear that Jesus' resurrection is not the resuscitation of a cadaver/corpse to a normal state of life. They are not saying that he was simply there for anyone to see, but rather that he showed himself to them and enabled them to perceive him and to recognise him as the same Jesus they had known on earth, but now raised from the dead. There is no account of the actual resurrection, but of the disciples' awareness of Jesus as alive in a new way.

And we can see the impact this had on their lives and their behaviour.

There are differences of place, time and detail in the way the stories of the appearances are told, because the writers were influenced by their own perspectives, by the situation of the people they were writing for, and by problems that may have arisen in the life of the community. But there is a fairly common pattern running through this fundamental experience.
a) The circumstances of the appearances are the same in that the followers of Jesus are sad and disappointed. 'But we had hoped ...' (Lk 24:21, Jn 20:19)
b) The initiative for the appearances comes from Jesus: 'Jesus came and stood among them.' (Jn 20:19; Lk 24:15; Mt 28:9,18)
c) There is some form of greeting from Jesus: 'Peace be with you.' (Jn 20:19; Mt 18:9)
d) A word of recognition follows: 'It is the Lord.' (Jn 21:7; cf, Jn 20:20, Mt 28:9,17)
e) A word of command from Jesus concludes the experience: 'Go therefore and make disciples.' (Mt 28:19, cf. Mt 28:10, Jn 20:21; Jn 21:15ff; Lk 24:26ff)

'They physicalise the apostles' experience with the Risen Lord in a way that reflects more the artistry of effective narration than the literal description of what really happened.' (Dermot Lane, page 53 ff.) 'There is an effort to show Jesus as the same but different and that 'seeing' him depends on faith.

2. What was its significance then?
a) It shows God's confirmation of Jesus' concrete way of living – his preaching, his deeds, his death. His way of life was certified, guaranteed, sealed, approved, confirmed and established by God.
b) It shows that God is truly a liberating God who is on the side of those who live for the values of Jesus: dignity, equality, love, justice. Because the resurrection confirms the life of Jesus, we are all offered the possibility of living a particular way of life in the following of Jesus. He shows us the humanity to which we are called.
c) If we live in communion with people now, we are in communion with God.
d) It shows that we can live the Kingdom in faith and hope now, as it will be at the end of time.

3. What is its meaning for us today?
1. That if we struggle against the forces of death and injustice now, in order to fulfil God's dream, we can live in the hope that there will be a breakthrough to new life.
2. Living the values of Jesus, despite the difficulties, means that death will disappear, light will triumph.
3. The Spirit of life, which was shown in Jesus and is present in us, cannot be put out, even by death.
4. No love is ever lost, over the face of the earth.
5. The last word is not death, it is life. It is not 'No' but it is 'Yes'.
6. Tears, pain, and death are overcome and only love re-

mains.

7. We are free to be as Jesus was, and to stand for what he stood for, in the power that the Spirit has given us. To stand and act as he did, is already the Coming of the Kingdom and the Resurrection.

Alleluia.

Much of the above is based on a CTS pamphlet by the late Archbishop Kevin McNamara.

SESSION TWENTY-FIVE

The Spirit Experience

Aims
• To enable participants to recognise the signs of the Spirit active within us, among us, and around us.
• To reflect on our journey through the course and begin to name the action of the Spirit in our personal lives, our team and in the other teams.

Materials
Poster of Steps in Group Method for Action
Six cards for Guided Reflection, with key words
Music (Taizé chant: Veni Sancti Spiritus)

Time-table
1.	7.45	Welcome.
2.	8.00	Focusing Activity.
3.	8.10	Guided Reflection on the Spirit.
4.	8.30	Personal Reflection.
5.	8.45	Team Reflection
	9.05	BREAK
6.	9.20	Shared Reflection in Prayer Room.
7.	10.10	Conclusion.

Suggested Procedure

1. Welcome and Introduction
Welcome the people and describe this session's aims and time-table.

2. Focusing Activity
All of us are called to live by the Spirit of Christ. We'd like to approach the question of the presence of the Spirit, and our relationship with the Spirit, through reflecting on our experience together on the course and especially during the Method for Group Action. Let's look briefly at the steps we took:
These can be put up in poster form.
1. Listening to each other's concerns
2. Sorting the concerns into themes.
3. Choosing the theme for which each group would be responsible.
4. Working together to pose that theme as a problem; making codifications.
5. Leading the investigation sessions and picking up what people wanted to do.
6. Setting our aims.
7. Planning and doing our research.
8. Designing the learning event.
9. Sharing the leadership.
11. Reviewing what was done
12. Participating in the work of the other groups.
You can use this to recall all that happened in the experience of the course.

Open Question
Are there other aspects of the course you'd like to mention? - team tasks, humour, happenings, visits, etc.

3. Guided Reflection on the Spirit
Noticing the Action of the Spirit
As the key phrases are mentioned, cards are placed on the floor around the central symbol. (see diagram)

We can form an image of the Father, because we have experienced fatherliness and motherliness.

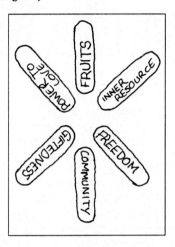

We can form an image of God the Son, because we have experienced sonliness and daughterliness.

But we come to knowledge of the Spirit from our experience of the Spirit's living, loving action in our lives.

The Hebrew word for spirit is *Ruah*, the Greek word is *Pneuma* and the Latin word is *Spiritus*, and they all mean *breath*.

Breath is so common to us that often we don't notice it.

But being unnoticed doesn't mean not being there.

When we are learning to pray, we have to learn to concentrate, to become quiet and peaceful. There are three methods used for concentration and they all come down to *becoming aware of the unnoticed experiences we have.*
For example:

Our breathing goes on all the time, so now, for a little while, become aware of your breathing. Sit down comfortably, close your eyes and pay attention to your breath. Is it very fast? Slow it down to notice it better. Is it superficial? Make it deep. Control it. Become aware.

Our hearing never leaves us, so become aware of your hearing. Sit comfortably, close you eyes. Listen to every noise you hear. Let those noises penetrate you, deeply and freely. Become aware.

We feel bodily sensation all the time. Become aware of these feelings. Close your eyes. Sit comfortably. Feel the touch of your clothes on your back. Feel your back touching your chair. Feel your hands resting on each other. Become aware and peace will set in.

Without some concentration, the presence of the Holy Spirit, the fruits of Pentecost, will remain as unnoticed to us as our breathing, hearing and bodily sensation.
- If I ask you whether you have noticed the work of the Holy Spirit in yourselves, and in others around you, over the past weeks, you will need to concentrate.

Let me remind you of some of the experiences which reveal the work of the Holy Spirit within us.

The Spirit is
Inner Resource (*place card on floor*)
Have you experienced resources deep within yourself that you didn't know you had? And were you surprised at what you could come up with when it was needed?
Scripture: 1 Cor 2:10-12:
'These are the very things that God has revealed to us through the Spirit, for the Spirit reaches the depths of everything, even the depths of God. After all, the depths of a person can only be known by their own spirit, not by anyone else and, in the same way, the depths of God can only be known by the Spirit of God. Now instead of the Spirit of the World, we have received the Spirit that comes from God to teach us to understand the gifts that God has given us.'

The Spirit gives us that sense of
Freedom
When we can overcome our fear, based on things within us and things around us, we feel we can choose freely to act despite the difficulties.
Scripture: 2 Cor 3:17:
'Now this Lord is the Spirit, and where the Spirit of the Lord is there is freedom.'
Rom 8:14:
'The Spirit you received is not the spirit of slaves, bringing fear into your lives again; it is the spirit of sons and daughters and it makes us cry out, 'Abba!''

Power To Love
When you feel yourself capable of going out of yourself, and being interested in other people and caring for them, that is when you experience the fire of the Spirit.
Scripture: Rom 5:14 and 9:
'These sufferings bring patience, as we know, and patience brings perseverance, and perseverance brings hope, and this hope is not deceptive, because the love of God has been poured into our hearts by the Holy Spirit which has been given us.'

Community
When you feel yourself entering into unity, fellowship and support with others:
Scripture: Phil 2:1-3:
'If your life in Christ means anything to you, if love can persuade at all or the spirit that we have in common, or any tenderness or sympathy, then be united in your conviction and united in your love with a common purpose and a common mind.'
1 Cor 12:13:
'In the spirit you have all been baptised and made one body.'
2 Cor 1:13:
'The grace of the Lord Jesus Christ, the love of God and the fellowship of the Holy spirit be with you.'

Giftedness
When we notice the different gifts of our companions and how we can co-operate to put them at the service of others.
Scripture: 1 Cor 12:4:
'There is a variety of gifts but always the same Spirit. There are all sorts of services to be done, but always to the same Lord, working in all sorts of different ways in different people. It is the same God who is working in all of them. The particular way in which the Spirit is given to each person is for a good purpose ... Now you together are Christ's body, but each of you is a different part of it.'

Fruits of The Spirit
When we use that inner resource and overcome fear, when we discover our gifts and put them at the service of others in love, when we support one another in doing the mission of Christ through the Spirit, we experience something new.
Gal 5:22:
'What the Spirit brings is very different: love, joy, peace, patience, kindness, goodness, trustfulness, gentleness and self-control ...'

Since the Spirit is our life, let us be directed by the Spirit.
2 Cor 13:
'In the meantime, we wish you happiness. The grace of our Lord Jesus Christ, the love of God and the companionship of the Holy Spirit be with you all.'

4. Personal Reflection
Ask the people to take time quietly to reflect on the following:
Recall the life of the course in recent weeks,
especially the steps you took
to plan and do the learning events.
Ask yourself:

1. How have I experienced the Spirit active in *my own life* during our work together?
2. How have I experienced the Spirit active among us as a team?
3. How have I noticed the Spirit active in the team from ...?

5. Team Reflection
Each team meets, appoints a co-ordinator, and shares their reflections. They agree on some statements in response to questions 2 and 3, to be shared in the celebration which follows.

BREAK

6. Shared Reflection in Prayer Room
The groups gather in the oratory. Some Taizé music is playing. The celebration calls for improvisation by the leading learners. In accordance with the mood and statements, the leaders weave in some words of prayer. The basic format is:

1. Music playing

2. Leader 1 introduces the celebration: gathered to acknowledge and celebrate the presence of the God's Spirit among us. I call on the group from ... to share their reflections.

3. Representative from Group A shares their statements.

(Leader 2 lowers music)

4. Leader 2 increases volume of the music for a short while, then lowers it again.

Leader 1 responds spontaneously to the first contributions and invites the next group to give their thoughts.

Leader 2 works the music again.

This format continues until all groups have given their thoughts. It is done in a quiet, relaxed manner, weaving reflection with music, with prayer and responding to the creativity of the Spirit.

7. Conclusion
Remind about team tasks.

SESSION TWENTY-SIX

Small Christian Faith Communities

Aims
• To propose Small Faith Communities again as a way of being the Church.
• To examine practical ways of being a Small Faith Community.
• To reflect on the Gospel as a Small Christian Community.

Materials
Elements of small faith community written on cards.
Handout 33: Small Christian Community Meeting
Video/Slide Show and recorder or projector

Time-table
1. 7.45   Welcome.
2. 8.10   Introduction and focusing activity.
3. 8.30   Presentation on Small Faith Community.
          Break
4. 9.15   Small Christian Community meeting.
5. 10.00 Reactions and rota for next week.

Suggested Procedure

1. Welcome
Prayer:
Begin with a short hymn, e.g. 'The Light of Christ has come into the world.'
Read Matthew 5:13-16.
Short reflection on the gospel text.
Invite spontaneous prayer.
Repeat hymn.

2. Introduction and focusing activity
In this session we are looking at Small Faith Community as a way of being Church. As we saw in our first session, the main elements of small faith communities are:
1. Mutual support.
2. Faith sharing.
3. Gospel reflection and prayer.
4. Study.
5. Outreach.
Please think about those elements and try to recall how you have experienced them in *Partners in Faith.*
Buzz and feedback.

3. Presentation on Small Faith Community
Use either presentation A or B.

Presentation A
Use a video, e.g. *Creating Small Faith Communities*, Arthur A. Baranowski, available from St Anthony Messenger Press, 1615 Republic Street, Cincinnati, Ohio 45210.
Ask teams to reflect on:
1. From listening to those people, what are the benefits of small faith community?
2. Can you see yourselves becoming a small Christian community?
OR
Ask the participants, 'What are the characteristics of a small faith community?' As they respond, write their replies up on a large sheet of newsprint, arranging them, unknown to the participants, in five columns, one each for the five points made above in the introduction (Mutual support, Faith sharing, etc). When the people are finished, highlight for them the fact that their replies correspond to those five points.

Presentation B
A slide show linked to prepared statements with questions for the groups (See Supplementary Material 1).
Ask the teams to consider:
1. What strikes you from the slide show?
2. Why would people participate in small faith community?
3. What would you need in order to be a small faith community?

BREAK

4. Small Christian Community Meeting
Leader invites the parish groups to use the material in Handout 33 to hold a Small Christian Community meeting.

5. Reactions and rota for next week.
Take reactions: How did you find the experience?
Rota for next week.
Concluding prayer.

Handout 32
Small Christian Community Meeting

People gather, sit down and chat. A piece of music is played to calm us all down. Then the leader opens the meeting:

1. Happenings of the week
Leader

Let us pause for a moment and think about the past week. Is there anything that happened during the week that you would like to mention briefly to the group?

Give people a chance to chose something and talk about it.

2. Prayer
Side A

Lord, make me know your ways,
Lord, teach me your paths.
Make me walk in your truth and teach me,
for you are God my Saviour.

Side B

Remember your mercy, Lord,
and the love you have shown from of old.
In your love remember me
because of your goodness, O Lord.

All

The Lord is good and upright.
He shows the path to those who stray,
he guides the humble in the right paths,
he teaches his way to the poor.

3. Leader
The gospel for this week is taken from Luke 12:22-31.
Slow reading of the gospel

Then he said to his disciples, 'That is why I am telling you not to worry about your life and what you are to eat, nor about your body and how you are to clothe it. For life means more than food, and the body more than clothing. Think of the ravens. They do not sow or reap; they have no storehouses and no barns; yet God feeds them. And how much more are you worth than the birds! Can any of you, for all his worrying, add a single cubit to his span of life? If the smallest things, therefore, are outside your control, why worry about the rest? Think of the flowers; they never have to spin or weave; yet, I assure you, not even Solomon in all his regalia was robed like one of these. Now if that is how God clothes the grass in the field which is there today and thrown into the furnace tomorrow, how much more will he look after you, you men of little faith! But you, you must not set your hearts on things to eat and things to drink; nor must you worry. It is the pagans of this world who set their hearts on all these things. Your Father well knows you need them. No; set your hearts on his kingdom, and these other things will be given to you as well.

'There is no need to be afraid, little flock, for it has pleased your Father to give you the kingdom.'

4. Picking out words and phrases and meditating on them.
Each one choses a word or phrase which strikes him/her and repeats it out loud prayerfully. Keep silence in between. *This is 'savouring' the text together.*

5. The text is read again
After a time in silence, we share what we have heard in our hearts.
No discussion, but respecting each one's contribution.

6. Focus on ourselves as a group
We ask ourselves as a group:
What task is our group called to in the year ahead?
As people share thoughts and ideas, someone keeps a note of what is emerging.

7. Praying together spontaneously
Leader invites people to pray spontaneously and the session ends with a familiar prayer or hymn.

Supplementary Material 1

To focus our attention on this theme we will show a short series of slides with a brief commentary.
(Copies of slides could be made available from our original set or you could make up your own set to fit the commentary.)

WHAT HAPPENS IN SMALL FAITH COMMUNITIES

1. People decide to come together to keep faith alive and active, to keep in touch. This means being together in a particular place, at a particular time, as often as we need to: weekly, fortnightly, monthly, whatever.

2. By doing this we are supporting one another in trying to follow Jesus today.

3. One of the things we do when we come together is talk about ourselves, our lives, what's going on.

4. We listen, support and challenge one another.

5. We read a part of the Bible to keep in touch with God and what God wants.

6. We see what that says to our own lives and to what's happening around us.

7. We share with each other our different angles on things Sometimes we decide to study a particular topic.

8. We take time to be quiet, to reflect and to pray; to listen to what God is saying and respond.

9. We celebrate our efforts to live the values of the gospel and are strengthened by the celebration.

10. We look at how we can influence life around us.

11. It's a question of expressing our faith in action.

12. The first level where we live the gospel is in our personal lives, by what we are, by what we say, what we do and by how we relate to others.

13. This of course applies to our work situations where we can try and live the gospel values of respect, freedom and equality.

14. Another area is in the family by the way we are for each other and our children.

15. We can also gather our friends and neighbours together in Advent and Lent to experience small faith community.

16. Or we can arrange a learning event with people based on a theme we have unearthed in the area.

17. Or we can simply decide to support those who are struggling for change.

18. For example, young people who are trying to get a start in life ...

19. What keeps us going, and true to the gospel, are the regular meetings between ourselves and with other Small Christian Faith Communities.

20. The more we keep our own faith alive the more we can be light and warmth to those around us:
    'A city built on a hill-top cannot be hidden.
    No-one lights a lamp to put in under a bowl;
    they put it on a lampstand
    where it shines for everyone in the house.'
    Matthew 5:14

21. Small Christian Faith Communities help us to be better what we are and enable us to:
    act justly,
    love tenderly,
    and
    walk humbly with our God.
    Micah 6:6

Supplementary Material 2

Integration of Different Aspects in Small Faith Community
(Derived from 'Creating Small Faith Communities' by A Baranowski, St Anthony Messenger Press.)

Many parishes are setting up liturgy, religious education and ministry teams but they do not offer ways for people simply to be together to reinforce each other in the struggle to live Christian life.

A parish, in its efforts to fulfil the mission of Christ, needs to foster the experience of love and the experience of faith.

Experience of Love
Parishioners themselves do not notice each other all that much except for involved people and people in critical situations. We don't manifest ordinary everyday care for each other because parishes are not structured to help us get to know each other. We preach caring but don't bring people together in a way that they can easily care about each other.

Experience of Faith
Secondly, people need an experience of faith. God and Jesus become more real for us when we share our faith – or lack of faith – with one another. Somehow God has to be found in everyday life. Most Catholics do not trust the faith that is in them. Most of us need help from others who care about us and know a little about our journey of faith before we learn ourselves to trust our experience.

Small Basic Faith Group / Small Faith Community
The way we come together as Church is key because it is the coming together that influences and changes us – not simply the programmes. Faith and love are experiences. The more these experiences are shared – and this can happen only in a small group – the more people notice God's call to be Church for one another and for the world.

To be a Christian experientially today needs a structure of support, faith, sharing and encouragement. That is why we need to provide opportunities and resources for people to participate as Church in this way, a way that is linked to parish, diocese and universal Church.

SESSION TWENTY-SEVEN

The Church in History

Aims
• To enable participants to appreciate afresh the origins of the Church.
• To develop a sense of the struggle of the Church to be true to Jesus Christ.

Materials
Three sentences written out large
Key words and dates on posters
Glasses of water

Time-Table
1. 7.45   Welcome, time-table, aims, tasks.
2. 8.00   Introduction.
           Focusing activity.
           Feedback.
3. 8.30   Church in history.
   9.15 (at latest)   BREAK
   9.30   Continue presentation and dialogue.

Suggested Procedure

1. Welcome, time-table, aims, tasks.

2. Introduction
This session is totally different from others, in that we are obliged to give, within the time available, quite a long presentation. In other years, we found that people have appreciated a historical presentation of the Church; it gives them a sense of rootedness and tradition and a sense of the struggle we have to keep true to the One in whose name we gather.

We will start at the beginning period and work our way up to the present. After each period we will stop and dialogue. You understand that we are not specialists and that we will be looking at the Church in history from our own perspective as *Partners in Faith*.

Focusing Activity
From Fr Enda Lyons' book, *Partnership in Parish*, we have taken three sentences which give us a good starting point to consider the Church in history.
Note: Weave some comments around the following sentences to be presented on posters.

How Christian Community came to be

Interest
What Jesus said and did and stood for made sense to people, struck deep chords in them – the very deepest chords – gave meaning and direction to their lives, gave them a new understanding of their life and death and destiny.

Association
People whose experience was enriched by Jesus, quite spontaneously felt the need to seek one another's company and to associate with one another. They wanted to exchange ideas about Jesus, to pray in his name, to celebrate together the new way in which they found him present among them after the Resurrection.

Organisation
People who were interested in Jesus of Nazareth would avail of whatever would help them to understand Jesus better and follow him more faithfully.

Ask people to buzz and these two questions: Imagine you are the disciples and the years are passing:
   1. What is it about Jesus you don't want to be lost?
   2. What 'things' would help you to continue to follow Jesus faithfully?

Feedback
Write up swiftly on newsprint what people say and prepare the way for what follows by your comments.

3. The Church in History

We will now present to you a broad overview of the Church in history. Sometimes, before each section, we'll ask you what you remember of the time in question and, afterwards, your reactions to what has been said.

What follows are the key words and dates from our presentation. Some relevant books are mentioned afterwards. However, the best approach is, keeping open our critical perspective, to dialogue with a teacher of Church history and make out a suitable presentation. We found that this section, with its emphasis on giving information, is out of kilter with the general approach of Partners in Faith *so we tried to present it in a dialogical way. We offered an impressionistic albeit accurate account.*

1. FIRST CENTURY
- Gathering of followers.
- Remembering; praying;
  sharing; breaking bread;
  serving.
- New Testament writings.
- Scattering.
- Persecutions.

2. CHURCH OF THE ROMAN EMPIRE
- Emperors:
  Constantine 313 A.D.
  Theodosius.
- Christianity: official religion
  of the peoples of the
  Roman Empire.
- Coalition of Church and
  Empire.
  Pope and Emperor.
- Structures of inequality
  within Church.
- Imperial values versus
  kingdom values.

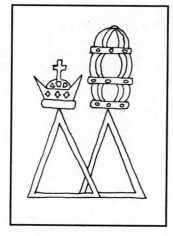

3. FOURTH AND FIFTH CENTURIES
- Faith problems - Arianism.
- 'Jesus less than God'
- Council of Nicea.
- Invasion of German Tribes.
  Arian faith v Christian
  faith.
- Church allied to Empire
  again.
- Baptism of Clovis (King of
  the Franks).
- Benedict and Monasticism:
  community 529 A.D.
  prayer - study.
  worship.
  works.

4. SIXTH TO TENTH CENTURIES: NEW VENTURES
- Gregory the Great:
  reforms:
    v simony.
    v property alienation.
    v lay investiture.
- Islam.
- Missionary outreach:
  cross.   Benedictines.
  book.
  plough.
- Irish missionaries.
  Tribes: 'cujus regio ejus et
  religio'
- Princes - these 'own' the
  people's faith, property,
  (chapels and monasteries)
  and lives.
- Feudalism.

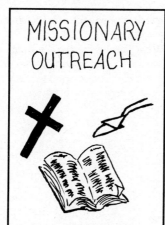

5. MIDDLE AGES: ELEVENTH TO FOURTEENTH CENTURIES
- Mendicant Orders.
  1200 A.D. = Dark Age for Papacy.
  Papal absolutism - imperialism.
  Rivalries.
  German Popes - French Popes (Avignon).

  Scholars and mystics.
  Need for reform.

Crusades - bloodbath scandal.
Heresies: Inquisition.
Demands for a believable Church.
- Dominic: democratic life.
- Francis:
  Rejection of wealth and power.
  Gospel rule.
  Simplicity.
  Small communities.

6. FIFTEENTH AND SIXTEENTH CENTURIES
- Renaissance, new thinking, laity, universities.
- Gutenburg, Printing Press.
- Columbus, Machiavelli, Copernicus.
- Abuses: appointments, taxes, indulgences, huge buildings.
- Martin Luther, prophet: 'You cannot buy grace.'
- Papacy.
- Wittenburg 1517 A.D.
- Protestantism: Knox, Calvin, Methodism, Anglicanism.
- Germans v Italian princes.
- Council of Trent.
- 'Roman' Catholic title:
  Formation of clergy and religious.
  Doctrine v Bible = catechism.
  Sacraments.
  Passive laity.

7. SEVENTEENTH TO NINETEENTH CENTURIES: ENLIGHTENMENT
- Rationalism: Reason v faith.
  Intellectuals v clerical domination.
  Science - arts - secularism.
- Devotion/ processions.
- Missionary outreach
  Far East.
  Jesuits in China.
- Revolution - France 1789.
  Goddess of Reason.
  Napoleon.
  Church loses power/property.
  Liberty-equality-fraternity.
- Poverty - religious orders get involved with poor.
- Social Conscience:
  Rerum Novarum 1890.
  Cardinal Newman - laity.
  Jansenism - individual piety.

8. TWENTIETH CENTURY
- World Wars One and Two:
  Destruction.   Search for meaning.
  Disillusionment.
  Despair.
  Darkness.
  Freud, Darwin, Marx.
  Disaffection.
- Between the Wars:
  Movements for renewal.
  Biblical, liturgical, social.
  Catholic Action.
  Young Christian Workers.
  Lay Apostolate.

- John XXIII: Vatican Two:
- Renewal: bible, prayer, theology.
- Liturgy: participation; vernacular.

- Community: people of God (basic communities).
- Mission in world - ministry - issues.
- Synod on Vocation and Mission of Laity:
    Personal holiness.
    Ecclesial community.
    Spread the kingdom.

Comment: The direction of this session needs to be open and flexible, giving people time to comment and to take a breather. A handout and references are recommended. In the middle, take a break as usual.

There may be more creative ways of doing this. We are still searching!